ayam

# discover your beautiful self

a

## LR

Leo Rastogi, PhD

# FIND YOUR AYAM: DISCOVER YOUR MOST BEAUTIFUL SELF

In most ancient wisdom systems, *maya* refers to the illusion of the world we see around us, created by the complexity of attachments and the ups and downs of our mundane human life. And they go on to say that through mindfulness and meditation practice, it is possible to break through this illusion, unveiling the true nature of our *'self'* and *'life'*, unfolding the natural human expression of joy, peace, right human relationships and fulfillment. This book refers to it as finding your **'ayam'** (aka '*I am*') and aims to start you on this journey.

*Ayam: discover your beautiful self* helps us craft a journey that is unique for each one of us. It brings us a collection of tools drawn from both ancient wisdom and modern science in a clear, easy to learn way. The aim is to enhance our awareness of new possibilities, new ways of living, working, relating, and being in our lives.

Deftly distilled from his hands-on experience spanning over two decades as a meditator and meditation teacher, and his professional career as a global CEO and entrepreneur, Leo Rastogi offers practical tools, insights and wisdom to help us step off the treadmill of life into a more vibrant, fulfilling and nourishing way of living in this world. Sometimes, he simply weaves them in as charming personal anecdotes!

From the basics of mindfulness and meditation and the more subtle wisdom of ancient cultures to the emerging science in the field of neurobiology, this book takes us on an evolving journey through these practices. Step by step, we are offered the insights and tools we need to grow from where we are and to begin experiencing the wholeness of this mystery called *'most beautiful self'*.

**This book is dedicated to**

My teachers, who shared their
wisdom so generously with me

My students, whose curiosity
inspires me everyday

# ACKNOWLEDGEMENT

I feel truly blessed that life has given me the opportunity to study with wonderful teachers around the world. This book contains but a few drops drawn from the lake of wisdom that I am blessed to have been immersed in over time. Were it not for their generous sharing of their mastery, I would not be the person I am today. To all my teachers, I am truly grateful.

Since starting this project and throughout, there were many times when I felt less than ready and the manuscript seemed less than adequate. Yet in all of those moments of vulnerability, I was lucky to receive a constant stream of encouragement from my partner in life, Dr. Richa Joy; thank you for nurturing me through this journey.

Thank you Javi for being the first to suggest that the ayam offerings include a book; your spiritual brotherhood, belief and vision for ayam, and your partnership in all we do together, made this project much easier and more fun than I ever expected it to be.

Over the years, I have been supported by a great team of colleagues and coworkers whose ideas have benefitted the book greatly. While I can't name them all, I must give a shout out to Charlie, Dan, Ale, Coral and Suzanne – thank you for our shared learning space.

This book is a small part of the larger ayam vision, which has the benefit of a great team of teams, whose work has brought ayam to life in the digital realm, with the ideas expressed in the book, making it a much richer immersion. Thank you Team Maaken, Alex, Gus, Ceci and thank you Team Zen, Gargi, Rohit, Rahul, Mili – it is always wonderful to work with you all.

A special call out to my superbly resourceful editorial and research team. Thank you Gillian, Wendi and Alina for your rigor, imagination and excellence!

Much of this book draws on my experiences in my formative years, which I could not possibly have immersed myself in if it were not for the support of my parents (Dr. A.P Rastogi and Dr. Rekha

Prakash). Thank you Mom and Dad for always allowing me to make unconventional choices in life. And to my Sister, Nirjhara, for reviewing my early drafts and coaching me to "lighten up" my writing!

Respecting the privacy of those involved, I have changed the names, places and particulars in several instances, as well as in the personal anecdotes mentioned in the book. I remain grateful to all those experiences and to the people I shared them with, for it has had a huge effect on shaping my vision.

Lastly and most importantly, I must acknowledge that this is just one step and the first of many that I envision to bring to the readers a synthesis of this timeless wisdom. The book itself draws liberally from the contributions of countless visionary souls, many of whom I haven't even met. I am most humbly grateful for having had the opportunity to put to pen their wisdom and I hope to continue this journey!

# CONTENTS

ayam

discover your
beautiful
self

a

**LR**

Leo Rastogi, PhD

# INTRODUCTION

Let me begin by sharing that I started the journey of writing this book with the intent that it was going to be essentially about mindfulness and meditation; an application-oriented DIY book, especially focused on some core ideas that I saw missing from mainstream discourse on the subject. As the project evolved and progressed, I noticed that I could not write meaningfully about the benefits of meditation without delving into processes of life that fill up our living experience – be it family, work, health or the eternal quest for meaning. This gave me a pause, which lasted well over a month, given I was clear that this was not meant to be a self-help book but a book that is focused on real-world practical applications but also rich in the contextual background.

Additionally, when writing a book about meditation one has to understand that its almost like writing a book about "swimming". No matter how well written the book is and how detailed and accurate the instructions are, its impossibly difficult to learn to swim by reading a book. For sure its possible to 'understand' how to swim from a manual, but that understanding does not give much skill of actually being a swimmer. So in this book while the context has been carefully presented and where possible practice exercises are provided, I chose to really rely on the ayam$^{(TM)}$ as the tool for readers to put into practice what they have learnt. You will not find long mediations scripts in the book (do they serve any purpose anyway - how could you be meditating while reading?) rather you will find references to meditations in the ayam platform that are recommended for the reader to experience, to allow the learning to truly integrate.

This was beginning to seem like a tightrope walk: to write enough about life to provide applications and relatability, but not so much that it became a self-help book. To go deep enough in meditation to enrich the context but not so deep that it becomes a spiritual or philosophical treatise – there are so many good ones already out there and I certainly have no aspirations to add to that list. It reminded me of a friend trying to describe what color she wanted in the office: she said something to the effect of; *"I want a light gray, not exactly a gray like ... you know the gray! But greyish enough that it looks like gray ... you know the grey I am talking about...."* Well no, I still don't know what she was talking about and I was glad I didn't need to choose, but yeah, my self-conversation was beginning to seem very similar to that. So I took a pause and decided to re-examine how I got to this place in my life anyway.

Ever since I was introduced to meditation at the age of 12 by a teacher in my school, I have had almost a daily practice. I have of course also dabbled in many different styles and forms and been immersed in diverse experiences ranging from monastic residencies and breatharian training to traveling around the world to learn esoteric and ancient meditations and healing techniques. No matter how different the experience was, I realized that at the core of it, I had common questions I was seeking answers to; something to the effect of; *How can I be a better person? How can I contribute best to those around me? How can I have a more impactful and fulfilling life?* While these are not questions that sound innately spiritual, as always, the journey of this inquiry for me had meditation as an important piece of the picture. And then I came across a quote somewhere that said: *"meditation is life, life is meditation"*, and suddenly the penny dropped into place and the shape and intent of the book became clear for me. It's essentially, therefore, a book about "life" and how "meditation and mindfulness" can bring more purpose, joy and fulfillment to it.

The book also coincides with the launch of the **ayam**™ app and platform, which has allowed me to make the book more immersive by being able to both point the reader to the digital resources that make for a great practice companion, as well as offering content around the subject in a digital world that does not have the constraints of the page count of the book. So to that extent, the **ayam**™ app and the book make perfect companions for each other. The app provides the daily practice companion, and the book is a great contemplative study resource – you may like to use both in sync to get the maximum value!

In the next few pages, I have attempted to provide you with an executive summary of the intent, design and ontology of the book. I prefer to call it the "white of the whiteboard" to have as the background context, in which each progressing chapter is a "new color marker" that will draw one piece of the picture.

And I do recommend you go through the sections that follow before you dive into the book – think of the rest of the chapter as the GPS map before the drive. I hope you find great experiences along the journey.

## Getting Back On Point

With roots that dig deep into ancient traditions and wisdom, mindfulness and meditation are two healing modalities that have become household names in recent decades. No longer is it considered unorthodox or strange to discuss the potential of these practices to enhance the quality of our lives. Since science has taken great interest in uncovering the underlying mechanisms that make these techniques so effective, mindfulness and meditation have found their place in mainstream conversation quite effortlessly.

Much of the focus of scientific research in this domain has been on what these modalities can alleviate. From stress and anxiety to depression, chronic pain, and addiction, researchers around the world have been conducting hundreds of studies to explore how mindfulness and meditation can restore our balance – both physically and mentally. From the breath's ability to bring us out of the 'fight or flight' response to the ability of mindfulness to shift our response to pain, there are a variety of explanations to cover why so many are turning towards these practices.

Using these modalities to mitigate pain and suffering is a very worthy and enlightening pursuit. For a long time, it was hardly fathomable that addressing the mind through awareness and wisdom teachings could have such a significant role to play in healing. Not only was it seen as incomprehensible to many, but to hold such views could have been ostracizing, depending on one's community.

Now, however, we largely accept that our mental state plays a role in creating (or detracting from) the experience of physical well-being. As our understanding grows about how these modalities interweave with the body's numerous physiological and energetic systems, our ability to explain this phenomenon is growing.

If we can agree on the findings that mindfulness and meditation can help us to restore our sense of equilibrium (such as by reducing anxiety, cravings, and difficult emotions), we might argue that so can a lot of other things. Cleaning up our diet, exercising, exploring bodywork, and other forms of therapy also have an impact on our sense of basic well-being. So what makes mindfulness and meditation different or unique?

## Expanding the Paradigm

The potential of these modalities runs much deeper and further than simply helping us to navigate the difficulties of life. These practices are not exclusively effective in restoring balance when we've lost it. In other words, they don't just bring us back to base; they create room for us to grow into entirely new ways of being.

Mindfulness and meditation expand what we might consider well-being to be. The deeper we dive, the more we come to realize that wellness is not just about mitigating the 'negative' or difficult experiences of life; it is equally about cultivating the good. Some of the 'good' that these modalities enhance, develop, and strengthen include:

- Feelings of harmony within ourselves, with others, and with the environment at large

- Feeling connected to a vision, sense of purpose, and meaning

- Our ability to communicate in ways that create harmony rather than division

- Feelings of joy, contentment, fulfillment, and gratitude

- Our ability to be with the paradoxes of life

- Our capacity to witness and nourish our shared humanity with others

- The frequency of our subtle energy body

- Our embodiment of additional virtues such as patience, compassion, and curiosity

In our modern way of living, many of us have unconsciously taken on a crisis management or crisis prevention attitude towards well-being. Since stress, poor mental health, loneliness, and lack of purpose have become pervasive challenges in today's societies (we will explore crises in Chapter 1), it makes sense that we are largely focused on what we can do to stave these things off.

However, what if you were to consider that mindfulness and meditation are pathways into an expanded paradigm – one within which you can both reduce the weight of these everyday challenges, while also opening yourself up to a fuller life with greater purpose, meaning, presence, and joy? Can you consider that the potential of your life is even greater than you presently imagine?

As we move further into our practice and exploration of these modalities, we find that they might stir up new questions within us, questions such as:

- Who am I really? What does it mean to be 'me'?

- Is there a way to see beyond duality – good and bad, right or wrong?

- What is the nature of these thoughts and feelings that I experience?

- What do I want to contribute to this world? What is my vision?

- What are my beliefs and how do they impact my life?

- How can I find common ground between differences of opinions, whether within myself or between myself and another?

- How can I best care for myself and others? What do I have to give?

When new questions start to arise within us, we open ourselves up to new insights and possibilities. Over time, with continued practice and exploration, our lives begin to grow in unexpected ways. Like a well cared-for plant, one that is given the full range of nutrients and love it requires, new shoots and blooms become possible where they weren't before – and each one is beautiful and unique in its own way.

## Bridging the Gaps

Within this process of discovery, we start to bridge gaps that may have previously held us back from experiencing fullness or wholeness in our lives. We start to see that life is more than just what appears through the lens we have been conditioned to viewing it with. By opening our minds and hearts to the unknown, we create space for new possibilities to take root.

Since mindfulness and meditation can be viewed through both a secular or scientific lens and one of ancient wisdom and tradition, the journey to truly understanding these practices comes from considering both approaches. This does not mean we need to force our beliefs to be any different from what they are; rather, it is a call for us to make room for seemingly opposing views or ideas we have yet to consider.

In reality, however, opposites need not be opposing. We can uphold and explore both the secular, scientific lens of mindfulness and meditation while remaining open and curious about the ancient. Held together, we soften the apparent division between the seen and the unseen, the known and the unknown.

Can we embrace the tangible and the intangible simultaneously? The measurable and immeasurable? The qualitative and the quantitative?

This ability to hold two different or opposing things at once is what helps us to soften division and embrace apparent contradictions – contradictions that can show up within ourselves, our relationships, and within life as a whole. It is here that we find greater wholeness amongst life's difficulties, as well as more space for nuance, mystery, and complexity.

> *"Only the paradox comes anywhere near to comprehending the fullness of life."*
>
> Carl Jung

Life is a great mystery – one that is constantly evolving, often challenging, and indeed miraculous. Through mindfulness and meditation, we can dive deeper into life itself, emerging with insights, skills, and perspectives we could not have uncovered without practice. This program and book is an invitation to start or continue this journey – to find out what is yearning to be revealed within you. Where does greater wholeness and fullness wish to be seen and expressed in your own life?

## What We Will Cover

This book outlines a range of practices, from the basics of mindfulness and meditation to esoteric teachings and the emergent findings of neuroscience. Including both lessons and practices, the intent is to empower you to deepen your cognitive and experiential understanding and to develop a personal practice that is unique to you and your life!

From the ancient roots of these practices to modern-day applications, we will explore complementary teachings through a broadened lens. Regardless of your background, beliefs, or interests, these modalities offer something to everyone as they impact every aspect of life.

As you journey through this book and the practices of the program, meet yourself where you're at. 'Where you're at' will undoubtedly change from day to day as life shifts and its flow moves through you. Embrace where you are in this moment, the next, and the next, coming to your practice with openness, curiosity, patience, and compassion.

Know that there is nothing you need to know already. Simply move forward with an open heart and curious mind, letting the wisdom and potential of these practices unveil themselves in ways as unique as you are.

Let life surprise you – it's the greatest gift of all!

# SECTION 1

Searching for Your AYAM:
Stepping Off the Treadmill of Life

AYAM is the reverse of MAYA. In Buddhist and Vedic philosophy, *maya* refers to the illusion of the world we see around us. As we take in the images, sounds, and other sensory aspects of this world, we tend to assume that it all 'is what it is' – or perhaps more accurately, that it is how it appears to be. The illusion suggests that the world is permanent and fixed when in reality, the only thing fixed is impermanence.

Stepping off the treadmill of life is about taking a pause from the busy activities, the noise, and the illusion of the world around us. Most of our engagements in this world keep us occupied with our experience as we perceive it to be. However, through the use of mindfulness and meditation, we are granted an opportunity to tune into the deeper layers of reality. We begin to break through the illusion of *maya*, unveiling its opposite – AYAM. It is here that we meet our true inner self: this subtle, ever-present sense of 'I am'.

To begin this exploration, we must start by taking a look at the reasons why so many of us are being called towards these practices today. Why is it that there is such budding interest in these ancient teachings and practices? Once we understand what motivates us, pairing that with the wisdom and opportunities of these ancient teachings, we start to realize that life can indeed be experienced in a much deeper, more nourishing way than it most commonly is today. This is how we begin: by witnessing where we are now and uncovering fresh possibilities of where we might go.

### Note:

*I have often been asked the question of "where the AYAM name comes from, or what it means, or how I chose it," etc.*

*In full disclosure, the story/explanation to the above is what we call "after the fact rationalization". As it really happened, the name **Ayam** presented itself through an intuitive download my co-founder Javi had one day when we were meditating together. He says it just appeared to him in front of his mind's eye. Prior to meditating, we had been* *discussing different choices of names, and once Ayam revealed itself, no other name ever sounded even close! Or as Javi says, "the project was ready, so we received the name."*

# CHAPTER 1

Why Everyone Is Talking About Mindfulness and
Meditation: Confronting the Three 21st Century Crises

Once upon a time not long ago, mindfulness and meditation
were explorations reserved for a certain subset of the population.
Spiritual seekers, yogis, and nomads were some of those you could
expect to delve into such unconventional sounding practices.

In this chapter, I am delving at some length into issues of modern
life that have ignited a greater interest in this subject. The reason I
start the book with this subject is not to literally *yell* about how bad
things are, but to do some confronting perspective sharing about
it for readers who may find an echo in their lives of some of the
conditions I describe here.

Let me begin by sharing with you a story from when I still had long
hair!

I remember when I first came to the US, my roommate would
often see me meditating – it really intrigued him what I was up
doing at 4:30 am on a New York morning! He would find me sitting
cross-legged on the living room floor with eyes closed and hands in
a spiritual gesture, finger pointing upwards, for a full 45 minutes.

Coming from a conservative catholic background himself, he was
no stranger to religious practices, but what really confused him was
the 'absence' of any deity or scripture around me or in my room.
He knew anecdotally that Hindus had lots of deities, so after a few
days when he couldn't hold himself back any longer, he finally asked
me which deity I prayed to and why I didn't have a picture.

It was difficult to explain to him that I wasn't praying, but meditating,
and I didn't need a deity for it. He was like, "*...you were what?*" I was

tempted to offer a more profound answer but, given that I had to get to the subway in 20 minutes, I shortened the conversation by uttering a word I knew he had heard before; "Yoga!" And yes, on hearing that, his eyes lit up – he could finally slot my practice! But this was a long time ago.

Over the past few decades, mindfulness and meditation have truly blossomed in western mainstream awareness. It would not be unusual now for a business leader, doctor, teacher, family member, or neighbour to bring up these practices in casual conversations. Neither, for that matter, would it be strange for a flight steward to tap me gently on my shoulder to get my attention, saying apologetically, "*Sorry Mr. Rastogi for interrupting your meditation, but what would you like for dinner?*" (In all fairness, I had a meditation book lying next to me so it was a good guess).

Something has shifted... but what?

To understand why everyone is now talking about the benefits, joys, and challenges of mindfulness and meditation, we have to consider what has changed in recent years. Since the dawn of the 21st century (and in the decades leading up to it), we have been faced with three major crises or epidemics:

- **The stress epidemic**
- **The mental health crisis**
- **Loneliness and lack of purpose crises**

Rising stress, mental health challenges, loneliness, and lack of purpose combine to create the perfect conditions for interest in mindfulness and meditation to grow. Why is that? As more and more people are crossing paths with any one or more of the above crises, we are starting to ask basic questions about how we're working, loving, living, and even breathing. It is clear that something about this 21st century fast-paced life is not working and intuitively, we can sense that it has to do with our emotional and mental well-being. Maybe mindfulness and meditation might hold answers to what we are looking for. It also helps that this case is actually being made continuously by thought leaders in mainstream media too.

Fundamentally, these crises directly impede our experience of health and happiness – two human experiences that are the fundamental 'quests' or 'goals' in life. Intuitively, we know that this is true; everything finally boils down to health and happiness. If you're not convinced that these are the fundamental yearnings of humanity, take a moment to consider something you long for. And why do you long for this object or experience?

Why are you yearning for a better job, a certain relationship, confidence, recognition, money, or anything else?

The answer is most likely because you believe it will make you happy, healthy, or both.

However, we also know that through all of our attempts to attain the objects, relationships, or states of mind that we think will lead to happiness, the experience of happiness itself is often just *fleeting*. When we get the job we wanted, we seek out the next promotion. On finally buying the house of our dreams, we start looking for ways to improve it... and so on.

So the key question remains: how do we access true health and happiness? Mindfulness and meditation unlock the doors to that answer, but first we must address the crises we face.

### The Stress Epidemic

Stress is far more pervasive than we often consider it to be. It is not just a heavy workload, lack of time off, or tension in an intimate relationship. Stress can be defined as 'pressure or tension on an object' and when we talk about human stress, we are the object in question.

And indeed, humans experience stress unlike any other living being on this planet. Yes, all animals have an innate stress response wired into their physiology and yet ours functions a bit differently. In his book 'Why Zebras Don't Get Ulcers', Robert Sapolsky outlines the difference between our response to stress and that of a zebra or lion.

> "But unlike less cognitively sophisticated species," he writes, "we can turn on the stress-response by thinking about potential stressors that may throw us out of homeostatic balance far in the future... Zebras and lions may see trouble coming in the next minute and mobilize a stress-response in anticipation, but they can't get stressed about events far in the future."[1]

Whereas animals respond to imminent, real danger, we respond to both the imminent and the imagined or the perceived *(the second dart we will talk about later in the book)*. This paves the way for a chronic experience of stress to overtake us and in the modern world, where infinite stressors are at our fingertips, we are more susceptible than ever.

The various types of stress that impact our modern day human lives are:

a.  Physical stress (physical strain anywhere in the body)

b.  Emotional stress (emotional overwhelm in response to any kind of stress)

c.  Mental stress (mental tension or pressure)

d.  Geopathic stress (the effect of the earth's energies on our well-being)

e.  EMF stress (exposure to electromagnetic fields)

f.  Environmental stress (toxins in the environment)

g.  Spiritual stress (lack of identity, meaning or connection with ourselves)

[1] Sapolsky, R., 2004. *Why Zebras Don't Get Ulcers*. New York: Henry Holt and Co.

As suggested, these stressors are amplified in modern society. As the pace of living increases, especially as we live far away from nature and natural rhythms, we are left with little time to rest and recharge ourselves. Furthermore, we are exposed to additional stressors that our ancestors did not have to face, such as electromagnetic radiation, eye strain from personal devices, and an abundance of toxins in the environment. Social media, constant updates and notifications, and less time spent outdoors are just some of the additional factors that increase the stress we encounter.

Another argument that is made about stress is that it's difficult to quantify it or measure it, although that is no longer true. There are now easily usable technologies like HRV (Heart Rate Variability) measurement that can give us a great deal of insight into the current level of stress we are experiencing and the prognosis of where we are headed. So stress is ever more real for us now...

This then begs the question: how will we manage?

## The Stress Response

To better understand how we can cope with stress, we need to have a basic understanding of what happens during the stress response. First of all, it is important to note that stress is complex and multi-factorial. For instance, if someone is having a hard time managing their workload, they may also be experiencing challenges at home, nutritional deficiencies or epigenetic imbalances that affect neuro hormones and make coping harder, as well as any number of other stress-inducing factors.

Furthermore, stress is personalized. What stresses you might not stress me – and vice versa. This is due to a wide range of factors, such as our beliefs, our conditioning, and our ability to adapt. Resilience plays an important role here, too. If you have harnessed skills to effectively recover from or process stress, you will be better off. Mindfulness and meditation play a big part in developing this resilience and adaptability.

In addition to differences in which specific stressors we each react to, the way in which we react varies from person to person. Some people internalize stress, which means it is kept inside. This can lead to any number of physical health conditions as well as mental and emotional challenges. What we keep inside (or in essence, what we sweep under the rug) doesn't just disappear; it eventually manifests elsewhere. Sometimes, it starts with mindful conditions like a tight jaw, grinding of the teeth during sleep or stiffness in the neck, before manifesting as more chronic conditions.

On the other end of things, some people have a tendency to externalize stress. This occurs when everything outside of ourselves is the 'problem'. The challenge here is that they never take responsibility for the way they interact with the world, which can lead to relational and social disruption.

Through mindfulness and meditation, we begin to harness the tools that help us to neither internalize nor externalize our experience. We gain the capacity to be with whatever our experience is, without blame, judgment, or suppression. We can still take responsibility and expect others to take theirs, but we do not unconsciously point the finger either inwards or outwards.

Now, whatever the stressor in question might be, our response to stress can take one of three forms:

a.  Fight

b.  Flight

c.  Freeze

Many of us are familiar with the *'fight or flight'* response – the name for the physiological reaction we have to a stressful situation. While this term indeed highlights two of the responses we can have when we feel threatened or fearful, it does not highlight the response that is now being intently explored by scientists: **the freeze response**.

For example, let's say we are put on the spot during a conversation at dinner. We express an opinion about a world event or other important topic and a loved one takes issue with it. We weren't expecting such a strong counter argument! We might do one of three things if we feel stressed about this unexpected interaction:

1.  We might fight, passionately defending our position at all costs.

2.  We might flee, backtracking on what we said or leaving the table all together.

3.  We might freeze, stopping cold in our tracks, anxious and unsure of where to go or what to say from hereon in.

Alongside these three responses, stress expresses itself through the physical body. Some of the signs that we are stressed include shallow or rapid breathing, unconsciously holding the breath, erratic or poor memory/recall, cold hands and feet, muscle tension or tightness, jaw tension, sweating, low energy, and poor digestion. We might not always relate these signs to feeling stressed, though through mindfulness and meditation practice, we start to connect the dots between our physical experience and our mental one.

My first encounter with freeze happened at a time when "stress" wasn't even a word in my vocabulary. During high school, I was participating competitively in a Maths Olympiad and I witnessed a surprising incident. In Asia, a Maths Olympiad is a very competitive affair that pits you against literally half a million other kids from around the country for a handful of scholarships. In the Olympiad I am talking about, for some parts we had to participate as a team. So I was representing my school along with a classmate, whom I will call Tina.

In the final round, we were required to solve as many questions as we could in 90 minutes. The first hour or so passed normally, with both of us working through the questions as best as we could, and then the bell rang notifying the start of the last 20 minutes – that's when it happened. I noticed Tina's breathing suddenly go shallow, almost like a hiccup, and then she laid down her pencil and just stopped. She didn't say anything, no loud scream, but just stopped cold and stared down at the sheet. I tried calling her name and shaking her a little bit, but nothing worked. She just kept staring at the sheet.

Needless to say, I tried to do the best I could in the time that was left and when the final bell rang, she just got up and left without uttering a word. I was left feeling partly angry about missing out on the opportunity of doing our best, but mostly confused as to what had happened.

For a while, in my mind, I blamed her for our abysmal performance in the final tally. It was much later in life, when I began to teach mindfulness practices to young adults on how to deal with examination anxiety, that I remembered this incident again and finally the penny dropped. Tina had simply "frozen" out of acute exam anxiety, and instead of yelling at her, I should have just asked her to "breathe... relax... and let go!" With this came a boatload of guilt and regret at not having been more understanding.

A few years ago, I made contact with her and apologized for my behaviour. She remembered the event and was very generous, telling me that afterwards, she decided that she didn't want to study science at all. Instead, she pursued a career in communications and then went on to write children's books! She still has some difficulty with stress but now regularly uses an app (which I won't name, lest it sound like an endorsement 😊) to relax. As they say in mathematics, QED!

## The Costs of Stress

We all know that stress doesn't feel good. When we are stressed, we are likely to feel physically, mentally, and emotionally depleted. All aspects of our being take a hit (whether we are conscious of it or not) when any one of the mental, physical, or emotional bodies reaches its limit of resilience.

However, beyond the general discomfort of stress, the tension that stressors place on mind and body run deeper than we often genuinely consider. Chronic stress weakens the immune and hormonal system[2], increases the risk of cardiovascular disease[3] (the new science of psycho-endo-immunology studies that in depth), increases gastrointestinal problems[4], and weighs heavily on mental well-being. It can also exacerbate certain underlying health conditions we might be struggling with.

When it comes to cancer, much of the research on the link between tumor growth and stress is still emerging. However, studies have identified various psychosocial factors such as stress, depression, and lack of social support to be risk factors in tumor growth[5]. Since chronic stress also alters immune function and increases inflammation, we might find ourselves at increased risk of developing certain cancers when suffering from it.

Furthermore, stress activates the hypothalamic-pituitary-adrenal (HPA) axis in the body, which is a central part of the body's stress response. HPA activation is associated with sleep deprivation[6], and when in a state of daily chronic stress that is not processed effectively, it impedes our circadian rhythm (or our wake-sleep cycle). As poor sleep quality and sleep deprivation impact the energy we have the following day, a vicious cycle is created. Stress creates sleep challenges, which leads to greater stress upon waking. And so the cycle continues, until we mindfully intervene.

Now, in addition to all of this, stress also has an impact on gene expression. As we look towards a relatively new field of research called epigenetics, we come to understand that genes can, in essence, be turned on or off. They are not as static as we once believed.

---

[2] https://www.ncbi.nlm.nih.gov/pmc/articles/PMC1361287/
[3] https://www.urmc.rochester.edu/encyclopedia/content.aspx?ContentTypeID=1&ContentID=2171
[4] https://pubmed.ncbi.nlm.nih.gov/18004186/
[5] https://link.springer.com/chapter/10.1007/978-3-030-16996-1_6
[6] https://www.naturalmedicinejournal.com/journal/2010-06/role-cortisol-sleep

One particular study that looked at the brains of mice found that exposure to a stress hormone caused modifications in their DNA[7], the implications of which are astounding. For instance, research suggests that neurological and psychiatric disorders are not due to mutations in one gene but rather, are the result of molecular disturbances and the signalling that controls the expression of multiple genes[8].

Epigenetic modifications can also interfere with enzyme production[9] (impacting various bodily systems) and metabolic function[10], leading to a wide range of complications and cause for concern. Needless to say, reducing stress in mindful ways is an important step in ensuring healthy gene expression.

All of this might sound pretty grim, and indeed it doesn't paint stress in a pleasing light. However, we can be grateful for the signs of stress that send us the signal that we are out of balance. Stress is a wake-up call, inviting us to tune into both body and mind with curiosity, care, and compassion. It is not an ending; it is the entry point into a new way of being.

> *"The physiology of stress eats away at our bodies not because it has outlived its usefulness but because we may no longer have the competence to recognize its signals."*
> Gabor Maté

## Coping With Stress

In addition to the fact that we each react differently to different life stressors, and that we tend to do so either by internalizing or externalizing, we each have our own coping mechanisms. Some of us cook or eat, some of us drink or smoke, some of us go to the gym or practice yoga. We might shop, gamble, or distract ourselves with

---

[7] https://www.nih.gov/news-events/nih-research-matters/stress-hormone-causes-epigenetic-changes
[8] https://pubmed.ncbi.nlm.nih.gov/17453016
[9] https://www.ncbi.nlm.nih.gov/pmc/articles/PMC3118659/
[10] https://www.ncbi.nlm.nih.gov/pmc/articles/PMC6153363/

social media, but rest assured; we each have our own conscious or unconscious stress management habits.

And indeed, some of us might turn towards mindfulness and meditation as a way of coping with life's stressors and the daily grind of living. We do so for good reason – both mindfulness and meditation indeed help to lower the stress response. However, it is important to understand that 'coping with stress' is not the highest purpose or greatest potential of mindfulness meditation, as we discussed briefly in the introduction.

We might use mindfulness and meditation as tools to make ourselves feel better, and yet both of these practices can open us up to so much more than a brief moment of respite. They can drastically shift the relationship we have with ourselves, with others, with our work, and with the world at large.

As we begin to navigate the stressors we are facing, we can indeed turn towards mindfulness and meditation practices to help. However, we will want to dig up the root cause of the problem, too. There are a variety of sources of stress that we tend to overlook, such as nutritional imbalance, digital exposure, and small, everyday stressors that eventually add up. Even physical scars from accidents or injuries can create regulatory stress in the body. Neural therapy is one practical intervention that can help to manage this type of stress.

What is most important here is a willingness to face what is causing that imbalance and to address it in whatever ways are the most nourishing for us. Mindfulness plays a key part in this as it helps us to be entirely present with, and compassionate towards, our experience. As we start to unravel the underlying reasons we are as stressed as we are, we begin to uncover ways in which we can improve our health and happiness.

As one of my teachers, a Tibetan monk and the Abbot of a monastery I studied at, often told us, *"when you leave these walls and go back to a householder life, stress is inevitable, I offer you no path to escape it. I do,* however, give you the tools to grow resilience and hope they remain your companions long enough for stress to give up on you."

One day, Bhante, one day..., I hope to experience that!

## Creating A New Normal

In my twenties, I volunteered as a program leader for an American training and development company. One of their core training tenets was that: it's possible to get used to almost anything in life and often, the reason why people don't work to make their life better is because, what to others seems very obviously a bad situation, has been accepted as normal by the people concerned. And they would have a rather rustic way of expressing it by saying, *"if you live long enough in the gutter, eventually you will also be OK about the sights and smells of the gutter."*

While the idiom of language used is a little far-fetched, the main point is actually true.

It is important to be mindful of the fact that stress can become so pervasive that we may actually consider it to be normal. Psychologist Dr. Daniel Siegel has suggested that stress can actually come to dominate the normal resting state. When an abnormal state becomes normal, we find ourselves caught in a trap. Stress can become who we are, what we do, how we cope, and how we operate. It becomes a part of our identity.

> *"We know in different psychological disorders you can see some variations in parts of the brain that are active in the default state, that tells you something interesting. In people who have anxiety, and some of those people who've been traumatized, you'll see an increased activity of areas related to stress, worrying, and rumination—that is, part of how they define who they are is through the act of worrying."* [11]
>
> *Dr Daniel Siegel*

[11] Dr Daniel Siegal, NICABM, 2019

Another point I must make here is one that I encounter a lot in my work with clients, where they mention that they have *"accepted this"* or *"made peace with that."* I want to note that, while unconditional acceptance is a very powerful quality, it's completely different from *"resignation"* or worse still, *"resigned cynicism"*, which can often sound innocuously like *"...well it's not going to change so I have accepted it."*

True acceptance is a state of non-attachment or being liberated (sometimes called *Aparigriha* in yogic practices) from something, and leaves us with a sense of peace and serenity on the other side. So it's always worth examining "acceptance" and distinguishing it from "resignation". Resignation will continue to accumulate stress in ways you don't immediately notice and can lead to chronic health conditions, as well as challenges in behavioral health – a subject we will look into in the next section.

Through mindfulness, we become more aware of what we deem to be 'normal', empowering ourselves to consider new views of reality. The transition takes time when what we have known has embedded itself into our identity, and yet transformation is possible. We can start by committing to this exploration of the unknown, slowly awakening to what is possible in an awakened, mindful life.

### The Mental Health Crisis

One of the greatest challenges of the 21st century has been the steady increase in behavioural health issues. While their causality is very complex and stretches across a wide range of factors, including epigenetic factors, toxin exposure, lifestyle issues, etc., it's the crises dimension that we need to understand a little bit empathically.

First and foremost, let's be clear that the stress epidemic and the mental health crisis go hand in hand. Evidence suggests that stressful life events often precede the onset of conditions like depression and anxiety[12], and chronic stress alone is no less of a concern. Researchers at the University of California in Berkeley discovered that chronic stress creates long-term changes in the brain that may explain the development of anxiety and mood disorders[13]. While the clinical dimensions of this subject have been dealt with very wonderfully in books on MBSR (Mindfulness Based Stress Reduction) and MBCT (Mindfulness Based Cognitive Therapy), I will delve into these from a more "as lived" perspective as a conversation starter for the readers.

As we've discussed, there are countless forms of stress, any of which can contribute to the development of mental health disorders. Substance abuse issues, trauma, hormone imbalance, lack of community, and conflict are just some of the stressors that can cause the state of our mental health to suffer. These factors are not new to the 21st century and yet, as our sense of community, purpose, and connection to nature declines, we lose our ability to cope and find balance. And without the tools to look at our current state of well-being with curiosity, compassion, and care, we move into patterns of avoidance. We find ourselves turning a blind eye.

## Turning A Blind Eye: Doing vs. Being

One pattern of behavior that is prevalent in the 21st century is our focus on 'doing' rather than 'being'. This inability to 'be' with what is present becomes a pattern of avoidance. We find ourselves incapable of mindfully sitting with the mental health challenges we face both personally and collectively to a large degree. This is avoidance coping, which the American Psychological Association defines as:

*"Any strategy for managing a stressful situation in which a person does not address the problem directly but instead disengages from the situation and averts attention from*

---

[12] https://www.ncbi.nlm.nih.gov/pmc/articles/PMC2568977/
[13] https://news.berkeley.edu/2014/02/11/chronic-stress-predisposes-brain-to-mental-illness/

*it. In other words, the individual turns away from the processing of threatening information."* [14]

We avoid our negative or uncomfortable feelings, which diverts our attention away from the issues that hold us back – whether individually or collectively. Perhaps we hope that this will make the issue go away, though as most of us can attest to, this is never the case.

But where does avoidance come from? Why do we manage our challenges this way? There are likely to be a number of factors that play into this, but two that stand out are stigma and the very complexity of the problem.

Mental health stigma still pervades in our society, despite the increase in campaigns such as 'mental health awareness' month. In our own private worlds, we can intuitively sense that an incredibly high percentage of the population struggles with emotional and psychological issues (whether manageable or debilitating). And yet, we still find sharing our challenges uncomfortable and daunting. Perhaps this is because we don't know what to do about them, or maybe it is because we fear the multitude of entangled contributing factors that lead to poor mental health in the first place.

If we do decide to face our mental health challenges with an open mind and heart, we quickly realize the complexity of the issue. We start to sense that the modern way of living creates mental suffering in countless ways, through lack of community, loss of natural landscapes, socioeconomic inequality, and increasing technologization. This realization can indeed be overwhelming, making it feel easier for some of us to avoid it all together.

Of course, discomfort is another reason we turn a blind eye to our suffering. In the modern age, many of us were not taught how to *be with* our emotions – how to honor the pain, refrain from creating extra suffering, and effectively and compassionately move forward.

---

[14] https://dictionary.apa.org/avoidance-coping

We were largely taught that certain emotions are 'bad' while others are 'good', leading us to suppress, deny, or fear the ones deemed to be undesirable.

> *"People have a hard time letting go of their suffering. Out of a fear of the unknown, they prefer suffering that is familiar."*
>
> Thich Nhat Hanh

I am reminded of a friend and colleague of mine, a very bright guy who hit a rough patch in his relationship – hardly a rare scenario in modern marriages. While under social and economic pressure to stay within that marriage, he chose the "avoidance route" about the whole situation. He started taking on so much responsibility at work that it would keep him away from home for days at a stretch – up to 25-28 days at a time. I was still working in the IT industry then, so our paths would often cross at industry conferences and every time I saw him, he would be a little more jaded, a little louder and drinking just a little more than the previous occasion.

Finally, one day I decided as a true friend that I needed to raise this issue with him so I invited him to my room after the conference we were at and brought up the subject, which I saw as a "ticking time bomb" of stress and alcoholism in his life. On suggesting to him that he should seek help, he brushed me aside by telling me how he was meeting and exceeding all of his goals, both professionally and financially. He basically questioned me; *"If I were really stressed and tired and needed help, how could I put in a stellar performance, quarter after quarter?"* I summed up by telling him I cared, and that I was there for him if he ever needed to talk or for references about resources to seek help.

Fast forwarding to 9 months later, I heard from a common acquaintance that my friend had been arrested for domestic violence, and spent a couple of nights in jail, lost his job, got divorced and literally had to leave the country to find employment overseas due to all that he now had on his record. It's been about 16 years since then and he has not been able to work his way back into the

US. I recently met up with him in Turkey and he said something which I thought we could all do well to keep in mind, and I quote:

*"....you know how the story of boiling the frog goes... you keep turning the temperature up slowly... and the frog keeps hanging on, saying to himself that he can handle it. All the way to the point that he just cooks alive, no longer able to jump out. I was like that. But you know that the funny thing is, I even had the temperature control in my hand. I could have saved myself and my family but I just didn't see it that way then, and now it's too late."*

So, the moral of the story is: don't boil yourself to death, metaphorically speaking of course, especially if the temperature control is in your own hands. It almost always is!

This is where mindfulness and meditation come in. Through mindfulness of our thoughts, feelings, and emotions – and through formal meditation practice – we begin to develop a new relationship with our human experience. Rather than avoiding the challenges we face, we are able to *be* with the painful aspects of this human experience. Ironically, this helps us to better witness, revel in, and experience gratitude for the good.

Mindfulness and meditation are often mistakenly considered to be practices that make us feel 'good' and while they often do in time, this is not their purpose. The objective of both mindfulness and meditation is to help us be with what is *right here* – good, bad, painful, or pleasant. Because as Carl G. Jung said:

> **"One does not become enlightened by imagining figures of light, but by making the darkness conscious."**

The value of course lies in the "how" of the assertion above, which we will address in the next several sections. Right now, my goal is for you to "form an intent" and "have the context" for all the practices we will deepen as we go along.

## The Pursuit of Perfection

Another underlying characteristic of our 21st century way of living is the expectation of perfection. When we are unable to hold our perceived darkness, we reinforce the belief that we must be free of it all together – absent of any struggles or flaws. Perfectionism leads to feelings of shame as we question our innate worth and goodness. In the words of Brené Brown:

> *"Perfectionism is the belief that if we live perfect, look perfect, and act perfect, we can minimize or avoid the pain of blame, judgment, and shame. It's a shield. It's a twenty-ton shield that we lug around thinking it will protect us when, in fact, it's the thing that's really preventing us from flight."*

A psychological profile that goes hand in hand with the pursuit of perfection is called the **imposter syndrome**. A term coined in 1978 by clinical psychologists Pauline Clance and Suzanne Imes, imposter syndrome describes a pattern of behavior in which people doubt their achievements and have an internalized fear that they are a fraud. Those with this pattern of perception have a sneaking suspicion that they are not good enough as they are, and that at any minute their inadequacy will be revealed by their peers. This leads to self-directed shame and a fear of humiliation.

Studies have found that imposter syndrome often presents itself alongside depression, anxiety, and low self-esteem. Interestingly though not surprisingly, it has also been associated with impaired job performance, decreased job satisfaction, and burnout.[15] At the same time, many high-achievers experience this syndrome too, suggesting that the way we navigate or cope with self-doubt can vary. If we recall the three possible stress responses, we will remember that in the face of stress (in this case, internalized doubt and shame) we either fight, take flight, or freeze.

Yet in our most objective moments, when the veil of self-doubt clears even if only for a moment, we are all able to acknowledge that the greatest opportunities for growth are found in our struggles. Attempting to live flawlessly and without error means missing out on the chance of developing our skills and accessing greater insights.

It may be helpful to note that imposter syndrome can and does effect very successful and seemingly confident professionals. I have worked with clients that run large enterprises, some of whom are even in senior positions of leadership in running a country, and I have found strands of this affecting them in subtle ways, constantly nibbling at their inner peace.

Both mindfulness and meditation can help us to witness and lovingly embrace our yearnings for perfection that contribute to shame, depression, anxiety, and other mental health disturbances. Embracing these yearnings does not mean we make them 'right'; it simply asks us to honor that they are there and to bless them with our compassion. Through offering ourselves this gift of acceptance, we pave the way for greater well-being.

## Loneliness and Lack of Purpose

This crisis is almost entirely a gift of our increasingly individualized lifestyle and what makes it very difficult to address is that while it is "felt" by a large number of people, the profession of mental health has not yet developed a rigorous diagnosis for it. It is often categorized as depression or anxiety – which may simply be side effects of much more complex ontological issues that underpin the lived experience of many.

Some aspects of this loneliness and lack of purpose have been touched on in earlier sections. As you can intuitively gather, the three epidemics are highly interwoven, each one impacting the other to certain degrees. For instance, poor mental health can lead people to isolate themselves, increasing the likelihood of experiencing loneliness or compounding mental health concerns. Stress can lead to physical and mental exhaustion, resulting in poor mental health and a lack of motivation to maintain and nurture supporting relationships.

The same interdependency can be considered for our individual well-being: our physical health impacts both our emotional and mental state of well-being, and vice versa. Mindfulness practice helps us to intuitively understand this interconnectedness, which can empower us to better care for all aspects of our being – mental, physical, spiritual, and emotional.

When it comes to the rising sense of loneliness and lack of purpose in modern day life, we can consider two key contributing factors: the disruption of social constructs, families and communities, and the rise of technologization – distancing us from our own inner self.

## The Breakdown of Families and Communities

Cohesive family units and communities have been disintegrating over the past few decades. In 2018, 35.7 million single-person households made up 28 percent of all residences in the United States. That's a considerable increase from 1960, when only 13% of all households were occupied by single persons[16]. In Sweden and Finland, more than 40% of households are now single occupancy.[17] It can be noted that this trend towards a greater percentage of single-person households is more prevalent in affluent countries.

Now, it must also be remembered that living alone is not the same as loneliness. That being said however, research does suggest that living alone may be associated with an increased risk of emotional loneliness. One study found that those who lived alone did not experience an increase in social loneliness, yet they did feel more emotionally alone and isolated from family members.[18]

Is living alone a predictor of loneliness then? It seems that the answer isn't clear as we experience a different type of connection and support from colleagues, friends, and family members. However, the concern of increased loneliness and isolation is worth considering as our lives center more around technological connections and less

---

[16] https://www.census.gov/newsroom/press-releases/2018/families.html
[17] https://www.ncbi.nlm.nih.gov/pmc/articles/PMC4985072/
[18] https://www.sciencedirect.com/science/article/pii/S0167494318302462

around true face time. These two ways of connecting with our support networks are not one and the same.

One very strong argument that goes against living alone being a predictor of loneliness is the "hermit" or "monastic" argument – where you would find monks and hermits living in near total seclusion but still profoundly connected with everything around them. And when you meet them, you can feel that their presence is completely warm, welcoming and reassuring. So what makes this difference?

While I am no psychologist, I would venture to speculate that loneliness is often seeded by lack of connection "with our own inner self", which begins with our thoughts, emotions and even the physical body.

If we can profoundly connect with our own 'self', mirroring this in our relationships in life can be that much easier.

There is another aspect that is somewhat ignored in the modern world, which is the increasingly limited interaction we have with nature. It's the beauty and warmth of nature, which is inherently meant to nurture us like a mother, that we share with all of humanity. But this facet of modern life has been somewhat under-appreciated – let's delve into this briefly.

Alongside the increase in single-occupant households in the last century was a decline in traditional rural communities, a key driver of which was the agricultural revolution[19]. As agricultural systems became increasingly mechanized, urbanization boomed and people began flocking to the cities. A new form of community developed, of course, as people continued to gather, share, and do business.

Yet something was lost in the movement towards the cities, and that was the care for and connection to the earth. Our sense of community is not complete when we only consider it to be imperative that we have our friends and loved ones near to us; our community

---

[19] https://graylinegroup.com/urbanization-catalyst-overview/

must include the earth we stand on, the water we drink, and the air we breathe.

In his book, The Unsettling of America: Culture and Agriculture, poet and author Wendell Berry writes:

> *"The soil is the great connector of lives, the source and destination of all. It is the healer and restorer and resurrector, by which disease passes into health, age into youth, death into life. Without proper care for it we can have no community, because without proper care for it we can have no life."*

It is no wonder that our concern for the state of nature is rising in collective consciousness now. Our own well-being depends on the well-being of the earth, and our communities suffer when we are not centered around that principle.

Furthermore, our lack of holistic, healthy communities makes it difficult for us to understand our role or purpose in this life. Many of us trudge to jobs we feel uninspired by or disconnected from, unable to envision any alternative. Does this mean we must return to the farm and tend to the land to gain a sense of purpose? No, but it does invite us to consider:

*How can we cultivate a stronger sense of community where we live and work?*

*How can we put our personal gifts, interests, and talents to best use?*

*How can we contribute to wholeness and healing, both within and around?*

Through mindfulness, we can start to connect the dots between ourselves, our work, and nature once again, realizing that everything is indeed interconnected. As we support, nourish, and mindfully explore any one aspect of our lives, we support and nourish the rest.

In subsequent chapters, we will look into some mindfulness practices that enable us to form this bond again, especially through Mindful Eating and Mindful Walking.

## The Rise of Technologization

We can say that in many ways, technology has supported our well-being. Yet as our pursuit of unending technological advances has consumed us, we've started to realize that much of it is contributing to our new age 'suffering' or as Buddha would call it, *'Dukha'*. It's a double-edged sword as we can see that society is now dependent on the very technologies that threaten to disconnect us from our innate capacity for peace and presence.

Social media is a front-running technology that has contributed to an epidemic of loneliness and lack of purpose. As social connections move online, we spend more time glued to our phones than we do face-to-face. In becoming increasingly dependent on virtual communication, our in-person social skills are neglected, contributing not only to loneliness but to anxiety, too.

*In my conversations with my young clients, I find that many of them have thousands of Facebook friends but would struggle to list a handful that they see more than once a month. Interesting, right?*

Studies have demonstrated that excessive screen time has negative effects on self-control, curiosity, attention, emotional stability, and task completion in children[20]. It has also been discovered through research that increased social media usage results in a decrease in individual self-esteem[21]. None of this is likely to come as a surprise. Intuitively, most of us can sense that social media and excessive use of personal devices results in a decrease in presence, inner peace, and vitality.

Furthermore, the increase in technology and automation leaves us wondering: what is our human role in all of this? As technological advances make more and more jobs obsolete, fewer of us are working with our hands and finding meaningful employment. What this calls for is a mindful return to the values and aspirations that are innately human: culture, creativity, curiosity, and compassion.

---

[20] https://www.ncbi.nlm.nih.gov/pmc/articles/PMC6214874/
[21] https://eujournal.org/index.php/esj/article/viewFile/9815/9318

As we make a mindful commitment to harness these capacities within us, we redevelop a sense of belonging. What is the culture we long to be a part of? How might we use our creativity to build a better world? What can we get curious about? What calls for our compassion? When we ask ourselves these questions with heartfelt concern, we may be surprised at the insights, ideas, and solutions that emerge.

## Where Mindfulness & Meditation Can Take Us

What these three modern day epidemics are is a wake-up call; an invitation to return to the presence, beauty, love, meaning, peace, and compassion that lives within each of us. Though many of us might feel overwhelmed by stress, mental health challenges, loneliness, or a lack of meaning and purpose, all is not lost. We can consciously choose to see our challenges as opportunities and strive to overcome them.

Mindfulness and meditation are often considered to be an antidote to our woes, which is somewhat paradoxical because in mindfulness and meditation practice the intention is not to 'fix' things. They help us to be right here, right now; not in some idealized vision of the future.

Having said that, these practices offer us tools of resilience, adaptability, insight, wisdom, and compassion that can help us to forge a more harmonious way forward. Their benefits do not arise overnight, but if you are in it for the long haul, you will come to see the depth they have to offer.

Beyond helping us to 'feel good', mindfulness and meditation offer us the opportunity to reconnect with who we really are, with the world beneath and around us, and with a greater sense of community and purpose. As we dive into these practices, we realize that they influence every aspect of our lives – from physical and mental health to work dynamics and personal relationships. At their core, mindfulness and meditation are about cultivating the virtues that make life all that it can be – all that it is.

As you delve into this work, note the difference between the quantity and quality of your practices. Pushing yourself through a 30-minute seated meditation without full presence is likely to have less of a grounding, restorative effect than a few 5-minute, heartfelt, daily practices. At the same time, remember that it is okay if you do not feel present during a practice. This 'non-presence' or mental scattering can be observed along with anything else that arises for you. Maintain curiosity and compassion towards your experience, regardless of what comes up.

Depending on your present state of being, you might gravitate more towards mindfulness practice than meditation, or vice versa. Neither is better than the other; what matters is what works for you.

For example, people with tight muscles, painful conditions, or attention deficit disorder might prefer body scan and progressive relaxation practices. Those with high adrenaline, increased sympathetic nervous system function, or copper toxicity (which can result in poor focus, anxiety, and other challenges) might gravitate towards mindfulness practices such as MBSR (mindfulness-based stress reduction).

Meditation, on the other hand, requires a relatively deeper concentration and is often preferred by people who have a more passive frame of experience or who do not get easily overwhelmed by sensory experiences (i.e. sounds, movement, smells). Meditation is also frequently sought after by those who are looking for a transcendent experience.

Regardless of which practices you feel inclined towards, you will begin to experience the benefits when you are committed to and focused on the work. As you begin this exploration, note where the mind might attempt to grasp at some desired state or attempt to avoid what is uncomfortable. Harness patience and compassion as you explore whatever arises, trusting that the gifts of these practices will be revealed over time.

**Suggested ayam$^{(TM)}$ practice:**

Mediations :  Calm, Sleep Well

Essentials : Peace and Calm, Breath Awareness

# CHAPTER 2

Horizontal Axis and Vertical Axis

I must admit, I was conflicted about starting the book by talking about challenges and crises, which are not really happy subjects. But I eventually concluded that it was perhaps needed to convey the sense of urgency. Now with that behind us, I wish to pivot in this chapter to the more aspirational and inspirational part of the journey through this book.

Actually, just before we do that, let me make one last point. The major lesson of Chapter 1 was that none of the 3 epidemics we discussed represent a *healthy state of being.*

If we agree with that, then the question arises: what is the heaviest cost that these epidemics exact on us?

I have personally felt that the greatest casualty of the three epidemics is our aliveness: our experience of being fully awake to, and integrated with, the 'wholeness' of life; having the presence of meaning, light and joy!

So what does this *'being fully awake'* mean? What does the *'wholeness of life'* look like?

Especially beyond our immediate experience, our opinions, our stories, our likes and dislikes, as well as our emotions, what is that more profound understanding of life that awaits us? An experience that is not limited by our own identity or individual history. These are eclectic pursuits with no fixed answers. But let's begin by asking ourselves:

*What is my relationship with macrocosm?*

*What is my role in the social fabric of life?*

*How can I thrive in all aspects of life?*

As we contemplate what the bigger picture of life might include, we realize that mindfulness and meditation have the power to take us beyond psychopathology, which is the scientific study of mental disorders and commonly used as a way of measuring the benefits of mindfulness and meditation. Under this lens, these practices are reduced to their quantitative ability to decrease markers of depression, anxiety, addiction, stress, and other mental health concerns.

While this is indeed a worthy use of these practices (and though quantitative analysis certainly has its place), it does not cover the full spectrum of what mindfulness and meditation can offer. This lens does not take positive psychology into account, which is the study of the positive aspects of life that contribute to flourishing, happiness, and meaning. These things are harder to measure (though not impossible) and tend to be overlooked.

But is life only about managing and mitigating pain and suffering? Or might we ask ourselves:

*How can I live in such a way that makes me feel fulfilled?*

*How can I cultivate more meaning in my life?*

*What is my purpose in the broader picture?*

Let's explore this by jumping into the two planes of reality that help us to better understand the goal or purpose of both mindfulness and meditation.

## The Horizontal and the Vertical Life: Mindfulness vs Meditation

Earlier in the book, we were introduced to two dimensions of life: the horizontal plane and the vertical one. If we were to put them on intersecting axes (see image at the end of this section) and mark our current 'location' on both the vertical and the horizontal, the space inside the lines would represent the fullness of our lives. As we grow in both domains, our life becomes more whole.

As I briefly mentioned in the Introduction, one of the common threads of conversation I have with participants in my classes is around distinguishing between *Mindfulness* and *Meditation*. In popular culture, the terms have been used interchangeably and, in some ways, one could argue that there is nothing wrong with this synonymous usage as both are equally important for the well-being of humanity. And this would be OK, as long as they don't have the constraining effect of limiting what tools, techniques and paths of self-mastery become available to the learners.

In the West, the modern context of Mindfulness has been dominated by the MBSR (Mindfulness Based Stress Reduction) framework and techniques, which were earlier popularized by the work of Dr. Jon Kabat-Zinn in the healthcare setting. Dr. Kabat-Zinn is a pioneer in every sense of the word, and laid the foundation for organized training, exploration, research and most importantly, popularization of MBSR or other ancient systems.

That being said, it must however be noted that while the foundational principle of MBSR draw on Buddhist underpinnings, especially the Vipassana meditation anchored in the *Satipatthana* method, both MBSR and MBCT offer a fairly limited set of practices and not the immense richness as propounded by *Sama Sati* practice by Buddha in the Noble Eightfold Path.

MBSR and MBCT both use Body Scan, Progressive Relaxation and Breath Awareness as their anchor practices and are great interventions for countering stress and several other health conditions. While that in itself has a great outcome, it is not the original goal of *Sama Sati,* or Right Mindfulness, as anchored in the Buddhist doctrine. Within the larger context, the aim is the realization of the impermanence of the body, thoughts and feelings, leading to 'liberation from suffering' and access to a much more peaceful experience of life.

So in some ways 'stress reduction' is a positive side effect of Mindfulness, although not its central pursuit. In simple terms, all I am saying is that 'much more is possible' with a disciplined Mindfulness practice, far beyond the gift of stress reduction!

Meditation (when engaging the *subtle body*), on the other hand one could argue is more effectively anchored in Vedic tradition, some of which has been integrated into Buddhist practices as well. The goal of meditation was also not aimed at stress release or the balancing of our mental well-being, but rather the *"unfoldment of our inner self"* and *"access to wisdom"*. Furthermore, there are many techniques and paths of meditation; the Buddhist path being only one of them, albeit a very powerful access in itself.

MBSR and MBCT both refer to their sitting practice as meditation which some puritanical scholars would argue, is not the same as in as understood in the Vedic context. Another myth that has taken hold more recently is that only the modern context of mindfulness has been studied scientifically for its positive effect on our neurobiology and heath at large. This is totally incorrect: over the last several decades, different meditation techniques have been studied and found to have a substantial positive impact For example, I would like to mention Transcendental Meditation as taught by Mahesh Yogi, popularly referred to as TM, which was extensively studied when it was made famous by The Beatles. Other notable systems include the Twin Heart Meditations of Pranic Healing, Zazen from Zen Buddhism, Kriya Yoga Meditations and many other eastern systems.

Summing up, I would like to quote one of my Tibetan teachers, who once told me, *"...practicing meditation or mindfulness solely for stress release is like becoming a parent for the sole reason of being able to buy and play with toys..."*

That being said, Mindfulness and Meditation are very intricately interlinked and in some ways arise together and complement each other. To illustrate this concept more generally, I would like to use the metaphor of the Horizontal and Vertical lives.

As you can see in the figure below, the vertical axis represents the path of meditation whereas the horizontal axis represents the path of mindfulness. Though we may focus on these pursuits separately and unlock a lot of value for ourselves, we cultivate the most joy, meaning, fulfillment and sense of connection to our lives when we explore them simultaneously or as I like to say, *synchronously*.

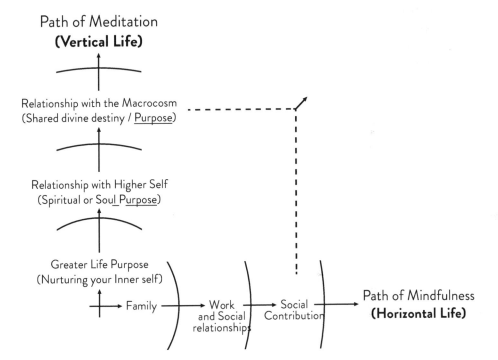

## The Path of Meditation

The path of meditation, corresponding with the vertical life, takes us on a journey within our consciousness beyond our physical body and sensory stimulus, to other levels of our 'being'. Along this path, we connect with our higher self, integrating ourselves into the macrocosm – the broader picture, the universe. This is the path of transcendence or self-realization, which is engaged through meditation.

Along this path, we connect with levels of 'being' - beyond the body, beyond our emotions, and beyond our senses. While we are still aware of our individual sense of self, we begin to see ourselves as a layered consciousness that is interconnected and shares purpose with other beings and the environment around us. This is the path where we nurture faculties like intuition, inner knowingness, psychic awareness, sensitivity to right choices, greater discernment and discrimination. We could sum it up as saying that we have a more intimate understanding of the nature of our life and the reality of macrocosm in which we live.

This concept of the vertical axis, which corresponds to the path of meditation, arises predominantly from Vedic tradition (though it's not exclusive to it, we can find parallels in several ancient lineages including esoteric Christianity, Kabbalah, Sufism, Paganism, etc.). In Patanjali's Yoga Sutras, eight limbs of yoga are outlined. The final three; dharana (focused concentration meditation), dhyana (awareness meditation), and samadhi (consciousness of union), together constitute samyama. When we master samyama, we attain a higher level of consciousness[22], much of which is fueled by the vertical axis.

Furthermore, when we turn to the Upanishads, which are ancient Sanskrit texts, we encounter the concept of Brahman. Brahman is understood to be the source of knowledge, encompassing the microcosm and a macrocosm[23]. The individual soul or self is called Atma, whereas Brahman represents the collective soul. And so, our individual soul is a part of the world soul[24].

We can also consider the very term yoga itself to gain a sense of what this body of knowledge is founded on. Though modern day yoga has become largely a practice for the physical body, its roots run much deeper than our individual personhood. Explored in its truest form, yoga is a practice of expanding consciousness.

---

[22] Naikar, C. (2002). Patanjali of Yogasutras (p. 82). Sahitya Akademi.
[23] Parthasarathy, A. (2014). Choice Upanishads. A. Parthasarathy.
[24] Frauwallner, E., & Bedekar, V. (1973). History of Indian Philosophy. Motilal Banarsidass.

The term yoga is derived from the Sanskrit root *yuj*, which means 'to yoke'. Various Sanskrit words derived from this root have meanings such as 'to be linked to', 'to meditate', and 'to recollect'[25]. Most commonly, 'to yoke' (as it is related to yoga) equates with 'to unite'. Yoga is therefore a practice of unity, bridging the perceived gaps between mind, body, and soul. In classical yoga, meditation, not postures, is at the center of the practice.

Various forms of meditation have risen out of Vedic schools of thought, largely focusing on this vertical axis. Transcendental meditation, chakra meditation, kundalini yoga/meditation, self realization meditation, self healing meditation and sound meditation are a few of the many. Almost all seek to unify one's ego (the lower self) with soul (the higher self).

So, another way to understand the above is that, when we explore the vertical dimension of life through meditation, we move away from our individual self to consider our place in the broader lens of life. We transition into the realm of soul. It begins with a turning inwards to nurture our innermost self and to connect with a greater life purpose. What is it we are here for?

This helps us to cultivate a spiritual purpose, or soul purpose, as we connect with our higher self, beyond the limiting confines of the ego. As we do so, we deepen our relationship with the macrocosm, connecting with the understanding that this earthly collective shares a common destiny. This is what unites us.

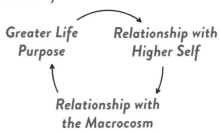

Greater Life
Purpose

Relationship with
Higher Self

Relationship with
the Macrocosm

All of this unlocks an intuitive impression of what our larger purpose in this incarnation might be. What lessons are to be learned here? What is my karma, meaning what am I meant to integrate, contribute, or understand in this lifetime? These intuitive impressions help us to uncover our soul purpose, which considers that our life is within a series of many. What we do now contributes to our collective evolution, which is where our relationship with the macrocosm comes into play.

As we grow in this dimension, we move towards greater meaning, liberation, and purpose in our lives. Life is no longer about overcoming hurdles; it is about living fully awake and being completely alive to this human experience.

This growth also enables us to access deeper levels of peace, kindness, compassion, creativity, focus and gratitude in life amongst many other virtues – all worthy pursuits for all of humanity!

## The Path of Mindfulness

On the horizontal axis, the path of mindfulness is a commitment to *present moment awareness – being fully alive in each and every moment.* This journey is one that liberates us from the pain of the suffering we experience when we engage too much in the impermanent aspects of life (such as thoughts, feelings, and emotions). It is a journey towards *'being present in the here and now'.*

In one way, it might not make sense to call mindfulness a journey or a path. Mindfulness in and of itself can only occur in the present moment, and yet the path is the continual unfolding of our ability to be present. Since, as humans, we tend to struggle with judgments, a racing mind, irrational fears, and other 'less than present' patterns of thought, mindfulness is something that we cultivate more and more overtime.

Buddhist doctrine leads us along the path of mindfulness, including through related meditations. Various techniques of mindfulness are referred to in the Satipatthana Sutta, such as mindfulness of breathing, walking, eating, and drinking[26]. Buddhism also introduces us to the four foundations of mindfulness:

- Mindfulness of the body (kaya)

- Mindfulness of feelings (vedana)

- Mindfulness of mind (citta)

- Mindfulness of mental objects (dhammas)

In addition, one of the core teachings of Buddhist philosophy is that of the five aggregates[27]. These factors, or aggregates, expand upon the above foundations to deepen our awareness of our experience. The five aggregates are:

1. Form (*rupa*) – the physical world, consisting of the physical body and the rest of the material world

2. Sensation (*vedana*) – feeling or sensation categorized into pleasant, unpleasant, and indifferent (or likes, dislikes, and neutrality)

3. Perception (*sanna*) – recognition or interpretation of sensory objects followed by the labeling or conceptualizing of these recognitions

4. Mental formations and habitual tendencies (*sankharas*) – mental actions that are formed by volition or are a conditioned response, creating karma

5. Consciousness (*vinnana*) – awareness or cognizance with the ability to discern

Mindfulness of each of these factors (also referred to as aggregates of clinging) helps us to observe our experience with greater clarity. It enables us to witness our reactions to life from a place of non-attachment and non-judgment.

---

[26] https://www.accesstoinsight.org/lib/authors/soma/wayof.html#mindfulness
[27] https://www.accesstoinsight.org/lib/study/khandha.html

Though it is a personal practice, mindfulness impacts the way we engage with the external world – our families, our work lives, our social networks, and our community at large. Therefore, it is not a journey of self-realization but one of being in greater harmony with ourselves and our surroundings. As we become more mindful of ourselves, our family dynamics, our work and social dynamics, as well as our engagement with greater society begin to shift.

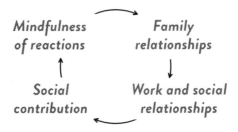

*Mindfulness of reactions*     *Family relationships*

*Social contribution*     *Work and social relationships*

Because of the ability of 'mindfulness' to help us become more attuned to the present moment (and to our reactions to life), it enables us to become more peaceful citizens as we engage in the social fabric of society. When we are mindful of how we respond to the world, we can no longer overlook the impact we have on the well-being of others around us. It becomes natural to consider:

*How can I live in greater harmony with my partner or family?*

*How can I have a more positive impact in the workplace?*

*How can I contribute to the well-being of those suffering?*

While these questions might start to come easy, changing our behavior is not quite as effortless. The mind is well-versed in creating excuses, quickly making justifications for our 'standard behavior'. This is not to say that our typical mode of being is 'wrong' or 'bad'. However, when we wish to evolve, stepping out of our comfort zone and our habitual patterns of thought requires commitment, courage, patience, and full presence.

The more we practice, the more aware we become of our habits of thought that impact who we think we are, what we think we are capable of, and what we believe about others and the world. Mindfulness in effect strips us of attachment to any thought, feeling, or emotion, helping us to witness whatever we are experiencing through a clear lens.

By training ourselves to be 'here now', we surrender our tendencies to reimagine or fix the past and to jump anxiously into the future that has not yet arrived. This ability to be present naturally ripples into all corners of our life, helping us to become more compassionate, attentive, nurturing, peaceful, and equanimous. It helps us to embody more of who we truly are in the physical world of relationships, exchanges, and experiences.

## Maximizing the Experience of Being Alive

As we grow along both axes, we naturally start to maximize our experience of being alive. Explored hand in hand, mindfulness and meditation help us to grow in both dimensions. Not only do we start to feel more whole within ourselves and in our community, but we also start to see the world through a broader lens. We integrate our individual consciousness with that of the whole.

Take a moment to look at the previous graph that shows the vertical and horizontal paths intersecting. Where do you sense you currently exist on each axis? Where would you plot yourself on the graph? If you were to draw two lines – one from your data point to the vertical axis and one to the horizontal axis, how large would the box be?

When you make this inquiry, know that maximizing our experience of life is not a race or competition. Each of us has room to grow, to develop along either or both axes. This is simply a tool for reflection; a useful check-in to see where we might be deeply yearning to grow.

As you journey further along both of these axes, the rectangular or square box created beneath your data point begins to grow. Life becomes more fulfilling, more harmonious, and more integrated.

To maximize your journey in the best way possible, aim to grow along both the horizontal and the vertical axis in synchronicity. This will help you to feel firmly rooted in both your human experience and in the universe at large. Much of modern day self-development focuses on the horizontal plane, helping us to function more harmoniously or successfully in our relationships, our work lives, and our communities. While there is nothing wrong with this approach, it lacks the bigger picture of soul and spirit.

On the other hand, a focus on the vertical dimension of reality can be witnessed in spiritual seekers who renounce the material world completely. While there is nothing wrong with committing wholeheartedly (and exclusively) to the spiritual world – to consciousness and transcendence – this approach hinders our ability to establish deep and meaningful relationships with the rest of the human community.

To be in this physical world while also maintaining a sense of the higher and more subtle realms of consciousness comes when we commit to both paths. It is an outdated paradigm to think we must choose one or the other. In fact, in order for us to thrive as a collective, we must learn to meaningfully grow in both realms, along both axes. This is the task that will guide us towards a rich, full, and expansive life.

While this is a simple and elegant pursuit, walking this path requires disciplined practice and the first step of this journey is exploring, discovering and acknowledging – *what is so* in our lives right now. We will discuss this theme in the upcoming chapter.

**Suggested ayam$^{(TM)}$ practice:**

Meditations: Joy, Abundance

# CHAPTER 3

Maximizing the 360 Degrees of Life

Nothing maximizes our life more than fulfilling our greatest potential and purpose. However it's not very easy to realize what our greatest potential may look like.

Let me share with you a story from my life.

I was training under a meditation teacher who came from a lineage of hermits, meaning monks that lived alone and renounced all forms of material life. Once, I travelled with him to Haridwar to meet with his teacher: I will call him Babaji (it's an honorific many old sages are given). While attending his *Kirtan* on the banks of the Ganges River, I made friends with a Brazilian woman, let's call her Claudia. She was on her way to Rishikesh, where she was going to spend a year in residency at an Ashram and train to be a breatharian.

A breatharian is a person who does not need to eat or drink to nourish their body: they receive all nourishment from the breath and use different breathing techniques to harness the energy of elementals to nourish all aspects of their being. I was very intrigued and fascinated by the idea and decided to accompany her to Rishikesh. On arriving there, I met with the teacher – a truly wonderful person and no doubt a highly evolved being.

I requested him to take me on as a student as well, promising him that I could return a year later for residency too if that is what was needed. He heard me out and then gently smiled and said he was going to tell me a story that I might have read earlier but which will make more sense now.

So he began the story:

*"There was a monk who was traveling through the plains of India when he heard of a very enlightened holy man who was rumored to walk on water. On arrival, the monk witnessed the walking on water ritual attended by hundreds, all applauding and bowing in salutation when the holy man emerged on the opposite bank of the river after having crossed it by walking over its surface. When the crowd dispersed, the traveling monk approached the holy man and requested permission to ask him a question.*

*The holy man consented but warned the monk that he could ask anything apart from how to walk on the water, because it had taken him his entire life to master, and wasn't something he could teach the young monk. The traveling monk immediately agreed, looking much relieved, and approached the holy man with folded hands, asking him most humbly: 'Oh, enlightened one, would you please tell me why a wise man like yourself invested his entire life in learning a skill, whose purpose and use I can fulfill by just paying 2 rupees (Indian currency) to the boat man ?'"*

Needless to say, I did not follow through with the full year residency, though I did stay long enough to learn some of the breatharian techniques – a story for another time. But the point I am making right now is that *"choosing your purpose of life"* is almost as important as working to fulfill it. While walking on water may be a great accomplishment, it has only so much use in modern life. Maximizing life begins with choosing a purpose that is worthy of you.

Now, getting back to our earlier conversation, to fully maximize our experience of life, we need to take a mindful look at every aspect of our lives at present – including the ones we have neglected. Though we might have adopted certain roles in life that prioritize particular domains over others, we need to tend to all facets of life in order to feel fully alive and truly balanced. Linear lives, focused on only one aspect of humanity, are limited; what we need is to awaken to the multi-dimensional nature of our experience.

There are seven corners of a multi-dimensional life we can take a look at to better assess how we can maximize our life in tangible ways:

a. Health and Wellness

b. Family and Intimate Relationships

c. Career and Professional Contribution

d. Social Relationships and Engagement

e. Self-Development

f. Contribution to Society

g. Spiritual Growth

Let's explore these in more detail and reflect upon how much of our own love, energy, and attention has been granted to each of these corners. Remember: there is no need to judge or condemn whatever realizations come to our awareness. Approach this as a process of compassionate inquiry, guiding you to tend more attentively to those areas that require your presence and care.

## Health and Wellness

*"Health is a state of complete harmony of the body, mind and spirit. When one is free from physical disabilities and mental distractions, the gates of the soul open."*

B.K.S. Iyengar

True embodiment of health and wellness is holistic, reflecting the well-being of mind, body, emotions, and spirit. It is a state we experience when we are not only absent of illness but also in optimal, vibrant condition. We fuel our experience of health and wellness through the foods we consume, the people and ideas we surround ourselves with, the strategies of self-care we adopt, and movement.

For each one of us, the inputs and outputs we require in order to thrive in this dimension of life are unique. For instance, some of us might thrive on a protein-rich diet, while others feel more alive with a greater intake of carbohydrates. Likewise, some of us might feel at our physical 'best' when we practice intense cardio, while others might find more balance in slower movements, such as Tai Chi and yoga.

Some questions we might mindfully contemplate or register in order to better assess where we stand in this dimension at present include:

- *Are my food choices contributing to a sense of health and vitality?*

- *What physical nourishment do I intuitively sense I might be missing?*

- *What inputs – food, drink, or other substances – are weighing me down (if any)?*

- *Do I hold any thoughts or beliefs that limit my sense of well-being?*

- *What forms of physical movement nourish me?*

- *Is my physical body getting what it needs?*

- *Is my mental body getting what it needs?*

- *How do I practice self-care?*

- *On a scale from 1-10, how would I rank my present moment aliveness in this dimension of life?*

Use the space below to make notes of any insights or reflections that arise upon reflection of your current state, needs, and desires for health and wellness.

_____

_____

_____

_____

_____

_____

_____

_____

## Family and Intimate Relationships

*"Love in such a way that the person you love feels free."*
Thich Nhat Hanh

Another dimension of life that reflects how well we are thriving is the realm of our family and intimate relationships. How strong are our connections to those closest to us? To flourish in this corner of life does not require that we have a 'big, happy family' or that we are in an intimate partnership at all. Feeling nourished by this corner of our lives simply asks us to consider honestly and courageously what the current state of our closest relationships are. It might also include reflection on what we yearn for if there is a key relationship missing from our experience.

Practically speaking, what each of our relationships require is unique, as we all find ourselves in different circumstances that shift throughout our lives. However, some of the fundamental values we can look out for when we are assessing the health of our intimate and family relationships include compassion, patience, kindness, openness, acceptance, curiosity, and care.

Some questions we can reflect upon to gain a better understanding of how well we are doing in this dimension include:

- *Do I feel safe to express my feelings, needs, and desires with those closest to me?*

- *Do I provide a sense of safety to my loved ones, assuring them through my actions that they can be open and honest with me?*

- *Do I honor my partner and other family members as individuals entitled to their own dreams, visions, and goals?*

- *Do I feel unconditionally accepted by those closest to me?*

- *Where might there be room to improve my current relationships? What qualities might my relationships be yearning for?*

- *On a scale from 1-10, how would I rank my present moment aliveness in this dimension of life?*

In the space below, write down any reflections or insights that arose from this contemplation.

_____

_____

_____

_____

_____

_____

_____

_____

_____

_____

_____

## Career and Professional Contribution

*"Strive not to be a success but rather to be of value."*

Albert Einstein

To thrive in our career or professional life means to feel fully integrated with the work we are doing. At the workplace, we embody a role. How well does that role suit us? Does it make us happy? Does it push us to be all that we are? Many people struggle to find a sense of ease and contentment in their work, so tending to this dimension of life is important for many of us.

In order to feel good about what we do, we want to feel (whether consciously or unconsciously) that there is a purpose to what we are doing. Sometimes, in order to find the purpose and meaning we are after, we feel a call to pursue a new job or career entirely. At other times, we are required to shift the relationship we have with the workplace itself. Only we ourselves can know what the best course of action is in these moments.

Some of the questions we can ask ourselves to better assess how integrated we are with the work we are doing include:

- *What type of contribution does my soul yearn to make through professional work?*

- *What value do I add to my organization and its products or service?*

- *What are my skills, gifts, and unique talents?*

- *Is there room for me to grow in my profession?*

- *Does the work I do make me feel alive and connected?*

- *Am I giving my professional life and career aspirations the best of me?*

- *On a scale from 1-10, how would I rank my present moment aliveness in this dimension of life?*

Use the space below to reflect upon any of the above questions to better assess how well this dimension of life is contributing to your aliveness.

_____

_____

_____

_____

_____

_____

_____

_____

_____

_____

## Social Relationships and Engagement

*"Each friend represents a world in us, a world possibly not born until they arrive, and it is only by this meeting that a new world is born."*

Anaïs Nin

Engaging in the social nature of relationships reminds us of our interconnectedness with all living beings. When our social relationships are supportive and nurturing, we start to develop the web of community. It is not enough to be self-sufficient; we all require social bonds to thrive.

What we each gain from, and share with our social networks, varies to some degree. However, the basic principles remain the same. Some of the values and characteristics of a thriving social dimension include respect, care, support, joy, gratitude, and trust.

To gain a better sense of how well we are being supported and nurtured by this dimension of life (and how much energy we are granting to it), we can reflect upon questions including:

- *Do the social relationships I have nourish my mind and soul?*

- *Am I able to express myself in my social networks?*

- *Is the direction of energy in my social relationships a two-way street?*

- *Do my social connections inspire me to learn, to grow, and to be all that I am?*

- *Are my friendships based on kindness, compassion, support, and respect?*

- *On a scale from 1-10, how would I rank my present moment aliveness in this dimension of life?*

You can use the space below to reflect upon the current state of your relationships.

_____

_____

_____

_____

_____

_____

_____

_____

## Self-Development

*"What we fear doing most is usually what we most need to do."*

Ralph Waldo Emerson

While our intimate relationships, our families, our work lives, and our social circles can all be agents that contribute to our growth, self-development is a private affair; it must come from within. Self-development (not to be confused with spiritual growth) requires a willingness to learn and a commitment to pushing our own boundaries. It is the process by which a person's character, skills, or abilities develop overtime.

Some examples of self-development include mastering a skill, cultivating and embodying a particular virtue, and developing greater control over our habits. It's about seeing where we can grow as a human in this life and then taking steps in the direction of our highest pursuits.

Some of the questions we can ask ourselves to determine how well we are flourishing in this dimension of life include:

- *What skills or virtues am I committed to or interested in developing? How committed am I?*

- *Am I aware of the self-limiting thoughts and behaviors I hold and am I willing to explore these?*

- *Do I believe it is possible to grow, change, or live in a different way?*

- *Am I curious about my thoughts, my beliefs, and my assumptions about myself and the world?*

- *Am I excited to see who I can become or what I can achieve?*

- *On a scale from 1-10, how would I rank my present moment aliveness in this dimension of life?*

In the space below, take a few moments to reflect upon how attentive you currently are to the dimension of personal development.

_____

_____

_____

_____

_____

_____

_____

_____

_____

## Contribution to Society

*"A healthy social life is found only when in the mirror of each soul the whole community finds its reflection, and when in the whole community the virtue of each one is living."*

Rudolf Steiner

Another dimension of our lives is the contribution we make to society. We each have a role to play, whether seemingly small or large, all of which have powerful ripple effects. The contribution we make to society can be found in everything from parenting and tending to the earth to offering goods and services or donating our time to causes that matter to us. Our societal contributions ultimately come from the totality of our actions.

When we consider our contribution to society, it is important to think about not only the tangible offerings we make – such as our professional lives or our volunteer work. It is equally important to consider what values we add through more subtle ways of being. What values do we promote through our interactions with friends and family? How do we share the love that lives within us? Every action resonates and so we all have an impact on our communities, whether we are conscious of it or not.

Some questions you can reflect upon to consider your own contributions to society include:

- *What impact does my work life have on the community and the world at large?*

- *What impact do my words make on the world around me?*

- *In what ways do I express my love, care, and consideration for all of life?*

- *What do I yearn to offer to this world?*

- *How might I expand my societal offerings in ways either subtle or strong?*

- *On a scale from 1-10, how would I rank my present moment aliveness in this dimension of life?*

Use the box below to jot down any reflections that arise when you consider how much care and attention is being granted to your societal contributions.

_____

_____

_____

_____

_____

_____

_____

_____

## Spiritual Growth

> *"The only journey is the one within."*
> Rainer Maria Rilke

The degree to which we grow spiritually occurs along the vertical axis. This is the spiritual wisdom dimension of our lives that is intimately connected to the path of meditation and insight. Mindfulness fuels this growth too, but ultimately it is the path towards transcendence that strengthens our understanding of our innate spirituality.

Whether we connect with religious, energetic, or secular understandings about our existence, spirituality is alive within all of us. We do not need to believe in specific deities or dogma to understand that we are all intimately connected. Our spiritual journey is the recognition of our interconnectedness and the realization that there is more to life than meets the eye.

To assess how much energy is being granted to our spiritual dimension of life, we might consider the following questions:

- *What is my relationship to or understanding of the word 'spirituality'?*

- *How much attention do I give to pondering the mystery of life?*

- *Do I have teachers or resources that I can turn to in order to explore a deeper meaning of life?*

- *Do I have a spiritual practice? How committed am I to this practice?*

- *Do I nurture my spiritual well-being and growth?*

- *On a scale from 1-10, how would I rank my present moment aliveness in this dimension of life?*

You can use the space below to write down some notes about your current level of care for and attention to spiritual growth.

_____

_____

_____

_____

_____

## Finding Multi-Dimensional Balance

Chances are, there is more energy flowing into certain dimensions for you than into others. If this is the case, it is entirely natural. We all have certain inclinations, needs, or interests at various times in our life that tend to take up a greater share of our time and energy.

That being said, finding multi-dimensional balance is crucial to our holistic well-being. An unbalanced life can lead to a meaningless, lackluster, or 'bankrupt' success. For instance, we might have a great career life but feel little connection to our loved ones or our social network. Likewise, we might feel great devotion to our family but lack a feeling of personal growth or greater purpose.

When we have dimensions that are starved of our attention, we often encounter crises later in life. Since everything is subject to change, we strengthen our inner foundation and resilience by ensuring that we are attentive to all corners of our life. Examples of common turning points that can lead to this inner experience of 'starvation' include:

- Grown children moving away from home and parents now seeking new meaning and purpose

- Midlife crises when the reality of having an 'ordinary career and life' sets in and other dimensions of life have not been tended to

- Experience of loneliness in later life if relationships have not been nurtured

- Experience of feeling lost in life if there is no connection to or even consideration of a greater purpose

- The ending of an intimate relationship where a strong social network has not been cultivated

- The loss of a job, leaving a 'career person' to question what else fulfills them

The list could trail on for quite some time. Whichever dimensions of life we fail to give our care and attention to can result in a sense of starvation when we reawaken to the value of this dimension (which often occurs through painful circumstances). All of this is why mindfully assessing our contribution to each dimension is crucial to building a full and vibrant life.

## Creating a Life Scorecard

After you've reflected on each of these dimensions with care and curiosity, you can go on to create a life scorecard to gain a more tangible sense of where your attention is required. Scorecards can be created in a number of different ways and do not need to be empirical (though sometimes numbers can help us to assess where we're at).

What scorecards ask us to do is to consider how we will measure our lives and what legacy we wish to leave behind. They ask us to consider the question: what is most important?

Take a moment to reflect upon each of the seven dimensions once again, considering what you wish to achieve or experience in relation to each. Every aspect of your life will need to be fulfilled differently. Having this range of aspirations helps us to keep ourselves in balance.

To assess how you might bring greater balance to your life, make note of the areas that are currently lacking sufficient care, attention, time, and energy. You might refer back to your previous reflections if you ranked how alive each dimension felt on a scale from 1 to 10

| Dimension | How will you measure your life? What impact do you yearn to make? What legacy will you leave behind? |
|---|---|
| Health and Wellness | |
| Family and Intimate Relationships | |
| Career and Professional Contribution | |
| Social Relationships and Engagement | |
| Self-Development | |
| Contribution to Society | |
| Spiritual Growth | |

Write down these areas in the space below and make a few notes about how you will offer yourself to these areas. Note that sometimes this means that other dimensions will have to give up some of the energy they take from you. This is all a part of the balancing process.

| Dimension that requires my attention | Ideas about how I will nurture this aspect of my life |
|---|---|
| | |
| | |
| | |
| | |

When you are finished, take a moment to connect with your heart as you close your eyes and take a few deep breaths. Ground yourself into this present moment for two to three minutes and then read on.

## Developing Purpose and a Deeper Meaning in Your Life

I invite you now to consider that today is the first day of the rest of your life. Why? Simply because it is. Starting now, you can choose all over again what you want this journey to be about. Set aside any ideas about who you were, who you think you should be, or what barriers hold you back from experiencing a full and radiant life. Connect with the highest self within you that knows who you *really* are and what you are capable of.

## Personal Vision, Mission, and Goals

Establishing our personal vision, mission, and goals in life is crucial to creating the one we so long for. These three concepts act as guiding lights to keep us focused on what it is we most yearn to experience and contribute to in this lifetime. Though there may be some debate about how each of these three notions are defined, what is important is that we think in all three categories. So, let's consider how we might interpret these terms.

Firstly, let's consider that your **vision** represents the larger landscape of your life. It takes an overarching view of the values and virtues you wish to be aligned with. Your vision is thematic and qualitative, and therefore not easily measured. It is something that only the heart is able to assess with accuracy.

Next, your **mission** is the distant goal you long to achieve. It clearly reflects your vision but also includes tangible achievements you hope to one day make. It is not necessarily something you are actively working towards now, but it is something that your present steps will naturally guide you to overtime.

Lastly, your **goals** are clear, actionable, and driven by your vision of the nearer future. They can contain both qualitative and quantitative aspects. They are things you can work towards in tangible ways now even if it might take some time to achieve them. Your goals embody the energy of both your vision and mission and yet they require that you take concrete steps today.

To clarify these, let's consider an example. Take Sally for instance. Sally is a nurse with three young children. Driven by her longing to care for those who can't care for themselves, her vision is to bring greater patience and compassion to this world. She believes in the power of kindness and generosity. Her vision is to run her own care facility that interweaves medicine and spirituality to bring holistic healing to those who are ill. Her present goals are to deepen her knowledge about Buddhism by studying with a teacher and to practice patience with her growing children each and every day.

Now, consider your own personal vision, mission, and goals as if you are starting from scratch. Nothing is impossible; your life awaits you. Take some time to reflect on what it is you want to experience and share in this lifetime and then construct a personal vision statement, a mission statement, and a set of three goals.

As you reflect upon your vision, you might consider questions such as:

*What values and virtues are nearest to your heart?*

*What does your innermost self long to contribute to this world?*

*What do you think the world needs more of that is aligned with your gifts?*

As you reflect upon your mission, you might consider questions such as:

*Where do you long to be physically, mentally, emotionally, and spiritually in 20 years?*

*What tangible contributions do you want to offer to this world?*

*What image of the future reflects your overarching vision?*

And as you consider your goals, you might reflect upon questions including:

*What will get you to where you want to be in 20 years' time?*

*What steps can you take today that will serve your mission and vision?*

*What do you wish to achieve by next year?*

Take as long as you need to reflect upon these questions and whatever else comes to mind. When you are ready, write down your statements below.

## PERSONAL VISION STATEMENT:

_____

_____

_____

_____

_____

_____

_____

_____

_____

_____

_____

## PERSONAL MISSION STATEMENT:

_____

_____

_____

_____

_____

_____

_____

## THREE GUIDING GOALS:

1. _____

_____

_____

2. _____

_____

_____

3. _____

_____

_____

## Global Consciousness

*"Our deepest fear is not that we are inadequate. Our deepest fear is that we are powerful beyond measure. It is our light, not our darkness that most frightens us. We ask ourselves, 'Who am I to be brilliant, gorgeous, talented, fabulous?' Actually, who are you not to be?"*

Marianne Williamson

As you move towards your overarching vision, remember that you are intricately interwoven into this global consciousness. What you do matters since everything – even the smallest of actions – has a ripple effect that eventually moves through the entire collective consciousness. What you do now is not inconsequential. You hold a power far greater than you know.

By bringing your life into multi-dimensional balance and by forging your way along both the path of mindfulness and the path of meditation, you broaden your understanding of both yourself and the world. Each step you take along this journey contributes to the evolution we are all yearning for, whether we realize it or not.

This is not a revolution, which would forcefully overthrow our existing beliefs and existing structure. It is a mindful and natural transition into a new way of being. Nothing needs to be forced because our hearts are already yearning for it. Each day we have a choice: to contribute to our personal (and therefore collective) evolution or to remain the same. What choice will you make today?

## Leaving a Legacy

None of us will be here forever, but the ghosts of our actions in this lifetime will remain. Everything we do today and in the days to come, counts for something and so, by committing to this evolution, we inspire all the lives that are yet to be lived.

When we truly come to recognize the impermanence of life, we have the opposite reaction of what we might expect. Many of us fear this impermanence, thinking that to embrace it would mean that nothing we do matters. However, it is to the contrary: *everything we do matters.*

*Your* life matters, so make it count. Continually refer back to your vision, your mission, and your goals (editing or readjusting them as needed) to reconnect with what it is you want to both give and receive in this lifetime. Why? Because life is about more than overcoming our difficulties or simply coping. It is meant to be lived fully; it yearns to see us thrive.

Mindfulness, or present moment awareness, will help you to stay focused on what matters. It will enhance your clarity of the worlds within and around you. Meditation will help to nurture your inner self, deepening your connection to the universe and to your soul purpose. It will help you stay aligned with what is most important to this highest self, helping you to progress further along the vertical path.

As you journey through this book, you will learn the tools and techniques you require to impact all of the dimensions of your life outlined above. Cultivate continued patience, compassion, courage, and a deep willingness to learn as you explore the practices and insights ahead. The fullness of your life awaits.

### What has Meditation and Mindfulness got to do with it

I am going to take some creative liberty here and surmise that what I have understood as the purpose of the journey of mindfulness and meditation, very simply said, is: *crafting the greatest life possible.* A life of joy, great health, service, self development and spiritual unfoldment. While the insights and moments of illumination will arrive for us in deep contemplation, we must bridge them into action to fully manifest their impact. This now becomes the domain of *'intentional action'* – not when our eyes are closed but then we are fully checked into life. This is why, before immersing in learning the 'techniques and practices', I have attempted to provide you with a framework and broaden the scope of how you might think about your life and all it contains!

As they say, well begun is half done or, as we say in meditation, *it's your intent that is important.*


**Suggested ayam<sup>(TM)</sup> Practice:**

Meditations:  Joy, Vitality

Essentials : Breath Awareness, Gratitude, Goodwill

# CHAPTER 4

The Hygiene of Learning: How to Use This Book

Most of us have had that experience of recommending a book or a practice that touched us deeply to someone, only for them to have a lackluster response to it, at best. When things move us, we want to share them, but what another person takes from what we share is beyond our control.

Let me take a moment to share a recent experience I had. About a couple of years ago a former colleague of mine was going through a relationship transition. He was deeply disturbed and highly self-critical about what he called "failing at the relationship" and was beginning to develop a short temper as well. In one of our conversations over coffee I recommended to him, very predictably I might add, that he try meditation to access peace and develop resilience. He seemed genuinely interested and promised to follow through. After a few months he called and left me a very grateful voicemail about how his life had completely changed by following my advice on meditation. I was of course very happy for him and immediately felt that is a testimonial for meditation I should probably ask for and with that intent in the background, I called him the next morning.

And I opened by asking him the leading question of *how his meditation practice was going* and he stunned me with his answer; *"...oh, I am not meditating any more! It never worked for me, I could never focus for more than a couple of mins,"* so now I was thoroughly confused and I guess he sensed it and continued:

*"...meditation didn't work but your advice did. The studio where I signed up for a meditation class also offered a class on Buddhist chanting...and in the chanting class the participants told me I have a great voice so I*

decided to go to a Karaoke bar to give it a try. And at the Karaoke bar I met a girl, we really hit it off. And we are now engaged. Thank you so much for recommending meditation to me... or I would have never met Alice! And now I am happy, I no longer need meditation!"

Needless to say, I didn't quite know what to reply to him at that moment except for, "I am so happy for you!"

So the point remains, people get what they get from the advice you share with them or experiences you recommend to them. There are a variety of reasons why this happens. Personal beliefs, expectations, attention level, attitude, as well as curiosity about the subject matter are just some of the factors that influence how a certain reading or teaching is perceived. And while we can't dictate what another person brings to any given resource, we can be mindful of our own attitudes and beliefs as we move through the material that interests us.

If you've arrived at this page of the book, chances are you are ready to learn about how mindfulness and meditation can empower all facets of your life. In order to get the most from this material – to maximize your learning potential – there are a few different mindsets and perspectives you can cultivate. First and foremost? The beginner's mind.

## The Beginner's Mind: Beginner vs. Expert

> "In the beginner's mind there are many possibilities, but in the expert's there are few."
>
> Shunryo Suzuki

Regardless of where we find ourselves in our personal journey, we are all beginners. Even experts are beginners from the point at which they stand. Since no one ever truly 'arrives' at the end of the journey of self-discovery, it is safe to say we are all on the path. The next step for each of us is always a new beginning.

The beginner's mind is a Zen concept that refers to an attitude of openness to the present moment, without preconceptions or assumptions, just as a beginner would hold. No matter how many times we've practiced a particular meditation, we are always coming to it from a new place and in a new moment.

Consider, for example, a mindful eating exercise. Typically, such a practice invites us to investigate a small piece of food (sometimes a raisin or a berry) with all of our senses. We step into this practice each time with complete openness to what the experience will be like. Have we eaten a raisin or a berry before? Of course. But have we eaten this particular berry, in this particular moment? No, this is the first, and so at this moment, we are beginners.

Likewise, we may be accustomed to performing body scans, having developed a regular, formal practice of checking in with how the physical body feels. However, each time we perform a body scan, we come to it in a moment we have never experienced before. Each body scan is therefore an invitation to explore how the body is presenting itself *today* and each day, each moment, provides us with a newness to be fully present to.

Maintaining this degree of curiosity and openness is crucial to staying fully awake, receptive, and present to our experience. I have frequently seen long time meditators struggle to maintain this beginner's frame of mind. It is not uncommon for those who have studied a specific type of meditation, such as Vipassana or Transcendental Meditation, to approach a practice from a place of knowing. A thought like, "Oh yes, I know how this works. I have been meditating for 20 years," can stand in the way of being fully open to the present moment.

When we hold onto the feeling that we are an expert, we might find ourselves comparing teachers and practices or critiquing certain techniques. This inhibits us from fully opening up to whatever the present experience or technique might offer. As we evolve, we become mindful of even this tendency, and so there is often a return back to the beginner's mind, when this sort of inner attachment to being an expert has arisen.

One encounter I had many years back that wonderfully exemplifies how even experts can cultivate a beginner's mind was when I met with a well-renowned yoga expert in the United States. At that point in time, I was hardly any expert; I was still learning the basics of meditation and was attending his training to increase my knowledge and deepen my practice.

In a private meeting with this long-standing teacher and 'guru' to thousands of other established practitioners, I shared a few breathing techniques that I thought might help him with a health issue he was experiencing at the time. Indeed, he found it to be of great benefit, so much so that he went on to refer to it in public during the training I was there to attend. He shared that he had learned something new from me that would accelerate his healing and that he hoped I would let him teach it someday.

I was surprised to say the least. His openness and receptiveness to the knowledge of someone who clearly had far less experience than himself was touching. But when I think about it more, why should I have been surprised? All he cared about was learning, and he was pleased to have been introduced to a 'new technique' that made him feel far better than he had in a while. To this day, I consider this to be one of the most inspiring examples of humility: a world-renowned expert who had powerfully cultivated the openness and unknowingness of a beginner's mind.

## What to Bring to Each Section and Exercise

As you move through this book, I invite you to do so with the following five principles in heart and mind. Being human, you will likely falter somewhere along the way, perhaps judging your racing mind or becoming frustrated with the process. This is entirely natural and entirely okay. Simply do your best to note where you drift away from the following suggestions and then come back to the way of thinking and being that will be most supportive of your journey.

### 1. Non-Judgment

As you move through each section and exercise, cultivate an attitude of non-judgment as much as possible. This does not mean you will never have a judgmental thought about a particular notion, exercise, or your experience; rather, it is an invitation to become more aware of the judgments you make.

There are many things you might adopt judgments about. For instance, you might consider a particular practice to be impractical or silly. You might judge yourself for not being 'good enough' or for feeling certain emotions. Or, you might assign 'negative' labels to some of the ideas put forth in this book. Whatever is the case, see where you might notice judgment arising and where you might soften those assumptions to become more receptive to the power of these practices.

### 2. Patience

Another virtue I invite you to cultivate while reading and practicing is patience. Patience is the capacity to be with the process as it unfolds rather than wishing for it to move faster than it yearns to naturally. Most of us will experience impatience somewhere along the way. This can happen because the mind is usually quicker than the heart and body to understand a new principle or practice. We might rationally grasp an idea first, but that principle can take some time to fully incorporate itself into the core of our being.

Trust that as you move through this book (and as you move through life for that matter), you are always where you need to be. This can be difficult to accept when we are in the midst of inner chaos, and yet there is always something to be learned, wherever we are. Adopting an attitude of curiosity and openness can help us to enjoy the ride – regardless of how fast or slow we appear to be moving.

### 3. Beginner's Mind

As mentioned, coming to this work with a beginner's mind (regardless of how long we've already been practicing meditation or mindfulness) is paramount if we want to get the most out of these teachings. When we believe we already understand how life, our inner workings, and these practices function, we will be far less receptive to new possibilities.

You can easily harness your beginner's mind by noting that each moment is a first. You have never been in this exact moment at any point in your lifetime. So, with that in mind, what is there to explore? Remember that everything we explore in mindfulness and meditation is in relation to this present moment. How does my body feel *right now*? What emotions are present *right now*? How can I better convey this message *right now*? Stay present and the beginner's mind will naturally rise to meet you.

### 4. Individualized Experience

Furthermore, it is important to remember that your experience of this book and these practices is entirely personal. That is to say, the way you experience a particular meditation will be different to the way I might experience it and, because life is in constant flux, these experiences for each of us will change from moment to moment.

There is nothing 'fixed' expected of you in these chapters and their practices. There is nothing 'specific' you must feel, gain, or adopt. What works for you is personalized, and this is free to change as time goes on. Honor your own present moment needs and intuition as you delve into this work.

### 5. Compassion for Yourself

Last but undoubtedly not least, hold compassion for yourself as you work through these chapters. Mindfulness and meditation are incomplete without this virtue, and so even if imperfectly, it is imperative that we remember to love and honor ourselves throughout this process. No one else can do that for us; it is up to us individually.

Some of the exercises here will be challenging. Some might even be provocative, depending on what we are presently experiencing and what beliefs we hold. Regardless of what rises (or what doesn't rise), remember that you are unconditionally worthy of love and acceptance. Be kind and gentle with yourself, minding as best you can the silent words you speak to your inner world.

## Tapping Into Our Unlimited Potential

The truth is simply this: *We each have unlimited potential to grow along both the horizontal and vertical axes.*

Whatever the mind might suggest as barriers to our growth are exclusively mental objects that need not hold the weight we think they do. When these mental objects are brought into the light of awareness, we are able to pass beyond the thoughts, habits, attitudes, and belief systems that would otherwise limit us. Much of this power is in your mind, and through practice, you will become increasingly adept at seeing the thought patterns that hold you back and superseding them.

There are no profound secrets you need to search for and no hidden keys you require to unlock the gifts of these practices. The core teachings of mindfulness and meditation are innately simple and are by no means reserved for mystics and monks. The mindfulness and meditation practices outlined in this book are enough to deepen and expand your world in infinite ways. All that is required is patience and practice.

Now, it is important to remember that knowing something intellectually, talking about it, or being able to describe its technical underpinnings does not make us an expert at it. Nowhere is this truer than in the realm of mindfulness and meditation. It is through practice – through the time we dedicate to being present for these exercises – that true transformation is possible. Just as art or film critics are not experts in the way that the creators of these art forms are, not all meditation researchers or neuroscientists hold the same depth of understanding as those who put the time into the practice.

What does this mean for you? That your commitment to showing up will deepen your practice in ways beyond what the mind can comprehend, explain, or rationalize.

Moment to moment, we are given the opportunity to show up in our practice – and that is where the magic happens. Start by letting yourself be present and watch these practices deepen and unravel in unexpected ways.

I wish you many happy days of practice and an amazing journey of unfoldment!

# SECTION 2

Living in the Here and Now: Mastering
the Basics of Mindfulness

Mindfulness is first and foremost about living in the here and now – in the only time and space we ever really experience. Sounds simple enough, but however counter intuitive to how it sounds, accessing the "present moment awareness" is not easy – it's a journey of experiences and disciplined practice.

As we commit to this journey of living life with greater awareness of the present moment, we begin to embody the benefits that these ancient and powerful (though simple) practices have to offer. But where do we begin? As the famous Chinese proverb goes, "A journey of a thousand miles begins with a single step."

Mastering the basics of mindfulness is where this journey starts. Though we might come to these teachings with a yearning to develop more harmonious work relationships or to learn how to communicate more effectively with our intimate partner, the work must begin within. As we harness our capacity to be mindfully aware of our own experience (i.e. our experience of the breath, the body, our words, and our thoughts), we strengthen our ability to apply these principles to the relationships we have with those beyond ourselves, specially along the Horizontal Axis we discussed in earlier chapters.

## Journey From Living With a Full Mind to Being Mindful

In this section of the book, we will learn about and practice the core techniques and principles of mindfulness. Through our understanding of and commitment to these basic practices, we will develop the groundwork from which ever-deepening mindfulness insights and applications can grow.

One of the first realizations we need to have in order to begin this work is something we each already recognize to one degree or another. That is, that the mind is full of thoughts, feelings, and emotions that are not easy to put down. None of us are immune from this fact. Each one of us has experienced the persistence, stubbornness, and enchantment of the mind.

The journey into a more mindful way of living is about transitioning from this place of living with a *racing mind full of thoughts*, to one in which we are *mindful (or aware) of the present moment* as it unfolds. This includes awareness of thoughts, emotions, physical sensations, the breath, and the world around us. These things are always present in the full mind, albeit hidden below the layers of noise in life. It would be great to notice how often we intentionally recognize *the raw nature of what is here.*

To exemplify this, we might consider a mind that is full of anxious thoughts along the lines of; "People will mock my creative work if I put it out there for all to see." Mindfulness of this full mind would invite us to notice the emotion underlying this thought (i.e. fear), the pattern of the breath, the way this fear manifests in the physical body, and the nature of the words we are speaking to ourselves.

As you become more aware of your experience in this way, you will gain a broader perspective of any situation you find yourself in. The full mind might still arise from time to time, but it's ability to control us (our thoughts, our words, our body, and our emotions) will be drastically decreased.

The more committed you are to the basics, the sooner the benefits of mindfulness will arise – and stick. Benefits are varied and vast, including but not limited to greater emotional regulation, improved communication skills, decreased stress and anxiety, increased sense of self-worth, increased immunity, improved cardio health and sleep quality. There is really no end to the reach of mindfulness.

The subsequent chapters in this section are laid out below to indicate what will be covered as we explore these core techniques.

- **The Breath and the Body**

    This chapter will explore the history of breath awareness and highlight the link between the breath and the body-mind vessel. Though the breath is not always in the forefront of our awareness, bringing our attention to it has a profound impact on our physiology. Body awareness practices, too, are influential in regulating various physiological processes, and so this chapter highlights core practices to increase mindfulness of both breath and body.

- **The Mindful Trinity: Mindful Movement, Mindful Eating, and Mindful Walking**

Though mindfulness is often associated with stillness, it is just as applicable when we are in movement. This chapter outlines how mindfulness applies to the three essential engagements of our day to day life: movement, eating, and walking. You will be introduced to some of the history of these practices before being guided to apply mindfulness to them in practice.

- **Mindful Language**

Expanding into the way we communicate with others, this section explores the power of the words we speak – both internally and externally. Like anything else, words carry their own energy frequency, and so they undoubtedly have an impact (either positive or negative) on ourselves and those we engage with. We'll look at how the tone, pace, and word choice itself impacts our physiology before moving deeper into how mindful language can be explored in the workplace. As in each chapter, this section will include practices to enhance your mindful communication skills.

- **Observing Your Thoughts and Feelings**

This final chapter of the section takes a look at how we can become more mindful of our thoughts and our emotions. It looks at the nature of our thoughts being rooted in the brain's neural network and explores one model, the Ladder of Conclusion, that can help us to be more mindful of our own biases, conclusions, and decision-making processes. Furthermore, it highlights how our thoughts have the capacity to increase suffering through the Buddhist notion of the first dart and the second dart.

As you deepen and expand upon your capacity to be present with each of these manifestations of experience, you will marvel at the capacity you hold to transcend outdated and limiting ways of thinking, acting, and living. We each hold far more power than most of us were raised to believe, and so through these teachings and practices, we bring to life that strength and vitality we were born to uncover.

Remember, the very act of living is experiencing the present "now", each moment as it flows from future to past.

# CHAPTER 5

The Breath and The Body

*Breath is the elixir of life, savor every sip. For it just flows through you moment by moment, you own nothing*

Dr. Leo Rastogi

A young student, *Duli*, is walking alongside his wise teacher, *Partho*, in the forest to a neighboring village. They come across a river they must traverse; it is shallow and the current is slow, so they quickly walk up to the shore. Just as they are a few steps away, they notice an old man lying at the bank of the river, not moving.

Partho walks closer up to the man to check if he is breathing, with an obvious intent to ascertain if the man is still alive. He quickly notices that while his breathing is shallow and labored, the man is surely breathing. Full of compassion and kindness towards him, Partho asks Duli to help him move the man under a tree for shade but just as they grab him, the man shoos them away.

Surprised, Partho asks; *"O my good man, are you well? We are but trying to save your life"*, to which the man lets out a sigh and replies. *"Would you please let me be, for I am awaiting the one from heavens to arrive and claim back the breath they sent me to this world with, for this is the last debt I must pay before I am liberated."* Taken aback by this utterance, Partho responds, *"Sadhu! Sadhu! Sadhu!"* and gestures to Duli to follow him across the river.

When on the other side of the river, Duli, who is amazed by this exchange, asks Partho the following questions:

*"Who gives us breath? And who decides how many we have left?"*

*Where does the breath reside in our body?*

*If breath is all that makes us alive, is it true we have no control of our life?"*

Partho smiles at his young pupil with twinkling eyes and responds, *"Welcome to the path of Nibbana – now we are searching for the same answers!"*

This story may sound much like an adaptation from a Vedic text or an ancient Buddhist anecdote. But, what if I told you I made it all up based on a conversation I had with my father (a Buddhist scholar) on a train ride while visiting his college, and the only thing true is the questions I (aka Duli) asked.

And what did my father answer? Well, it doesn't matter, but let's just say that a few years into the future, I found myself receiving training as a breatharian (I talked about it briefly earlier): training that prepares you to be able to give up all physical possessions, the need for clothes, shelter, food and even water, being able (and trained) to sustain yourself just on the *breath!* Truly out-of-this-world stuff, and seeming almost surreal to me now as I look back at that phase of my life!

That being said, the point remains that *breath* truly is the elixir of our life. In fact, the only *deterministic reality* of our life, as philosophers will call it, is that it begins with a breath, ends with a breath, and has a finite number of breaths in between.

So, the simple act of inhaling and exhaling is the profound experience of being alive; of living. Everything else that happens around it is what we could call our impermanent sensory experience. Sometimes, we mistake it as "life".

But most of us are so engrossed in the *Maya* of this sensory experience of taste, touch, sight, smell, thoughts and feelings etc., that the act of 'inhale-exhale' is relegated to a subconscious and automatic action. So much so that, within a few years, we begin to forget the art of breathing itself.

When I have new participants in my meditation classes or retreats, one of the first exercises I work on with them is 're-learning to breathe fully'.

Breathing is not simply the act of inhaling oxygen and exhaling carbon-dioxide, with some biochemical processes in between. It's actually a much more complex and multi-dimensional energetic process. It is an intentional act of rejuvenation and renewal, moment by moment, of our whole being, including our body right down to every cell, our vitality, energy, emotions and mind.

We inhale not only oxygen, but also the bio-plasmic life force of nature, which in yogic systems is called *"prana"* from the air. This is why we feel more rejuvenated when we inhale the fresh air of a setting in nature as compared to even pure oxygen in, let's say, an oxygen bar in Tokyo.

Most of our meditative and contemplative experiences have breath at the center of them, so we will begin our immersion into experiencing, nurturing and mastering the techniques of mindfulness and meditation, by beginning to cultivate a profoundly new relationship with our breath.

The techniques laid out in this chapter are easy and elegant. The value lies not in "understanding them" but undertaking rigorous practice so that they become just simply an innate nature for us.

Most of the practices I discuss in this chapter are also available as guided practices in the AYAM app, especially in the daily essentials section. So, let's begin by briefly exploring some ideas around it derived from ancient wisdom.

## The History of the Breath

As we discussed above, breath is perhaps the first sign of life! Right from the moment we were born, we take our first breath, expanding our lungs, and our breath has been and will remain our constant companion until our time is up in this life. It's central to the experience of being alive, in fact, ironically, so much so that we almost take it for granted, and yet we can't last a minute without it.

The art and science of breath as a subject is so wide and ancient that no one book can do it justice, never mind a chapter. However, in the next few pages we will explore it in the specialized context of this book and section specifically.

If we want to explore the history of the breath and the roots of this life force as it pertains to mindfulness and meditation, we need to keep an open mind. Often, our understanding of the breath in this context gets filtered into a single teaching or tradition when, in reality, no single culture holds ownership of this fundamental energy. Like ancient trees, the root system of the breath is complex and vastly interwoven.

The beauty of the breath in human life is that the *act of breathing* is pretty much automatic, not requiring any conscious effort or thought, so it keeps working, often silently, in the background as we go on with our day to day lives. And just herein lies its greatest irony.

While it does not *require* our attention to function, getting to know the techniques, science and art around it can tremendously benefit our well-being in numerous ways. Many of these benefits have been scientifically looked at in modern times, but ancient traditions and cultures understood the breath's importance long before the scientific revolution.

You may already have some idea about certain traditions and cultures where our understanding of the breath holds roots. From ancient India and China to Greece and Egypt, countless cultures explored and understood the power of the breath thousands of years ago. And of course, the breath itself is not a new invention; it's been with us since the dawn of time. So, it makes sense that people from all around the globe began to look beyond the mere physicality of it and into its energy force and healing potential.

To highlight just a few different traditions and practices of breathing, we can consider the Sanskrit term *pranayama* (intentional breathing practices), the Chinese practice of *Qigong* (involving intentional breathing, meditation, and movement), and the Egyptian term *Smai* (the science of breathing). While the specific practices in each of these traditions may have been different, they each harnessed the same underlying energy force.

Most of these cultures also speculated about 'breath' being an access or connection to the path of spiritual experience or illumination. Nearly all monastic practices in the last 5000 years have included rituals, practices and even disciplines intermediated by intentional breathing practices, for example: the use of Rosary beads (or their equivalent) in most branches of Abrahamic faith, the Vedic chants with breath as a count or modern Buddhist breath meditations.

Even within single cultures, breathing practices often broke off into varying branches. For instance, Buddhism gave rise to both Vipassana and Zen techniques that use the breath in different ways. To put it simply, Vipassana focuses on the physical sensations of the breath (expanding out from there) and one Zen breathing technique involves 'observation of breath count', or *sūsokukan*[28]. This type of observation is paired with abdominal breathing.

In the eastern esoteric systems at a crossroads of Hindu and Buddhist practices, we encounter the science of Kundalini yoga, which is yet another example of breathing philosophy/techniques, taking a unique shape and form as compared with other peer yogic branches. While there are certainly overlaps between Kundalini and those of other yogic branches, there are differences in the way these are practiced and explored. *Breath Holds* and *Mantras* are often used in Kundalini meditation to produce different effects and energetic awakenings. Furthermore, the intense and dynamic 'breath of fire' is a fundamental component of Kundalini practices and is said to strengthen the nervous system, purify the energy meridians, and increase energy and vitality.[29]

---

[28] https://plato.stanford.edu/entries/japanese-zen/
[29] Shakti Parwha Kaur Khalsa. (1998). *Kundalini Yoga: The Flow of Eternal Power.* New York: Penguin.

The larger point I am trying to make here is that regardless of the lens through which we view the breath, it's clear that no single culture, religion, tradition or region of the world can take credit ownership of it. The breath came before human consciousness could observe, label, and manipulate it. Then, through unique paths, each tradition uncovered different ways of witnessing, moving, and benefiting more fully from this dynamic life force.

## The Link Between Breath and Body-Mind

*"Breath is the bridge which connects life to consciousness, which unites your body to your thoughts."*
Thich Nhat Hanh

As Thich Nhat Hanh points out, and as many other traditions understand it, the breath is a bridge between the physical and the subtle. It connects that which is seen with that which is unseen. As such, the breath plays an important role in both body and mind and, both body and mind have a role to play in it. The breath is interwoven with every single part of us, so it's natural and graceful functioning helps to keep us flowing as we're meant to.

On the most profound level, breathing engages all physical organs, all energy layers (or auras), and all energy centers (or chakras). Though the breath begins locally in the respiratory system, its energy is felt throughout the entire body, as well as in layers beyond. It might be hard to wrap your mind around this broader vision as we often experience the breath within only the nostrils, the chest, and the belly. However, as all things are made up of energy, and all energy interacts with the energy next to it, the breath ripples out in all directions and influences the functioning of everything. Breathing well therefore has a deep cleansing and calming effect that can be harnessed as we tune into it.

Becoming more attuned to this vital life force is the work of breath awareness. It is the first step in exploring the balancing and healing potential of the breath because, if we are unaware of how the breath flows, we will be unable to meaningfully engage with it.

## Breath Awareness

Breath awareness is the simple, though profound act of paying attention to the breath. Moment by moment, we watch the flow of air into and out of the body, remaining observant of its path, its pattern, and any sensations it presents. We might start by noticing the *inner breath* (the breath as it circulates within the body) and then expand our awareness to include the *outer breath* (the more universal life force that supports the dynamic relationship of all living things).

This intimate knowledge of the breath is highly valuable because the breath says a lot about our present state of well-being. The way we breathe impacts our experience of peace and calm as it influences our nervous system functioning. When we breathe deeply, engaging the diaphragm, we unconsciously initiate (or maintain) the body's relaxation response. Discovered by Dr. Herbert Benson in the 1960s, the relaxation response is the body's innate response to both physical and emotional stressors.[30] Counteracting our fight-or-flight response, it helps us to return to a state of equilibrium when the mind and body are on edge.

However, as you likely know through personal experience, this relaxation response does not always kick in right away. In times when we're faced with imminent danger, it's natural for it to hang back for a while as we engage our senses and muscles appropriately so as to find safety. However, when we're in a fight-or-flight state due to mental or emotional stress and in the absence of a real threat, it can still be quite difficult to soften this stress response.

This is where the breath comes in. Numerous studies have shown that yogic breathing, mindful breathing,[31] and diaphragmatic breathing[32] help to lower the body's stress response. Cortisol levels decrease and

---

[30] Benson, Herbert, and Miriam Z Klipper. *The Relaxation Response.* Harpercollins E-Books, 2009
[31] https://link.springer.com/article/10.1007/s12671-019-01225-4
[32] https://www.ncbi.nlm.nih.gov/pmc/articles/PMC5455070/

all other signs of fight-or-flight move back towards a more natural, resting state: heart rate and blood pressure lower, digestion kicks back in, and the mind returns to a more relaxed space as well.

Now, the breath is not the only mechanism for easing the stress response and finding equilibrium. The body, too, is a useful tool for reconnecting us with the present moment and with our inner sense of peace. Body scans, for instance, help us to get back in touch with our inner tranquil state.

Can you recall a time when you've 'caught' yourself holding your breath, or when you've become aware of contraction in your shoulders, your abdomen, or anywhere else in the body?

Body awareness (whether through informal practices or formal exercises) enhances our ability to recognize when this happens. Specific techniques, such as progressive muscle relaxation, have been found to also be of great benefit in bringing about the relaxation response.[33]

Many of us don't have a great relationship with our bodies. It's not uncommon for most of us to chronically place mind over matter. We value the mind above our sensory experience, above the more subtle wisdom of the body, pushing ourselves until the physical body crashes. This crash presents itself as anything from chronic fatigue and headaches to autoimmune disorders and life-threatening illnesses.

So, the body scan is a tool just like yoga; a practice through which mind and body merge to reflect our innate wholeness. Yoga means unity, a merging of our lower and higher selves in divine union. Like yoga, body scans are a foundational part of bridging the apparent gaps within ourselves, playing an important role in the journey towards unity.

All of this highlights how interconnected mind, body, and breath are. When we become mindful of the state of one, or when we mindfully

---

[33] https://www.researchgate.net/publication/257795404_The_MBSR_body_scan_in_clinical_practice

begin to shift the state of any of these, the result is a ripple effect on the 'other' parts of us. Each of these parts are indeed a component of the whole. As one flows, the rest follow.

I would strongly encourage you to take a few moments to try out the Breath Awareness series of meditations in the AYAM app. For me, I wouldn't start my day without it!

## What Neurobiology Says

The breath-body mechanisms have been looked into at great depth in recent years by the scientific community as well. Research is finally catching up with ancient understandings to create additional reasons as to why these practices are so effective. It is now becoming clear that what we do with our breath and our bodies has a direct impact on our neurobiology.

When it comes to the brain and the breath, research has discovered – and continues to look at – a cluster of neurons in the brainstem known as the 'breathing pacemaker'.[34] These neurons affect not just our breathing but also our levels of alertness and emotions as well. Though the exact mechanisms of this 'pacemaker' are still being explored, they very likely contribute to why slowing our breath helps us to feel more at ease.

The breathing pacemaker aside, the breath also influences hormonal activity in the body as briefly mentioned through the relaxation response. To take this understanding a step further, we can consider the hypothalamic-pituitary-adrenal (HPA) axis. This axis regulates immunity, certain mental processing, and metabolism, as well as playing a direct role in our experience of stress. Diaphragmatic breathing helps to regulate this axis and decrease stress hormones including adrenaline and cortisol.[35]

---

[34] https://www.theverge.com/2017/3/30/15109762/deep-breath-study-breathing-affects-brain-neurons-emotional-state
[35] https://www.ncbi.nlm.nih.gov/pmc/articles/PMC5455070/

Now, progressive muscle relaxation and body scan techniques also regulate the brain and nervous system in similar ways. As we become more aware of the body, we are invited to consciously release tension where it feels safe and comfortable to do so. This too triggers the mind into relaxing. Like breathing practices, progressive muscle relaxation has also been found to lessen cortisol levels and promote our sense of ease.[36]

The benefits of breath and body practices are not observed in the mind alone. As the stress response lessens, immunity improves, risk of cardiovascular disease lessens, memory and attention span increase, and countless other markers of health and wellness are improved upon. The ripple effect of these practices touches all aspects of our lives, improving well-being in numerous dynamic ways.

**Breath and Body Mindfulness Practices**

There are numerous different breath and body practices worth considering in order to reduce stress, improve markers of health, and help you to achieve a greater sense of peace and overall well-being. Here are a few basic ones you can consider to get started. In later chapters, we will take a closer look at breath awareness for focus, breath awareness for peace and calm, and breath awareness as it relates to additional markers of well-being.

Any meditation or breath awareness exercise in general has the ability to give us that momentary refuge where the outside chaos of life does not matter, and we get profoundly connected to the peace within.

For the practices I am detailing below, an extended and expanded version of them is also available on the AYAM app in the Daily Essentials sections as : Breath Awareness – Peace and Calm, and Breath Awareness – Basic.

---

[36] https://www.tandfonline.com/doi/abs/10.3109/10253890.2015.1053454?src=recsys&journal-Code=ists20

## Breathing Exercises

### EX1: The Simple Mindful Breath (5-7 mins)

1. Begin by finding a comfortable seated or lying down position, ensuring that your spine is straight, and your shoulders are softly relaxed. Make sure there is one straight line throughout the back and neck and then gently close your eyes.

2. Start by turning your attention towards the breath. Deeply inhale through your nose, and slowly exhale from your mouth... and relax.

3. As you do so, simply notice what is present – any thoughts, feelings, emotions. Let them be. Gently bring your attention back to your breath, and continue to inhale-exhale, and relax.

4. If you mind wonders, it's ok. Just gently bring it back. Without judging, changing, or denying your present experience of the breath, observe its natural rhythm, depth, and any sensations it creates. Continue to inhale-exhale.

5. Follow the breath exactly as it is, paying attention not only to how it appears at any moment, but also becoming aware of how it shifts on its own as you settle into this practice. Continue to inhale... and exhale.

6. Now, gently settle into a pace and rhythm you find natural and spend at least three to five minutes here, focusing exclusively on the natural rhythm of your breath.

7. When you feel ready, before opening your eyes, take a few moments to notice what your experience of this was like and what state the mind is now in.

### EX2: Diaphragmatic Breathing (5-7 mins)

1. For beginners, diaphragmatic (or belly) breathing is most easily observed and practiced while resting on your back. Ensure that the spine is straight and the entire body is relaxed. Take a few simple mindful breaths to settle in.

2. Place one hand on your chest and one on your belly as you begin to breathe down towards the base of your spine. Notice the movement in both hands as they rest on your body, seeing if you can let most of the movement be in the hand resting on your stomach. The hand on your chest does not have to remain entirely still, but it should move only very subtly. This focus helps you to contract the diaphragm, a thin muscle that separates the abdomen from the chest, which engages the relaxation response.

3. Continue breathing in this way for three to five minutes. Let your breath return to its natural rhythm and take a moment to mindfully observe the state of both body and mind.

## Body Awareness Exercises

### EX3: The Simple Body Scan Practice (7-10 mins)

1. Begin resting on your back with your arms comfortably by your sides. Your feet can fall gently outwards. Take a few mindful breaths to settle in.

2. For this simple body scan, begin by drawing your attention to the top of your head and noticing it with your closed-eyed awareness. Then, draw your attention to various parts of your head as you scan downwards – your forehead, your eyes, your cheeks, your nose, your mouth, your jaw, and your chin. As you witness each of these areas, you might notice a natural softening. Allow this to occur where it is comfortable to do so.

3. Continue to be aware of your breath, as you continue to scan your body. If your mind wonders, don't fight it; that's just what minds do. Gently bring your attention back to your breath.

4. Continue scanning the body downwards, slowly and gently moving through the neck, the shoulders, the upper arms, the elbows, the lower arms, the hands, and the fingers. With every step, just notice what's present. There is nothing to change or fix – just notice. And relax and let go.

5. Then, return to the top of your chest and continue downwards from here. Witness (and soften where it is natural to do so) the upper chest, the upper back, the spine, the belly, the lower back, the hips, the pelvis, and the buttocks. Just notice what's present. There is nothing to change or fix – just notice. And relax and let go.

6. Always continue to be aware of your breath, and if your mind wonders, keep bringing it back to the breath and the body scan.

7. Continue down the legs, scanning your upper legs, your knees, your lower legs, and your feet. Just notice what's present. There is nothing to change or fix – just notice. And relax and let go.

8. Once you have moved through the entire body, hold your full being in your awareness with eyes remaining closed. Become attuned to whatever is here, without judging your experience in any way.

9. To move out of this meditation, return to your breath for a few gentle cycles and then slowly open your eyes when you are ready.

*EX4: Progressive Muscle Relaxation (Tense and Release) (7-10 mins)*

1.  Progressive muscle relaxation differs from a simpler body scan as it requires active tensing and release of various body parts. This helps to promote deeper relaxation by promoting a more conscious and complete degree of softening.

2.  To begin, come into a resting position on your back with arms comfortably by your sides and feet naturally falling outwards. Take a few steady breaths to settle in.

3.  Once you feel settled, gently move through the following body parts (or groups of body parts), taking a few moments to tense and then release each one. As you move through these, be mindful of the transitions – of what it feels like to tighten up and what it feels like to fully relax after contraction. Explore:

    •   The toes and feet, curling them inwards and then releasing

    •   Both legs, pulling them tightly in towards one another and then releasing

    •   Your hands, clenching them tightly before softening

    •   Your arms, pulling them in towards the body before release

    •   The chin and throat, tucking the chin into the chest and then softening

    •   The face, squeezing all facial muscles in towards the nose and then relaxing

    •   The entire body, pulling everything inwards for a few seconds and then softening completely

4. Once the entire body has returned to a resting state, ground yourself through the natural flow of the breath. Observe whatever is present in mind or body, noting how this practice may have shifted things for you.

## EX5: Gentle Spine Stretch (5 mins)

1. For another mindful body practice involving gentle movement, come to your hands and knees with your hands beneath your shoulders and your knees beneath your hips. The back should be flat. This is your neutral 'tabletop' position.

2. As you inhale, drop the belly towards the floor, creating a gentle curve of the spine. The shoulders open and the buttocks press up towards the ceiling. Let this be as subtle or as deep as what feels right for your body in this moment.

3. On the exhalation, create a counter stretch by moving in the opposite direction. The spine curves up towards the ceiling, the head drops, and the buttocks tucks in towards the pelvis.

4. Follow the natural flow of your breath as you slowly and gently move in-between these two forms. Notice each and every sensation that arises, remembering to stay mindful of the breath at the same time. Practice this for three to six minutes.

5. To finish, return to a neutral 'tabletop' position and then slowly come back into a seated posture. Take a few mindful breaths before gently opening your eyes. Notice what has shifted both physically and mentally.

## Workplace-Friendly Practices

When I was in the CEO role, I often had situations where one of my executives would come into my office with a really worried look on the face. It usually meant 'Houston – We have a problem!' And they ranged from an upset customer to a competitive bid or even the resignation of a key employee etc., etc. I would often begin by asking the employee to relax. Basically, gently bringing their attention to the fact that this was certainly not the end of the world and, when this crisis passed, the earth would still be spinning on its axis, the sun would still rise and most importantly of all, he or she would still have their job intact.

Then one day, my EVP walked into my office (let's call him Jim), very animated about an unreasonable request from a customer. I could literally see smoke coming out of his ears! Now let me describe him: six feet five inches tall, well built, former college football player – I think you get the picture. As he entered my office, he immediately broke into an animated and heavily gesticulated description of all that he thought was wrong with the customer. In moments like this, my primary concern was always the well-being of my team and in finding a way to quickly put them at ease. I firmly believe that a calm employee makes better decisions.

So, I did what I always did. I said, "Jim, first just relax". He continued, appearing almost desperate and I reiterated, "Jim, relax!" This time, he looked at me, visibly irritated, and yelled at me, "Relax? But how?"

Wow! That was a moment of enlightenment for me. I realized that while I had been preaching the "relax" doctrine to my team, it was within no context of advising them on practices around the "how" of the relax. After this realization, I instituted a practice of taking "3 minute breathing breaks" before we discussed any crises. I can tell you that it did wonders for the temperature in my sales and service teams!

In the paragraph below, I am sharing simple techniques that any organization and any team can implement to promote more calm and aligned conversations and engagements in the workplace.

**Relax – but how?**

Bringing mindfulness into the workplace has numerous benefits, both for the organization and the individual. Numerous studies are beginning to show this, suggesting that mindfulness practice may:

- Reduce stress and burnout[37]

- Increase productivity and focus

- Enhance job satisfaction

- Cultivate a more positive relationship to work[38]

- Reduce psychological distress and fatigue[39]

While each of these are certainly beneficial for the individual, they also contribute to more productive companies with happier and healthier employees.

Both breath and body exercises can be explored in the workplace with ease. However, they may need to be modified according to the space and time you have in the office or other work environment. Some of the variations you might consider include:

1. **5-Minute Breathing Break**

   These breaks could be explored numerous times throughout the day as either a preventative measure for stress or as an active way for easing anxiety, stress, or other difficult emotions when tensions are high. You might practice simple mindful breathing or diaphragmatic breathing.

---

[37] https://www.frontiersin.org/articles/10.3389/fpsyg.2018.00195/full
[38] https://www.apa.org/pubs/highlights/spotlight/issue-126
[39] https://www.ncbi.nlm.nih.gov/pmc/articles/PMC4569475/

## 2. 5-Minute Body Break

Similar to the 5-minute breathing breaks, these body breaks can be used at any point throughout the day and more than once where possible. They would ideally incorporate both mindful awareness and gentle movement, so I suggest you spend two to three minutes performing a simple body scan before gently stretching out any areas where tension is observed. You might consider the gentle spinal stretch, neck rolls, or any other safe and comfortable practices that suit your body.

Simple techniques like these can be explored quietly on one's own or, if you're involved in promoting employee health and well-being, you might consider hosting mindfulness practices as group sessions. Whether offering short, ten minute sessions during lunch break or more intensive mindfulness practices at the end of the day, breath and body exercises encourage wellness amongst employees of all levels. This makes for happy, healthy personnel and a vibrant, successful organization.

## Going Beyond Inhale and Exhale

The art and science of breath is exactly that – part art and part science. What we have covered in the chapter so far are simple, yet powerful techniques. The science of breath is however a very deep ocean and there are many other techniques that can not be summed in this book or even a collection of volumes.

Over the years, as I trained in different systems of breath-based practices, including the Yogic *Pranayama*, the Mental Physics breathing of Ding Le Mei, *Susokukan* in Zen, Sexual Alchemy in Tibetan Tantra, *Sukshma* Yoga, Tai Chi, Qi Gong, etc., I realized that there is a lot of wisdom in these ancient techniques that can be used to deepen meditative practices without requiring one to necessarily learn the whole system.

In service of that, I have included some advanced breathing techniques in Section 3, where we will use hand positions (mudras) and combine them with breath-holds (bandhas) to harness the power of the inner breath for modern day needs of stress relief, energy boosting, increasing vitality calm and deep sleep.

In the Chapter on Ontology of Advanced meditations, we will also revisit the connection between the breath and the body and this time we will address the relationship with the subtle layers of our body or the energetic body and harness that for self healing meditations.

So as they say, this is just a beginning – there is much to come, so watch this space! And keep on breathing.

*Deeply inhale.... and slowly exhale... relax... and let go!*

**Suggested ayam(TM) practice :**

Meditations : Calm, Sleep Well, Focus

Essentials : Breath Awareness, Vitality

# CHAPTER 6

The Mindful Trinity: Mindful Movement, Mindful Eating, and Mindful Walking

*"Sensei AJ, may I ask you for a favor?"* requested a well-dressed businessman with folded arms, having presented himself to the morning meditation gathering of a young teacher. *"Sure Jay, what's on your mind?"* responded the teacher.

This was a practitioner-teacher, leading daily mindfulness (sitting) practice in public parks every morning, before changing into a corporate attire and heading to his CEO job in an international company. Jay was a professional affiliate who had recently developed a curiosity about mindfulness,

*"I want to learn how you find time to integrate these practices into your life. I am so busy every day that I just don't get time to practice. Can I shadow you for 1 day and learn?"*

*"Sure"*, the teacher replied, *"if that is what you would like, let's do it today if you are ready!"*

*"I am ready,"* was the answer.

It's now 7:30 pm. Jay and AJ are driving back from the office, and Jay asks AJ in a confused manner:

*"So, it seems that today was not a good day to shadow you as you were also too busy with meetings, a business dinner and the quarterly review. Shall I come back tomorrow?"*

*Replying, the teacher said; "Sure, if you like. But tomorrow, don't just be there but be present, it will be more useful."*

Jay was confused: *"What do you mean?"*

*"Just that"*, came the reply. *"Next time, notice the 3000 steps I walked today, where you were faster than me and were on the phone, the 2 meals I ate in silence while you watched and commented on the news, the 4 times I got up to stretch between my meetings. And every moment I listened to you without interrupting, without judgement, and most importantly, the 1000s of full breaths I took today, relishing each one.*

*Life is the longest meditation my friend. From the first breath to last. Don't let it pass you by, unlived, while you are busy trying to fix the past or worrying about the future."*

It was time for Jay to get dropped off at the parking lot and walk to his car, and he walked just a little bit slower.

Let me end by saying that the story is real, and I was either AJ or Jay. I will leave it up to your imagination to guess, but in the larger context it does not matter. The principle I am introducing here is that *present moment awareness* is just that: "awareness of the moment that is here", the one that we are living now, and being aware of what that moment contains, be it an intent, act, thought or feeling.

Expanding this capacity of being present is the fundamental goal of mindfulness.

In this chapter, we will explore some acts we perform every day, sometimes without even being conscious of them. But with the techniques we learn, we will aim to bring to them our 'present moment awareness'.

This is how living mindfully begins.

## The Mindful Trinity

Mindfulness goes far beyond the way we engage with our thoughts and feelings. While it might be practiced during formal meditation, it is not limited to stillness, nor to silence. Instead, mindfulness is a way of being authentically present with our environment, both inner and outer, as we move through each moment of our lives.

From the conversations we engage in to the first movements we make as we climb out of bed in the morning, mindful attention can be granted to any experience – big or small. It is completely unconditional in relation to our circumstances and so requires no meditation pillow, no dim lighting, and no special gear. Eyes open or closed, we can tune in mindfully to each moment to enhance our sense of presence, peace, and contentment.

While each action, experience, or engagement is a moment for mindful awareness, the Mindful Trinity highlights the three essential, most practical moments where we can enhance our present moment awareness:

*Mindful Movement*

*Mindful Eating*

*Mindful Walking*

These three 'activities' are the practices most easily integrated into our everyday lives, as most of us engage in all three. Even those that are unable to walk in the most direct or literal sense have some way of moving through the world – a way that can be tuned into with greater awareness. We can also consider walking to be a metaphor, as it is expressed in the Buddhist scripture Vinaya Pitaka. When we expand outwards from the most literal sense of this action, we see that walking is the way we interact with the world around us – the way in which we move through life.

Whereas body awareness practices and mindful breathing exercises have us explore our present moment through stillness or relaxation, these three practices invite us to let awareness be present *within* action. The goal is a dynamic state of calm, which has a profound effect on our ability to find inner peace amidst the flow of life.

While anyone can practice 'mindfulness in action', these sorts of exercises are particularly helpful for those who find it difficult initially to stay still. Whether this is due to ADD/ADHD, hypersensitivity to the environment, or a mind that has not yet become accustomed to slowing down, the Mindful Trinity invites us to gently explore mindfulness through everyday activities. These are also perfect for those with busy schedules as 'special time' does not need to be set aside for practice.

One immeasurable benefit of these dynamic mindfulness exercises is that the results can be witnessed and felt immediately. Consider, for example, how often you have paused to be present while eating or walking. Most likely, not too often. When you practice mindfulness during any of these simple actions, the contrast between the 'mindful way' and your habitual movements will be stark. You will immediately gain a felt understanding of what it means to slow down, to tune in, and to be 'in' the present moment.

These techniques are not new to the modern world. While many of them may just now be arising in collective, modern-day consciousness, they are steeped in ancient wisdoms and traditions, as we'll explore in each of the following sections.

## Mindful Movement

*"Life is a dance. Mindfulness is witnessing that dance."*
*Amit Ray*

Humans have been moving mindfully for centuries across various traditions. Yoga, for instance, took root in India over 5000 years ago.[40] And while its development in Western cultures has become increasingly modernized and focused on the physical, it is – at its core – a mindfulness practice that unites mind and body through self-awareness and the breath.

---

[40] Shally-Jensen, Michael. *Alternative Healing In American History: An Encyclopedia From Acupuncture To Yoga.* ABC-CLIO, 2019, p. 245.

Similarly, Qigong is a dynamic practice of ancient Chinese culture that involves aligning the breath with movement. Mindfulness is a central component of this practice[41], dating back over 4000 years. The purpose of the practice is to circulate *qi* (or 'life energy') through the body to help maintain, promote, and replenish health and wellness.

Just like the breath, increased scientific attention is being granted to these types of mindful movement practices. Studies reveal that yoga helps to:

- Increase physical strength and flexibility

- Improve respiratory and cardiovascular function

- Reduce stress and anxiety

- Reduce depression

- Improve sleep patterns

- Promote recovery from addiction

- Reduce chronic pain

- Improve overall well-being[42]

Likewise, Qigong has been found to be of benefit in a wide range of conditions, including anxiety disorders, depression, fibromyalgia, and chronic fatigue.[43] As Qigong helps to restore the natural balance of qi in the body, it promotes homeostasis throughout both mind and body. As it does so, it helps to improve both physical and mental health, just as yoga does.

Exploring mindful movement does not have to be elaborate. In fact, the simpler you make it in the beginning, the more focused and present you will be. And, since the difference between mindful

[41] Baigent, Patrick. *The Path Of Relaxation*. Lulu Press, Inc., 2016.

[42] https://www.ncbi.nlm.nih.gov/pmc/articles/PMC3193654/

[43] https://www.researchgate.net/publication/247719331_Qigong_as_a_Mindfulness_Practice_for_Counseling_Students_A_Qualitative_Study

movement and more customary forms of physical exercises is the attention we grant to the practice, focus and presence is what we're really after.

Once you become accustomed to a particular mindful movement, you can expand outwards by incorporating more dynamic flow to our movements. You might gravitate towards practices similar to yoga, qi gong, tai chi, or dance, or you might develop a practice that blends styles and traditions. Mindful movement does not need to look a certain way; it's about our attentiveness to the action.

To get started, you might consider these four simple practices to help you become more familiar with what it means to move mindfully.

### EX1: Lying Leg Lifts

1. For this practice, I invite you to begin resting on your back in *savasana*, or corpse pose. Your arms can rest naturally by your sides and your feet fall comfortably outwards. Take a few deep breaths to ground yourself here, letting all muscles surrender into the floor beneath you. Allow your eyes to close.

2. From this resting position, begin to slowly raise your right leg off the ground so that it hovers just about a foot or two above the floor. Before and as you lift it, note:

   o The areas of the body that engage as you prepare to raise your leg

   o The sensations associated with these areas that activate

   o Any resistance, pressure, or force observable alongside this movement

   o The way the breath changes, if at all

o Any other observations that filter into your awareness

3. Hold your right leg in the air for just a breath of stillness before slowly lowering it back down with the same slow speed and attentiveness as when you lifted it. Note any sensations that arise with this movement, alongside gravity.

4. Repeat the practice with the opposite leg, and then repeat the whole series two or three more times. There is no rush with this. Take your time to witness what moves through breath, body, and mind as you practice these leg lifts.

## EX2: Neck Rolls

1. To practice neck rolls mindfully, find a comfortable seated position on the floor, on a bench, or on a chair. Straighten the spine, soften the shoulders, and close your eyes. Take just a few grounding breaths to help you settle into this space.

2. When you feel ready, slowly lower your chin towards your chest, noting the sensation of this gentle stretch through the back of the neck. Expand your awareness to scan whatever else is present in the body, perhaps observing some sensation in the mouth, the forehead, or elsewhere.

3. Now, depending on the condition of your neck, you might decide to form half circles with the top of your head or full circles. If there are any injuries present, avoid dropping your head backwards at all, and if you observe any pain during this practice, slowly come out of the movement and explore whatever feels safe for you.r

4. To start, slowly draw the top of your head towards your right shoulder, moving even slower than you might like to. Notice the shifting sensations within the neck and anywhere else in the body.

5. If it feels safe for you to do so, you can continue this circular motion by moving along the back of the neck over towards the left shoulder before arriving back in the center of the chest. Otherwise, slowly draw the top of your head back along the front, your chin passing your chest once again as you make your way to the left shoulder.

6. In any case, let this movement be slow and steady, drawing your attention to the direct sensations associated with this flow. You can also expand your awareness to note:

   o Any contraction or release that occurs elsewhere in the body

   o The state and underlying energies of the mind

   o The depth and pace of the breath

7. If you are forming full circles through the neck, take a moment to pause with your chin at your chest after two or three minutes. Then, repeat the motion in the opposite direction for about the same length of time. When you are finished, you can safely come out of the practice by gently lifting your chin when it is in a neutral, forward position.

### EX3: Seated Side Stretch

1. For this practice, you'll want to find a comfortable seated position. Cross-legged works best, though sitting with your buttocks on your heels will work as well. Ensure that the spine is straight and the shoulders are relaxed. Take a couple of deep breaths to ground yourself as you close your eyes.

2. Moving slowly and with full awareness of each movement, inhale as you raise your arms up and overhead. Let your breath be slow as you watch this steady movement against gravity. Notice any sensations observable through this movement.

3. As you exhale, slowly extend your left palm down towards the earth as your right arm extends over top of your head towards the left. The left side of the body contracts as the right side stretches open. Explore this gentle bend through the side of the body, noting:

   o   Any observable sensations that arise as you move and as you find stillness

   o   The feeling of your left palm making contact with the earth

   o   The depth and pace of the breath

   o   The contraction in the left side of the body and the stretch in the right

   o   Any noticeable qualities or thoughts arising in the mind

4. Take a few full breaths here, observing any sensations that arise or shift within you. After four or five full breath cycles, reverse the motion on your next inhalation, slowly coming back up to center with arms overhead.

5. On your next exhalation, repeat the practice on the opposite side. Maintain the same degree of open attention to both physical sensations and mental or emotional currents. Stay compassionate and curious as you explore, and after four or five breaths, transition back to center mindfully. Exhale to lower your hands, noticing the gentle movement alongside gravity as you come down.

## EX4: Standing Arm Lifts

1. Begin in a neutral standing position with your feet hip distance apart, your chest open, and your shoulders relaxed. Close your eyes and take a few moments to ground through your breath. Let the breath be natural and steady.

2. Once you feel rooted, begin to draw your fingertips away from your sides. Slowly and mindfully, observe the sensations that arise as your fingertips slowly inch their way towards the ceiling. While you don't need to count this out, it should take at least 10-15 seconds for your fingertips to point straight upwards.

3. As you move, notice the muscles that become engaged, as well as any resistance that is felt in the arms. Open your awareness to observe anything else that is present in mind or body.

4. Hold your arms straight up overhead for two or three breaths, noting what this feels like without judgment and assessment. Then, slowly let your arms come back to your sides. Again, this should be slow and steady, lasting at least 10-15 seconds. Notice how it feels to move with gravity rather than against it.

5. Let your arms rest by your sides as you tune into any sensations that reside after this small and gentle movement. You may repeat the exercise three or four times, noticing what changes.

## Mindful Eating

Mindfulness of eating is another practice that has been with us for centuries. In fact, some say it was humankind's first act of worship.[44] Now, due to the rise in both environmental and personal health challenges that stem (at least partially) from the foods we are eating, returning to a more mindful manner of consumption is growing increasingly important.

Though you might consider mindful eating to begin when you take your first bite, it actually begins a step ahead of consumption. In

---

[44] Butash, Adrian. *Bless This Food: Ancient & Contemporary Graces From Around The World.* New World Library, 2013.

Christianity, this is known as saying grace before a meal to honor and give God thanks for the gift that has been provided.

However, this act of prayer, worship, and/or thankfulness is not limited to Christian traditions. In Jewish culture, Birkat Hazan is the grace given before a meal, recited before eating the first piece of bread.

In Vedic traditions, too, ritualistic offerings to the gods or to the ancestors[45] comes before humans take their first bite. Likewise, ancient Egyptian artwork in tombs depicts food as a common offering to deceased pharaohs and to the gods Osiris and Isis. These traditions help to deepen our connection to the life we experience and to the invisible realm of being, helping us to honor the natural cycles of universal energy.

> *"Living creatures are nourished by food, and food is nourished by the rain; rain itself is the water of life, which comes from selfless worship and service."*
>
> Bhagavad Gita

Mindfulness of the food we eat also includes enhancing our awareness of the love and the labor between farm and fork, of the wisdom and vitality of the soil itself, and of the intimate relationship we have with our food. As we increase our awareness of these factors, we enhance our sense of well-being both directly and indirectly. Not only do we gain an immediate sense of gratitude and contentment, but over time, we are likely to notice our food habits shifting in ways that are more nourishing and balancing.

Of course, mindful eating also involves the direct experience of consumption. Whether we are exploring our experience while sipping a cup of tea or taking the first bite of a warm stew, we can enhance our everyday mindfulness practice by noticing what happens in mind and body as we eat. By tuning into our five senses, into the thoughts that move through us, and into more universal

---

[45] Sayers, Matthew R. *Feeding The Dead: Ancestor Worship In Ancient India*. Oxford University Press, 2013, p. 111.

themes that sustain us, we deepen our connection to the food we are eating. This helps to:

o   Improve our digestion through enhancing the breakdown of food

o   Increase our awareness of hunger and 'fullness' cues

o   Enhance our awareness of cravings, empowering us to make our personal best choices

o   Increase our sense of gratitude and enhance our understanding of universal connectedness

o   Improve our relationship with food itself

As we practice this on a regular basis, we start to gain deeper insight into how our emotions are related to our consumption habits, how different foods affect both mind and body, and in which way we can better promote or maintain well-being. This growing awareness of our relationship to food empowers us to make choices that feel genuinely good for both mind and body. We start to ease up on habitual patterns of eating as we become more conscious of what works for us.

The following practice is a simple exercise to increase your awareness while you sip a cup of herbal tea. You might also practice this with a glass of water or fresh juice. The contents of your cup are far less important than the attentiveness you bring.

### EX5: Mindful Sips

1.   Before you begin, ensure that your tea is warm rather than hot so as to avoid burning your palate. If you're sipping juice or water, this shouldn't be a concern.

2.   Take a moment to find a comfortable seated position where you won't be disturbed for the next ten minutes or so. Hold your beverage in two hands and take a moment to close your eyes as you ground yourself into this practice.

3. Begin by considering (with eyes remaining closed) the contents of your mug. Take a silent moment of thanks as you note:

    o   The soil that nurtured the seed that grew into whatever herbs, fruits, or vegetables can be found in your mug (if drinking tea or juice)

    o   The fresh water that has been provided to you from the earth and through whatever systems are in place to deliver it to you

    o   The hands that were involved in preparing this beverage

    o   The nurturing properties of whatever rests in your mug (whether tea, juice, or water)

4. Eyes still closed, slowly raise the mug to your nose. Begin by observing how the aromas of this beverage mingle with your nose. Spend one full minute here.

5. Consider your sense of touch, noticing the temperature of this drink against your palms. Then, gently open your eyes for a moment as you examine this drink with your sense of sight. Is it colored or colorless? Is it difficult to tell in your glass? If you gently and safely wiggle the glass, how does the liquid change and move?

6. Close your eyes once again as you raise the mug to your lips. Soften the belly as you gently take a small sip, letting the liquid linger in your mouth before swallowing. Consider:

    o   The temperature of the liquid

    o   The sounds as you swish it around your mouth

    o   Any noticeable tastes, whether strong or subtle

o  Any other sensations in the mouth (i.e. jaw tingling, salivating)

o  What the mind might be saying

7.  After 30 to 60 seconds, swallow this single sip, noting again the sounds and other sensations as you observe the liquid moving through your throat and landing in your stomach. Take a few moments to rest here in stillness, observing the stomach and whatever else moves in you. Repeat with another sip.

You can repeat this practice with just about any item or you can explore it without an item of food at all. For example, you might close your eyes and imagine what it would be like to bite into a lemon. How would the jaw react? How would the face shift? What does the mind say?

Similarly, you could close your eyes and envision that you have your favorite flavor of pie or cake in front of you. What feelings or emotions does this stir? What does the mind say? What about the body and the heart?

The key to mindful eating is to remain compassionate and non-judgmental. Food is heavily tied to our traditions, our emotions, our stories, and our past, so challenging thoughts and feelings might be connected to a particular type of food. Explore this slowly and steadily, starting with foods that feel 'neutral' to you before diving into things that might be a bit more complicated.

## Mindful Walking

*"Walk as if you are kissing the earth with your feet."*
hich Nhat Hanh

The third of the Mindful Trinity (but no less important than the prior two), mindful walking is a practice that tunes us into both our localized body (our own physicality) and to the vast body of earth and space around us (the physical world at large). As mentioned in the introduction to this chapter, 'walking' is not only a literal, physical movement; it is also a way of moving through life and of being in intimate relationship with the world around us. Those that cannot explore the world on two feet can still engage in a personalized form of walking meditation.

Just as mindful movement and mindful eating are embedded into the teachings of ancient cultures and religions, mindful walking has its place in history as well. In the Shramana tradition, for instance, monks spent most of their time walking around the country. They settled in a single place for only short periods of time (typically during the rainy season).[46] Interestingly, this movement eventually gave rise to Jainism and Buddhism.[47] Though often overlooked in modern day takes on mindfulness, walking meditation is an important part of Buddhist tradition still today.

In Islamic traditions, too, walking has a special place in the sacred. A common practice is to pray while walking, whether on one's way to the mosque or as a pilgrimage.[48] In this way, meditation is not seen as separate from one's movements. It is not designated to stillness alone. The dynamic journey, too, is therefore made sacred.

The focus of walking meditation is two-fold. First, it is based on the direct experience of walking. As each foot rises and falls, moving through air to earth and back through air, we are invited to notice each sensation of this process. This helps to focus and still the racing mind by bringing it directly into the body.

Second, walking meditation is about reverence for the earth. It is an invitation for us to acknowledge and honor both the world beneath our feet and the world as it manifests around us. Whether deep in the woods or walking through a bustling market, mindfulness of our walk – our path – invites us into a more intimate relationship with our surrounding environment. This brings a deepening sense of trust, connection, wisdom, and peace.

---

[46] Fárek, Martin et al. *Western Foundations Of The Caste System*. Springer, 2017, p. 131.

[47] https://courses.lumenlearning.com/suny-hccc-worldcivilization/chapter/the-sramana-movement/

[48] https://www.middleeasteye.net/discover/umrah-islamic-religious-pilgrimage-explained-mecca-sau-di-arabia

So, as you practice mindful walking, I invite you to keep both of these aspects in mind. You might begin your practice by enhancing your awareness of your feet as they hit the earth and then slowly expand towards open awareness from there. These two phases are explained below.

### EX6: Walking with Awareness Practice

*Part One*

1. This practice may be done within your home or in a natural setting where it is safe for you to tune out the world around you for a short while. You might practice it in various locations over time, mindfully noting the difference in your experience according to your environment, to the day, or to whatever else might be going on in your life.

2. If in your home, you might walk around a room in a circle. If outdoors, you can practice this down a path or open field. The exact pattern is less important than the attention you are able to grant the practice.

3. From standing, start by slowly raising one foot off of the floor, noting the way the foot transitions. Which part of the foot lifts first? Observe movements in the joints and engagement of any muscles that are used. Let the movement be much slower than feels 'normal' or comfortable.

4. Then, observe the way this foot moves through the air, slowly letting it land on the floor in a natural manner. Notice which part of the foot lands first and which arrives second. Let this step be slow and steady so that you can witness all three phases – the lifting, the shifting, and the rooting.

5. Repeat with the foot now behind you. Watch these three phases of movement with close attention and curiosity.

6. Continue this slow and steady movement for three to five minutes. Stay focused on the direct sensations of your feet and your legs. In the words of Thich Nhat Hanh, "Walk as if you are kissing the earth with your feet."

7. You might also notice thoughts or emotions that arise. If so, acknowledge them gently and then return your attention to your movements.

Part Two

1. Once you have spent some time observing your feet as they meet the earth and as they transition through the air, you might explore a walking meditation with open awareness. This practice invites you to expand your observation to include the world around you.

2. Transition slowly from your feet by noticing the earth beneath you. Is it soil, grass, or sand? Is it wood flooring, carpet, or tile? Whatever the case, notice what rests beneath you before slowly letting other aspects of your environment filter in.

3. Notice the air and the temperature of it on your skin. Notice the plant life or lack thereof. Notice any insects or animals in your field of awareness. Notice the beauty and the comforts; the colors and the textures. Without judgment, take everything into your awareness. Spend five to ten minutes in this intimate communion with your surroundings to begin with. As you practice this, notice what feelings, emotions, or insights arise as well.

4. Again, you might explore this in different settings. What does it feel like to practice an open awareness walking meditation in your home versus at the beach or in a forest? Remain open and compassionate as you explore this practice, seeing if the world around you might have some wisdom to bestow upon you.

## The Parable Of The Mindful Stroll

Let me end this chapter with a story. It relates to a trip I undertook to Australia, where some friends had organized a meditation meet-up and workshops. In one of the them, there were some deep questions asked about several matters such as the *Shramanic* tradition of walking meditation, with some people even comparing 'mindful walking' to the widely different ideas of Jesus walking on water and the 'walking of the course' by an expert golfer, to getting into or staying in the zone (I still don't know how these two completely unrelated themes emerged in the same class discussion).

I had just wound up what I felt was a particularly ordinary lecture about Mindful Walking, that included walking around the lush golf course by the clubhouse, where the class had been organized. I somehow felt that my participants were less than inspired by walking barefoot on the grass!

And just as I was making a mental note of what to do differently next time, I saw a man, we will call him Adi, rushing towards me with a big smile on his face. Clearly, he had something to say.

He came up to me and shook my hand, stating:

*"Thank you so much for giving a new meaning to my favorite part of the day - the morning walk. I loved the exercise we just did. I am even more inspired now to feel my connection with nature with open awareness everywhere I walk."*

I have rarely felt this touched by someone's joy of discovering open awareness and mindful walking, I guess because Adi had come up to me in his wheelchair. Paralyzed from the waist down, his morning walks were about exploring the grounds of his assisted living facility in his motorized wheelchair.

Thank you Adi, my walk has never been the same again either.

# CHAPTER 7

Mindful Language

*"If only words could speak, they would cry out in pain of how much we use them to hurt others"*, was the title of a short monograph I once wrote for a book club I participated in. It was an emotional phase in my life and the topic was raw and ready for me when I wrote this piece. The intent was to provide a table topic for us to discuss on an open evening. It made for a lovely, good natured discussion in which many people shared their stories, and it turned out especially interesting towards the end when a lawyer humorously parodied the title – he was really good.

As we were leaving that evening, Sarah, a college student in her early 20's approached me and asked if we could speak briefly as we walked to the parking lot. I didn't know her well enough to call her a friend, as most of our previous interactions had been limited to a hello or a wave to acknowledge each other in the group – but I always appreciated her enthusiastic and animated participation in discussions. This evening she had been unusually quiet, so something instinctively made me say *"yes of course."*

She said that she loved what I wrote and that it rang true for her, as she had been more hurt by words in life than anything else, but she didn't want to talk about that. She had a different question all together and asked, *"I agree that words can hurt a lot, but can words heal… are they ever enough? Or wait, let me ask it another way,"* she continued. *"Why is it that hurt caused by words doesn't heal as easily with just words alone? Why do we always expect more?"*

At 8pm on a Saturday night, in the parking lot, I was not expecting this question. It made me speechless for a moment, because I had been struggling with this issue in my life too. And I ended up responding; *"It just seems that way. But words can also heal... it just takes more humility, compassion and patience. And practice!"*

The moment I said that to her, I felt lighter and looking back now, I realized that it was the beginning of my getting past my own emotional drama. She shook her head as if in agreement and repeated *"...patience... patience it is."* We talked for another 20 minutes or so, standing next to her car, and then exchanged a brief hug and went our separate ways. We never discussed this topic again and a few months later I changed cities and soon forgot about this interaction.

Four and half years later, I got a thank you email-card from her. When I received it, I didn't recognize the name initially, but on reading the content of the mail, the memory finally came to me. She wrote, and I am summarizing, *"...thank you. It's been a few years since we had that chat in the parking lot. Just to let you know, I kept at it. Four years into it, now I finally have my brother and mother back in my life. So words can indeed heal. Thank you! The journey started that night. You should share that essay with more people. Feedback: Write also about how words can help people heal".*

Now I have no idea what was going on in her life at that time as she never discussed it with me that evening, nor for that matter how our brief chat was in any way helpful. But she was saying back to me what I have since then adopted as a guiding principle in life: *"Words are powerful, they carry energy – choose carefully what intent you bring into existence in your life with the words you send out to the universe."*

This chapter walks you through some of the ways to choose your words Mindfully!

## The Power of Words

If you have been on either the giving or receiving end of harsh words (or both at various times in life), you can understand the power that language has on us. Words have the power to unify or to divide – to heal and nourish or to deplete. What we say and how we say it greatly influences the quality of our relationships with ourselves, with friends and family, with our partner, and with those we work with. There's no way around it; in many ways, language is what holds us together – until it doesn't.

Consider the state of the world today. How often is mindfulness of language sensed in the words we hear and read? You might consider the news, social media, and the interactions you have with those in your network. Chances are, while you may encounter experiences where language is used mindfully, you can also recall deeply polarizing language and particular tones of speech that feel less than fully aware. From politics to our private hours, we, as a collective, have yet to master the art of thoughtful communication. Our relationships feel the fallout of that, more so today than ever before.

Now, mindful communication not only impacts how we think and feel about our friends, family, work colleagues, and the world around us; it also impacts our actions and experiences. For example, when we use negative words and harsh tones, we send out energy of the same wavelength to those around us. This then impacts the opportunities and experiences we might be offered or come to enjoy.

We can also dive a bit deeper to consider how our words affect our inner world. For instance, when we use self-defeating or self-limiting language, we reaffirm beliefs that we are unworthy of whatever it is we desire. Our sense of self takes a hit, as do our emotions, resiliency, and overall mental health.

Furthermore, this type of language goes on to limit the actions we take in the outer world and the opportunities that come our way. Often referred to as the law of manifestation, our thoughts and beliefs directly impact the world around us.

> *"Everything is created twice, first in the mind and then in reality."*
> Robin S. Sharma

The law of manifestation might sound to some like a New Agey, unfounded belief in alchemy, but in fact, it's a lot more tangible than we might give it credit for. Manifestation is simply the natural process of translating energy from one form (or level of reality) to another.[49] Since both thoughts (internally-spoken words) and our actions are made up of energy, it is completely reasonable to expect that the characteristics of one will impact the other.

However, the ripple effect of our words (both inward and outward in direction) reaches even further than the opportunities and experiences we attract. Language – the way it is used and the specific words chosen – has an impact on our physiology as well. In more ways than one, our words support or deplete our sense of balance and well-being.

## The Physiological Effect of Language

From the pace of our speech to the words we use and the tone behind them, our personal well-being and that of others is deeply influenced by language. For starters, research has found that our speaking rate has a direct effect on nervous system activity.

One study in particular found that when speech rate increased, the parasympathetic nervous system (rest and recovery mechanism) withdrew and the sympathetic nervous system (fight or flight response) became aroused.[50] In other words, an increase in the pace of speech turned on the stress response and weakened the body's sense of peace and ease.

The tone of our speech, too, can influence our own state of well-being and that of those listening to us. For instance, when we feel angry, our words are likely to convey the emotion through the way we deliver our message. Anger sparks an eruption of hormones, resulting in cortisol secretion. This response speeds up our heart rate, increases blood pressure, and decreases digestive and immune system functioning.[51] When we are chronically angry and convey

---

[49] Spangler, David. The Laws Of Manifestation: A Consciousness Classic. Red Wheel Weiser, 2009, p. 56.
[50] https://www.ncbi.nlm.nih.gov/pubmed/27355761
[51] https://www.iahe.com/docs/articles/nicabm-anger-infographic-printable-pdf.pdf

this strong emotion through our words, we are likely to affect not just our own sense of homeostasis, but that of others as well.

You can probably understand all of this intuitively. It makes sense that certain speech tones and a quick rate of speaking would contribute to feelings of stress and unease. However, have you ever considered the implication of specific words? Simple words themselves do indeed have the ability to impact our physiology as well.

Let's come back to the parasympathetic and sympathetic nervous systems, taking a closer look at the mechanisms of each and the words that stimulate or suppress their functioning.

Firstly, the parasympathetic nervous system (often called our 'rest and digest' mechanism) is associated with the following:

- Managing the body while at rest

- Healing, rest, and repair

- Increased digestion

- Decreased heart rate

- Muscular relaxation

- Bronchial constriction

- Feelings of peace and calm

Words that are likely to encourage the parasympathetic nervous system (PNS) to rise to the foreground include:

o Allow

o Permit

o Let

o Be

o Guide

o Effortless

---

***Mindful Pause***

*Take a moment to consider your own experience of these words. Choose three words from the above list, close your eyes, and slowly repeat them (one after the other) for a minute or two. Rest in silence for another minute, observing any felt sensations within the body or any thoughts that come to mind.*

---

Conversely, the sympathetic nervous system (again, the 'fight or flight' response) is associated with:

- Managing the body during perceived threat

- Fight or flight (taking action)

- Decreased digestive function

- Increased heart rate

- Muscular contraction (body tenses up and quickens)

- Bronchial dilation

- Feelings of stress and fear

Though the difference might seem subtle as the words standalone, those that trigger the sympathetic nervous system (SNS) to kick in as opposed to the rest and digest mechanism include:

o Try

o Control

o Effort

o Work

o Hard

o Push

o Must

o Should

---

### Mindful Pause

*As you did for the first set of words, take a moment to consider your own experience of the words listed here. Choose three words from the above list, close your eyes, and slowly repeat them (one after the other) for a minute or two. Rest in silence for another minute, observing any felt sensations within the body or any thoughts that come to mind.*

---

The first set of words (those associated with the PNS) reflect a sense of ease, trust, and surrender. The second set (those associated with the SNS) reflect the opposite. Words like *try, effort,* and *should* reflect some type of struggle or difficulty. As we hear these words (whether self-spoken or from an external source) we associate them with either ease or difficulty – trust or uncertainty. These associations become thoughts, which send certain patterns of energy through the body. Whether we fight, flee, or settle restfully depends on the language we are infiltrated with.

With practice, we can master the use of the PNS encouraging of friendly words. I would like to invite you to try that out – it's one of the things that can truly impact the whole universe of your relationships immediately.

## Mindful Communication

> *"Kind words can be short and easy to speak, but their echoes are truly endless."*
> Mother Teresa

Now that you have a sense of the way that our words and the way we speak impacts our physiology and that of others, the next step is to put this growing awareness into action. How, through your words, can you support your own wellness and that of those in your home, community, or workplace?

First and foremost, it's important to remember that communication is a two-way street. It involves both speaking and listening and requires that we mindfully enhance our awareness of the role we play on both sides of any exchange.

When it comes to speaking, the first step towards mindful communication is awareness of our words, our tone, and the rate of our speech. We can practice this preemptively (such as before giving a speech or broaching a difficult discussion) by considering what we'd like to say and noting the key words we plan to use to convey the message. We might inquire:

*Will the words I use encourage trust and collaboration or will they suggest command, demand, or conflict?*

*How can I better choose my words to promote receptivity, open dialogue, and compassionate honesty?*

When in the middle of a challenging or heated discussion, we can also tune in mindfully by asking these same questions. It is never too late to shift the tone, language, or pace of a conversation. Where needed, moments of pause are also recommended. This helps us to reconnect with what we are really needing to say and gives us time to reflect upon the words, views, and needs of the other party.

*"The quieter you become, the more you are able to hear."*
*Rumi*

When it comes to listening, enhancing awareness of our inner dialogue is the first step to hearing more authentically. Where might you be pre-formulating a response to what is being spoken? Are feelings of defensiveness arising, impeding your ability to listen attentively?

Non-judgmental, attentive listening is an art of conscious conversation. This does not mean we deny our own views or opinions, but it does require that while listening, we set those aside to take in the feelings, needs, emotions, beliefs, and viewpoints of the other. We can soften our judgment by stepping back from the need to categorize things as 'right' or 'wrong', opening with patience and compassion towards whatever is being expressed.

Mindful communication is a dance that doesn't have an exact formula. Each exchange requires something slightly different from us, but at the root of any, true presence is yearned for. Keep the following notions and questions in mind to deepen mindfulness during your next conversation:

o **Non-Judgment** – Can I soften my analysis of, or assumptions about, the words being shared? Can I surrender the need to label things as 'right' or 'wrong', 'good' or 'bad'?

o **Inner Silence** – Where can I become a bit quieter, taking pauses in my own speech or softening my tendency to formulate a response while the other is speaking?

- o **Compassion** – Whether on the giving or receiving side of the conversation, can I imbue this experience with greater kindness, understanding, and support?

- o **Curiosity** – Can I remain open to the unknown, staying curious about the feelings of another, about my own experience, and about the possible steps we might take forward?

- o **Patience** – Am I rushing to reach a conclusion or am I interrupting the speech of the other? Can I slow down my speech and my mind, opening up to the natural flow of this exchange?

In summary, as my sister once reminded me, *"It's never what you say, it's how you say it, that gives it the true meaning!"*

## Language in the Workplace

Contrary to what business authors would have you believe, my decades as a corporate CEO have taught me that 'conversations' are the biggest cultural intervention in an organization, and the *'quality of conversations'* is the most reliable measure of the organizational climate. So, for all of you corporate or other workplace creatures, please listen to what the "network of conversations" in your organization are about. They will invariably define the experience people are having of working there.

Mindful communication is something we can apply to any relationship or interaction. We might start by applying it to how we communicate within the privacy of our own minds and then extend it outwards to influence our interactions with friends, family members, work colleagues, and strangers. Wherever there is language, there is an opportunity for more mindful dialogue.

While the benefits of mindful communication are universal regardless of where we practice them, results manifest themselves in different ways according to the environment. For instance, mindful communication applied to the inner world can help an individual explore and address subconscious belief systems and unhealthy habits. In families, language used mindfully can, for example, bridge gaps between the predominating needs of children and parents.

When it comes to the workplace, some of the specific benefits of mindful communication include:

- Greater transparency and trust within the organization

- Improved relationships between colleagues and different levels of management

- Greater clarity surrounding needs, goals, and the vision of the organization

- Improved conflict management and negotiation skills

- Fewer misunderstandings and conflicts

- Increased collaboration, engagement, and creativity

- More successful team meetings

Ultimately, this leads to enhanced productivity, a stronger sense of unity, and happier employees, from the bottom up.

It doesn't mean it will be easy, or that seamless conversations will take root overnight. Mindful communication is not something that is second nature to most of us – yet. And, where there are already high tensions in the workplace, things will have to come to the surface before they work themselves out.

However, if we are patient, compassionate, and non-judgmental towards ourselves and those we work with, the learning curve is an intriguing and enjoyable one. It offers us the chance to take a closer look at our own beliefs, behaviours, and short-sightedness, granting all of us an opportunity for meaningful growth.

Mindful language can be introduced into the workplace through a variety of means. From casual conversation to important team meetings, every interaction is an opportunity to communicate with greater awareness and compassion. Some specific situations where mindfulness is of great benefit to the workplace include:

1.  **Performance Reviews**

    Performance reviews typically involve a wealth of feedback, some of which might be challenging for the receiver to embrace. Most of us have a hard time receiving feedback, so if you are the one delivering constructive criticism, be mindful of this. Before the one-on-one meeting, thoughtfully consider the words you will use and the tone of your voice. Ensure that your language is infused with compassion and that your words help to build trust. Furthermore, be open to what the other side might like to contribute. Ask questions and remain curious.

    If you are on the receiving end, be mindful of your unconscious or habitual reactions to suggestions or feedback. Take a pause where needed before reacting too quickly. You might even share that it's difficult for you to hear certain things. For instance, you might say something like: "I know I tend to rush things at work, but it is difficult for me to hear that this has been also noticed by my colleagues." This helps to remind everyone involved of our shared humanity.

    For most of my life I was a CEO, and in that job, feedback comes mostly from Board Members or 360 degree feedback from your peers and reports. In both cases, it is in some way 'flavored' by the company's economic performance. I had gotten quite used to that. Midway through my career I started serving with a Non-Profit, and here the feedback content initially simply shocked me – most if it was about how people 'felt' in my presence. I learned a lot about the power of communication when you are able to avoid 'power of position' biases and tried my best later to integrate this process in my company.

## 2. Team Meetings

Before team meetings, consider how you might convey the message that needs to be delivered more clearly and compassionately. Are the words you are planning to use the language of trust and collaboration or command, demand, and conflict? See where you can lessen up on words that spark the fight or flight response, opting for more of those that promote 'rest and digest'.

Also, remember that mindful communication is not just something we can prepare for; it's something that requires openness, flexibility, and adaptability. For instance, if an employee raises difficult questions or shares their frustration that wasn't anticipated, how can you facilitate thoughtful dialogue around the topic? Remember that silence is an alternative to quick reactions, providing us time to digest and reflect upon the thoughts and feelings expressed.

Most importantly, team meetings must be safe places where people can engage in healthy conversation, respect diversity of opinions and even air disagreement and grievances. None of this has to require heated debates or elevated voices, if we follow simple mindful principals of *"listening and speaking with compassion and non-judgement."*

## 3. Mass Communication

With a growing amount of work and meetings happening online, mindfulness principles can also be applied to our emails, web-based meetings, and other online communications. Some points to consider include:

- Is online communication a two-way street? Are questions, thoughts, and feedback being encouraged the way they would be in a more traditional method of communication?

- Are web-based communications clear and concise? Are they adding to clarity or creating confusion?

- What types of words tend to reappear in your emails to employees? What type of environment or energy do those words create?

**4. Unforeseen Circumstances**

Illness, injury or a death, changes in the economy, and organizational restructuring are just some of the less predictable situations that require utmost care when it comes to communication. During these times, we need to tap into our humanity so that we are conveying words that build trust, love, and support. These sorts of circumstances can bring up great amounts of fear, stress, grief, and confusion (depending upon the situation) and so reminding ourselves to connect from the heart helps to soothe everyone involved.

I recently read a letter posted by the CEO of a large internet company (in the travel and hospitality space); an amazing case study on communicating with compassion and humanity. Just as I was feeling good about the new leadership initiative of companies, I saw a post about another company laying people off with pre-recorded voice messages and video calls. I guess the example in these cases really needs to be set by the corner office and also inculcated into the culture of the company on an ongoing basis.

In summary, regardless of what arises at work, language is a key component in effectively navigating it. Through the words we use, we contribute to either a frequency of togetherness or separation. The more mindful we are, the more we veer towards unity.

So be mindful of your language – for that is what creates your lived reality.

## A Couple of Mindful Language Exercises

While there are numerous ways that we can explore mindful language, these are a few specific practices we might consider to begin with. As we become more familiar with what it means to communicate mindfully, we will naturally begin to embrace its principles in all of our interactions.

## Needs Evaluation

Whenever we find ourselves caught up in differences, we can enhance our understanding of what's really going on by considering that there are likely opposing needs at play. In his work on Nonviolent Communication (NVC), Dr. Marshall Rosenberg explains: "Judgments, criticisms, diagnoses, and interpretations of others are all alienated expressions of our needs."[52] When we consider this, we might get closer to mindfully solving the situation by inquiring: what is the need that underlies my complaint, criticism, or judgment?

To practice this:

1.  Take a moment's pause during a difficult discussion where finding common ground feels unlikely. Invite both yourself and the other to consider: what fundamental need(s) underlies this experience for me?

2.  Needs can include (but are certainly not limited to): safety, security, support, freedom, trust, compassion, meaning, respect, empathy, play, creativity, or autonomy. Take your time to explore the root of your concern.

3.  Once underlying needs have been assessed, bring them to the surface by sharing them. For example, the head of an organization might share a need for financial security, whereas an employee might express their need for trust or

---

[52] Rosenberg, Marshall B. Nonviolent *Communication: A Language Of Life: Life-Changing Tools For Healthy Relationships*. Puddledancer Press, 2015.

creativity. Once both parties have expressed their needs, consider: is there a way that both of our needs can be met?

This practice helps us to get to what often goes unsaid. Though seemingly simple, it helps to clear away the clutter that tends to impede our vision during difficult conversations. The needs evaluation is perfectly suitable for both personal and professional life, helping to bridge gaps that appear to divide us.

## Mindful Listening

An exercise we can explore quietly on our own or consciously with a team member, mindful listening helps to strengthen our ability to be fully present while another is speaking. If you are involved in planning team building events, this is a great exercise to consider for inclusion.

To practice with a partner:

1.  Choose one person to start as the speaker and the other to start as the listener.

2.  Once it is decided who will speak first, set a timer for one minute. When the countdown begins, the speaker will start talking about who they are, where they come from, what they enjoy doing on weekends, their favorite book, where they find inspiration, and so on. Whatever comes to mind is perfectly suitable for this exercise.

3.  When the alarm sounds, the listener then repeats back to the speaker as much information as he or she can recall. By repeating back the details of what they heard, the listener is encouraged to tune in with 100% attention.

4.  Swap roles and repeat.

This is a fun exercise that can be practiced again and again within the organization to serve as a reminder of what it means to truly listen.

## Being Yourself & Living with Yourself

I was initially hesitant and somewhat apprehensive about sharing this experience, but then a close friend reminded me about my own gospel of always being vulnerable, so here is something that I personally learnt much from.

Over my corporate career, I have been involved in multiple M&A, both regarding my own companies as well as companies I have advised. In one of those experiences, I ended up at a firm that was very well known for its people friendly practices – a tag it perfectly deserved. The top management was committed to cultivating and keeping the company a mindful place, and it was a very attractive feature that contributed heavily towards my decision to collaborate with that company.

However, a few months into the position, I started to realize my language had begun to change: it had gotten more aggressive, pessimistic and was combined with my increased stress level. I was frequently using the words from my inventory of SNS triggering words and I slowly saw how my world view began to alter. Initially, I chalked it up to 'performance issues'. I was clearly having difficulty adjusting and performing and the numbers of my group were dismal and looking even worse. In my mind, I made it mean that this deteriorating performance was causing all these negative changes.

Very quickly, I realized that even my meditations were shallower – that was a huge red flag. I had been at times down in life earlier too, and in much worse situations but my meditations had never been off. In summary, it was a 'basket case' emerging. And it hurt my self-esteem quite a bit because by this time I had been practicing meditation for well over a decade and had been teaching it for a while as well. So what was really going on?

One weekend, I sat back in introspection and came to the conclusion that it doesn't matter what the factors were – my performance, organizational culture, circumstances, weather, dollar exchange rate or super ball results – it was all irrelevant. Fundamentally, I was generating my own life and that I was becoming a person I did not want to be.

I could change most of the things around me but not the "network of conversations" I needed to live everyday in that role – I did not have influence on most of them as they were either inherited from before I arrived on the scene or continuously reinforced by other leaders around me.

So basically, should I stick around to "win" but in the process risk "losing" myself?

I decided to make changes before things went too far. These changes came at a huge personal cost, both financially and emotionally, including my leaving the company and later on the industry. One could always argue that maybe if I had been a better leader, I could have done things differently, or that I chose to leave it all because of my performance.

But my life is my own and my lessons are my own, so here are some things that I learned:

- Be objective about when the macrocosm you live in is beginning to make overwhelming changes to your emotional/mental well-being. The operating word here is 'overwhelming'.

- Words matter, conversations matter – they create a 'world view' that is very difficult to alter unless change comes from within.

- Persisting when you know you are not making progress can be 'resilience' or 'denial'. Invoke discernment to know the difference or ask a trusted advisor to help you see the difference.

- Mindfulness begins with 'noticing your lived experience'. When you notice a change there, take a moment to 'notice' where it arose, and how its persistence makes you feel.

Needless to say, within a few months my life was back on track. And in retrospect, I could see the contrasts even more. I have since then become even more selective about the experiences I populate my life with.

As Buddha explains in his sermons on the eightfold noble path of liberation from suffering, *Sama Ajiva* – right livelihood, *Sama Vacca* – right speech and *Sama Sati* – right mindfulness arise together (as well as the other 5 elements).

Profound!

## Another Anecdote

Over a decade ago, at 5:30 am on a winter morning, high up on a mountain in Asia *(to protect privacy of my companions, let's call it Mt ST)*, with lots of snow on the ground, we were walking to a clear space we had identified the evening before to meditate *(why was I there and with whom is another story for a different time)*. My legs were not moving as well as I would expect a healthy 20 something's legs to move and my hands were so cold that I was hesitating to use them too much, lest they just freeze and fall off! But I somehow managed to reach the clearing and sat down to meditate. Soon the cold was seeping in through all the layers we were wearing, and my co-meditator decided to head back to the hotel, mumbling something to the effect of not wanting to get sick.

I continued with my meditation, beginning with the Buddhist chant from the lineage of the teacher I was studying with then. I felt my breath become deeper and instantly I was 'pulled' into a state of deep meditation. I distinctly remember that in the middle of the meditation, I felt that I was being drawn into exploring the forest at the edge of the valley in front of us about half a mile downslope. It took me about twenty minutes of winded walk and on arriving there, my first recollection was of smelling the trees and noticing the mist on the leaves before I saw a group of Shinto monks meditating about 50 meters away. Immediately, two thoughts came to my mind: I guess I was drawn to the monks not to the forest, and why were there *Shinto* monks here in the middle of nowhere?

I must have made a noise and one of the monks sitting at the center opened his eyes and looked at me with a smile. He didn't seem surprised at all to see me, almost as if he had been expecting me to arrive and gestured to me to sit with them and join in the meditation.

Initially a bit unsure, I said to myself; "well, they pulled me in" and sat down quietly to begin meditating alongside this collection of monks. Just before I closed my eyes, I noticed that all the monks looked exactly alike and their soft chants were in a language I did not recognize. I had an amazing, very deep meditative experience, one that you cannot describe with words, and that you don't want to come out of. But not too much later, the monk who had invited me to join touched me on my shoulder and said *"we are done for today"* and I opened my eyes. It seems that all the other monks had already left except for this one. He then advised me to continue a daily practice and not limit myself to the system I was learning but to expand my horizon to deepen my knowledge, so I will be ready to teach one day.

I was a Tech CEO at that time, so *'teaching meditation'* was not exactly the next step for me, not even in my wildest dreams. But there was something special about this monk and I intuitively knew I needed to remember what he said. I bowed to him and before I could say anything, he spoke his last words to me; *'In time, we will meet again, and you will be ready'* and he walked off. Something about the meditation had left me empowered and touched. I couldn't put my finger on it, but it was different, profoundly different.

As I walked back up, a much tougher journey than coming down, I quietly mulled over what he had told me – it all felt surreal and made no sense. I was so tired by the time I reached my hotel that I just slept for the rest of the morning. By later afternoon, I woke up to the frantic ringing of my phone, only to hear my business partner on the other line ranting and raving about a mini crisis. To cut a long story short, the next morning I was on a flight back to work and within a few days I had forgotten about the monk and meditation, focusing right back on EBITDA and ROI.

Many years later, I was in the departure lounge at Frankfurt airport, returning back from having visited some Orthodox Christian monasteries hidden amongst the mountains in Meteora, Greece. It had been my first international retreat as a co-facilitator, and I was very excited about it and planning how to do many more of them. Just then a middle aged lady (Ruth) came and sat next to me and we struck up a casual conversation, which in some mysterious way worked itself to a discussion around inheriting from parents.

Ruth then shared with me how her father had briefly lived as a monk in Thailand and before he passed, he had given her a book he greatly treasured. This book was in turn gifted to him by his mentor, the abbot of the monastery where he trained, at the time of his leaving and returning back to the UK. By coincidence, she happened to be carrying the book with her, wanting to read it to get to know her father better.

She showed it to me; it was frayed at the edges and almost falling apart, printed in an old style and dated to 1966. The dedication page had the picture of the authors' teacher along with a note hand scribbled below it which read: *"Here we meet again, and you are now ready'*. The picture of the teacher, though an impression, left me in no doubt that it was the same monk who I had met years ago in the forest on the mountain and meditated with. Even the picture looked like it was situated in the same forest, with the same trees, and all of it came rushing back to me, with goose bumps appearing all over my body. I was about to tell Ruth about it when I noticed the note below the picture was dated 1842-1910. So clearly, I could not have met the teacher in the picture in flesh and blood, and yet I did.

Right in this instant, the words monk spoke to me came rushing back to my mind, bringing alive for me my own journey of life up to this point. In that instant something in me shifted. For a long time I had been telling myself that basically I am an entrepreneur but now engaging in my 'sabbatical vocation' as a meditation teacher. This duality, would sometimes hold me back in ways I never realized. In this surreal moment I was able to finally let go of my 'identity' from the past, making room to acknowledge and accept my true self expression. Yes in that moment I realized, that "...I was now ready...". Just saying that to myself felt so liberating that I don't have words to describe that feeling. Life for me since then has never been the same.  In a gist - words are powerful, be mindful of not only what you say to others but also what you keep telling yourself. Words literally create the scaffolding of reality we live as our lives!

## Language and Community

In the history of the evolution of Homo sapiens we all are (*assuming we all belong to the same species, barring a few aliens that may be hiding amongst us* ☺), the evolution of language gave us a multiplied ability to communicate, and was therefore a major milestone.

In many ways, this milestone was the beginning of the 'community'. Over time, as we have evolved, our ability to communicate has become increasingly sophisticated and we are able to express complex emotions, ideas and phenomena. Sometimes in ways when skill fully deployed can mobilize us into powerful actions.

So we must appreciate that language is also at the core of 'communication' and 'community' – both being pillars of modern society.

The simple act of being mindful of our choice of words and the intent with which we deliver them can have a profound impact on our immediate communities and by implication, the larger society.

Over time, as the means of communication have increased, there has been some degree of laxity with which we have started viewing it. For example, in the days of the telegraph, we needed to send a message and pay "per word", so we very carefully chose what they would be. By the same token, there must have been an awful lot of pressure on the earliest writers who wrote on sheep skin – they could neither edit nor go on forever. The choice of words was very intentional.

While we can now send endless texts and have reams of paper, the fact remains that the power of our words also multiplies with the extent to which we can "say exactly what we mean" and its converse of "mean what we say".

So use words wisely; to build bridges and not divides, to heal and not to hurt, to include and not to separate, to explain and not to complain, to bring a smile and not to cause pain, to express love and not indifference, to honor and respect your soul and others. While words may not seemingly cost anything, they can empower you to manifest nearly anything in your life – joy, health, abundance, and peace included!

May the grace of words be with you!

# CHAPTER 8

Observing Your Thoughts and Feelings

It was a crisp December morning and I had started the day really early at 4 am, as I set out to meet this well-known scientist whose research on 'consciousness' has been at the forefront of the bridge between science and spirituality. I had read a lot of his work around consciousness and was really keen to see if I could get some deeper insights from the research he had not published earlier.

I dutifully arrived to meet him after driving for a few hours and he seemed genuinely excited to see me. We had a wonderful exchange of ideas well into the afternoon, and topics we engaged in ranged from the quantum nature of consciousness to the precise mechanisms at subatomic level, where, he theorized, matter *arises from consciousness*. I had been keeping myself updated with the latest research also coming out of CERN and we also discussed what that meant to his work.

Finally, towards the evening, the subject veered towards *'different states of consciousness'*. I was especially interested in those that arise in deep meditation. He proposed to me an elaborate framework of how he perceived 'enlightenment', 'thoughtlessness', 'samadhi', etc. I must admit that we had a substantive debate, given my own background both in the scientific enquiry and meditation practice. As it got to the time that I would need to leave, I posed to him a question that had been on my mind for a while: *"What is your personal meditation practice like?* and his answer astounded me. He responded, *"I don't have one!"* I then followed up with him, *how can he attempt to describe or model experiences that he has never tasted?* He responded by saying that he had read enough that he understood them better than *'experts'* and concluded by stating, *"After all, meditation is just a thought experiment."*

Needless to say, another couple of hours of spirited conversation ensued which ended with my invitation for him to actually practice some guided meditation to have at least somewhat of a 'lived experience' of what he was to eloquently write about and, to his credit, he readily accepted the invitation.

On my way back, I made up my mind that when I was going to write a book on meditation or mindfulness I will certainly include some content on the 'nature of thoughts' – after all, I very much believe that meditation is anything but *a thought experiment!*

Trivia – he never followed through on my invitation and has written several books since then, including on healing and meditation, without ever practicing or training on either!

## The Nature of Our Thoughts

Our thoughts are with us from the moment we wake until the second we fall back into a sleeping state at the end of the day and actually, sometimes they are carried by our subconscious into our sleep too. However, despite their presence throughout our entire waking lives, most of us grant them little mindful attention. Instead, we tend to take them for what they appear to be – 'somewhat real' – failing to realize that there's a lot more to our thoughts than would appear on the surface.

When left unexamined, our thoughts have a profound, unconscious impact on our lives – most of which we are not even aware of, including on our mental and emotional state, our physiology, and our experiences.

The father of the psychoneuroimmunology (PNI) program at UCLA, Prof. Normal Cousins, famously said in his book *Anatomy of An Illness* that "beliefs become biology." His book was drawn a lot from his own life. And he was not the first one to expound this; in fact, he readily acknowledged the work of the late nineteenth century scientist Dr. William James as a major influence on him. Dr. James was a Professor of Psychology and Physiology at Harvard and would often remark, "There is no clear dividing line between a person's philosophy and physiology."

But where do thoughts come from? What are they made of, and how do they influence the world of experience?

Thoughts are also 'energy in action'. Often referred to in esoteric literature as *thought forms,* they even tend to provide a matrix or scaffolding for different material realities to manifest. In fact, our subtle body (we will discuss that in the next section) has a layer of energetic bio-field called the *mental aura* where thoughts are supposed to reside.

On a physiological level, our thoughts are believed to be rooted in the brain's neural networks. This is where our beliefs rest – beliefs about ourselves, about others, and about the world. When something comes into consciousness (let's say it's the word 'money' or 'love'), engrained neural pathways are triggered, bringing to light our habitual thoughts. These thoughts impact our actions, thereby influencing the way we experience life.

These hardwired networks rise from the subconscious mind, founded largely in our early childhood experiences. Though deeply rooted, they are not impossible to change once we are aware of them. Mindfulness is the first step.

Now on a more esoteric level, our thoughts and emotions also contribute to karma creation. Whatever you think, intend, imagine, or consciously feel is like an action rippling out into the subtle world. Physical, mental, emotional, and even karmic results can be witnessed. So in this way too, what we think and feel, we create.

Before moving on from this session I also want to address an important distinction: while thoughts are 'powerful', they are not 'facts' – they are just 'thoughts'. We will explore this theme in later sections by examining how confusing our 'thoughts' with 'facts' can trigger a large number of stressors in our lives!

Furthermore, thoughts are a composite of both emotional and mental processes. Our thoughts (or our beliefs) work in tandem with emotional patterns in the body. Cognitive functioning and feeling arise together with our pure being, which results in both physiological changes as well as patterns in speech, behavior, and overall life experience.

Let's take a look at one simple example that reflects how our thoughts directly impact our biology. As you read through this, remain mindful of what occurs in the body:

*Imagine for a moment you are in the kitchen. You go to your fridge, swing open its door, and consider what you might like to drink or eat.*

*The fridge is nearly bare, but in the bottom drawer, you notice a lemon. You reach in and pull it out, rinsing it off under the tap.*

*Bringing it over to the counter, you grab a knife and carefully cut it down the middle lengthwise. You turn one half on its face, slicing it again so you're now left with two quarters.*

*You raise the lemon to your nose, breathing in the aroma of lemon oil off the rind.*

*Then, without much forethought, you dig your teeth into its flesh.*

*Notice what it feels like in the body to bite into this fresh, sour lemon.*

Without actually having a lemon in front of you, could you observe the way the thought of biting into a lemon alone created a physiological response in the body? You might have noticed a tightening in the jaw, a grimacing of the face, or some other reaction to this imagery.

Whatever the particular sensations may have been, this practice exemplifies how our beliefs become our biology. What we think – or what the mind processes – has a major effect on the physical body. Similarly, you might consider the body's response to a scary movie or to even just the thought of fingernails running down a chalkboard.

As noted, emotion, like thought, has a direct impact on our physiology. In the last chapter I touched on how anger triggers the body's stress response, resulting in the release of hormones like cortisol, adrenaline, and noradrenaline.[53]

Jealousy and grief too, instigate this response which, when prolonged, has a negative impact on well-being. When chronic, stress weakens the immune system, increases the risk of heart disease, and increases the prevalence of chronic fatigue, metabolic disorders, and depression.[54]

In addition to these emotions, any tendency towards excessive examination, rumination, anxiety, or worry will trigger the stress response as well. These tend to appear as 'thought spirals' – the same words and beliefs looping themselves around the mind again and again. If we don't have the tools and insights required to mindfully break the spiral, the body remains in 'fight or flight' mode. Unlike our rational cognitive functioning, the body can't differentiate between our thoughts and reality. If the mind is in fear, so too is the body.

So, it goes without saying that the thoughts and feelings we experience are worthy of our consideration if we want to improve

---

[53] https://www.iahe.com/docs/articles/nicabm-anger-infographic-printable-pdf.pdf
[54] https://www.apa.org/helpcenter/stress-body

our overall well-being. You've likely heard of the power of positive thinking – the notion that positive thoughts will bring us into a more positive state of being. Indeed, positive thoughts have a complimentary effect on the body, and as we've explored: we cannot underestimate the power of negative thinking. Mindfully addressing our negative thoughts is an impactful place to start if we want to harness the full power of the mind.

## Meditation and Thoughtlessness

Before we start out on this section, I want to address that there are many words used to describe a state of deep meditation or state during and after it. Some of the words that I have come across include emptiness, nothingness, *shunya*, tranquil mind, quiet mind, unconditioned mind, infinite consciousness, neither-perception nor non-perception, void etc.

You may note that meditation predates English language by thousands of years, so most of these 'words' are an approximate translation of profound experiential states or non-states.

For most advanced meditators, each of the above and many more represent varied and differentiable experiences, profoundly distinct from each other. However, for most people starting this journey, the jargon can feel like part of the same 'cloud' of peaceful feeling and I suggest not to overthink it but just allow the practice to grow and in time you will be able to find a place for each one as they arise in your consciousness. I have, for the purpose of this book, lumped everything together in an abstraction called 'Thoughtlessness' – I hope my teachers forgives me for taking this liberty 😊.

OK, so coming back on point, we spent a lot of time in the last section discussing positive and negative polarities of thought. That being said, at the end of the day, we are defined neither by our positive thoughts nor our negative ones. Beneath the surface, a deeper understanding can be probed. While we can examine and consciously influence the content of our thoughts through meditation, we might take our exploration a step further, eventually uncovering the greater power of 'no thinking'.

'No thinking', or the absence of thought, does not rely on our conditional experience to provide us with a sense of peace and contentment. This is one of the final stages or highest goals of Vipassana. At this stage, peace is present regardless of the nature of the mind: we've transcended the power of our thoughts.

Similarly, there also exists in Buddhism an even more advanced concept of 'no self'.[55] This doctrine emphasizes the impermanence of all things and the deeper understanding that there is no *separate* self. From this place there can be no attachment to thoughts or feelings – just a pure witnessing of whatever is present and how it arises.

We cannot force ourselves to arrive at this thoughtless state before we are ready; doing so would only be another mechanism of the mind. However, if we are willing to put a little bit of time in each day, earnestly devoting ourselves to this exploration, we will soon catch glimpses of what it's like to be without mind. Within this place, the deepest level of peace and contentment is felt.

While certainly I have attempted to somewhat describe the power of 'thoughtlessness' above, this experience is actually indescribable because any 'thought' can not capture that state. When you are thinking of that state, the very fact that you are thinking will withhold the experience of this condition in any meaningful way. The more you think about not thinking, the more that thought persists. It's an *uncertainty principle* of its own kind, simply implying that 'thinking' about'"not thinking' is *invalid ab initio*.

However, a deep state of meditation, one that we all can achieve, has the potential to bring us to this state of equanimity and tranquility, during which an experience of 'thoughtlessness' becomes possible.

---

[55] Humphreys, Christmas. *The Wisdom Of Buddhism*. Humanities Press International, 1987, p. 77.

## The Ladder of Conclusion

We mentioned that our thoughts and beliefs rest in neural networks that are formed through life experience – and primarily through *early* life experience. By the time we reach our adult years, much of what runs through the mind is already heavily programmed. These habitual or conditioned thoughts and beliefs influence the way we perceive the world – and the types of conclusions we come to.

The Ladder of Conclusion (sometimes referred to as the Ladder of Inference[56]) is a psychological construct that explores how we make conclusions, factoring in the data we collect and the biases we hold. These biases are largely rooted in our personal experiences and subsequent belief systems. Let's explore the ladder step by step, taking a closer look at why we conclude the way we do:

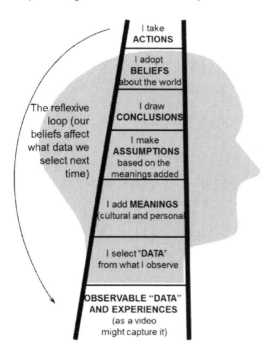

(Image from: https://thesystemsthinker.com/the-ladder-of-inference/)

---

[56] https://thesystemsthinker.com/the-ladder-of-inference/

The Ladder of Conclusion models the steps we take to make a conclusion – and also reflects what happens after we've made a particular mental decision. The steps include:

1. **Selecting Data**

   Of all the data available to us in any given moment, we consciously or subconsciously select what data points we will embrace and what we will ignore.

   *Example: You notice that Joanna yawned a handful of times during your presentation to the board.*

2. **Adding Meaning**

   To whatever collection of data we've chosen, we add our own dialogue to what is meant by this occurrence.

   *For example: You reason that Joanna is not as interested in where the company is going as the rest of the team.*

3. **Making Assumptions**

   Based on the meaning added to the data points collected, we make assumptions about the situation.

   *For example: You assume that Joanna is unhappy at work and is unable to pull her weight.*

4. **Drawing Conclusions**

   We use our assumptions and personal interpretations to draw conclusions about the situation at hand.

   *For example: You decide that Joanna is not fit for a promotion at this time.*

5. **Adopting Beliefs**

   Based on the meaning, assumptions, and conclusions drawn, we adopt (or reaffirm) beliefs about the situation.

*For example: You reaffirm your belief that to thrive in business, one needs to be 'on' at all times. If you're tired, you don't have it in you to lead a team. You might also develop additional beliefs about Joanna, such that she is not as valuable an asset to the company as others.*

6. **Taking Action**

From here, we take action based on the previous steps.

*For example: Joanna does not get considered for promotion.*

The 'reflexive loop' (as outlined in the diagram) reflects the fact that the beliefs we hold and the actions we take go on to influence the data we select the next time around. The cycle goes on as we continually reinforce our limited understanding of the world, of people, and of ourselves.

Before we explore some of the problems with this sequence, just take a moment to consider the example outlined through each step. What other possibilities might exist at each step? Consider:

---

*What additional data points might have been ignored?*

*What assumptions might someone else have made?*

*What alternative conclusions could have been drawn?*

*What other action steps could have been taken?*

---

**Problems On the Way Up**

When we consider this simple example, it is clear that there are some issues with the way the ultimate conclusions were made. And while our own thought processes are often more complex than this, the flow is much the same – unless we are mindful of the pattern.

Some of the problems with decision making according to this construct include:

1. **Biased Conclusions and Narrow-Sightedness**

   Personal biases play a huge role in decision making via the Ladder of Conclusion. As we climb the ladder, our biases, prejudices, beliefs and attitudes all influence the way we climb to the next rung. These can enter at any stage – from data collection to action – and are likely interwoven into the entire decision-making process. This unconscious tendency to project our inner world onto the outer world leads to narrow-sightedness, often resulting in decisions that do not reflect the whole picture of a given situation.

2. **Inability to Find Common Ground**

   Furthermore, when we make decisions this way, we often find ourselves at odds with others. It is difficult to find common ground if we are not open to exploring alternative viewpoints and realities. When we assume our thoughts to be true and our decision making to be 'the right way', we lose our ability to learn, negotiate, and connect.

3. **Negative Beliefs Reinforced**

   This pattern of thinking also reinforces negative or limiting belief systems. The conclusions we draw are often rooted in righteousness, which validates the stance we take on a particular issue. The more deeply ingrained our belief systems are, the harder it becomes to change them.

## Seeking Closure

If you're wondering why this streamlined thought process occurs, one of the main reasons is an interesting occurrence called 'closure' phenomenon. This cognitive construct notes our human desire to find an affirmative answer rather than hovering in ambiguity.[57] Driven by two tendencies – our sense of urgency and our desire for permanence[58] – we yearn to find long-lasting solutions as quick as possible.

This closure construct has us speeding up our cognitive processes in order to find 'the answer'. When we do this, we deny a more subtle unfolding of events and we certainly miss important information along the way. Our intense drive to reach the destination leaves gaps in our decision-making that can negatively impact our end result.

Seeking closure also helps us to make sense of the world definitively even though, on the contrary, the world is hardly definitive. Constantly changing and more complex than meets the eye, life circumstances often leave us with a certain degree of ambiguity. Rather than rejecting this, might we move towards it with curiosity? Can we inquire:

*Is it possible to sit with this as it unfolds, letting answers come rather than chasing them?*

## Minding Your Steps

Rather than unconsciously climbing from rung to rung as quickly as possible, we can positively and powerfully shift our decision-making by minding the mental steps we take. Slowing down the process is one way to start, but there are additional insights you might consider:

- **Acknowledge the gaps in the way you process information**

    Begin by recognizing that your perceptions of a situation are not an ultimate truth or reality. While your insights are certainly valid, they do not represent the entire picture.

---

[57] https://psycnet.apa.org/doiLanding?doi=10.1037%2F0033-295X.103.2.263
[58] https://www.tandfonline.com/doi/abs/10.1080/14792779643000100?journalCode=pers20

Acknowledge your own blind spots, your assumptions, your biases, and your underlying belief system.

- **Listen to others without judging**

  When in conversation or negotiation, practice non-judgmental listening. Rather than listening to respond, listen to understand. What data points are you overlooking? What alternative perspectives can be taken? Listening mindfully helps us navigate towards common ground and more integrated solutions.

- **Explore the steps that lead to whatever conclusion you come to**

  Whether internally or in discussion with another (and sometimes both), consider the steps you took to arrive at your ultimate conclusion. Where did you move too quickly to the next rung? Where did you grant the most time and attention? As you observe the thought process more closely, it will become easier to uncover information you missed or steps you rushed through.

- **Be open to input from others and remain curious about their own process**

  Placing assumptions and your own perception aside, remain open to suggestions that others might have. Stay curious (as opposed to judgmental or assumptive) about the way they come to conclusions. This will also encourage them to be more open and receptive with your own process.

- **Ask more questions before concluding.**

  Before drawing a final conclusion, see if there is more data to collect by asking new questions. We often limit our vantage point because we fail to ask the right questions. Get creative as you consider other ways of addressing whatever situation is at hand.

- **Understand that things don't have an inherent meaning.**

  Events don't have an inherent meaning, in and of themselves. 'Meaning' happens on our side of the equation – it's what we assign to the situation. Based on our own biases and past experiences, we assume that certain things have a particular significance. However, when we relax our assumed meanings, we remain more receptive to all possibilities.

## The First Dart and the Second Dart: The Mindless Spiral

*"Pain is inevitable. Suffering is optional."*

Haruki Murakami

In addition to enhancing mindfulness of this Ladder of Conclusion, there are other mental behaviors we can draw our attention to in order to shift our life in profound ways. A concept passed down from the Buddha that outlines how our thoughts impact our well-being is that of the first and the second dart. Together, these two create a mindless spiral that impedes our ability to move through our difficulties with ease.

In one translation from the Pali Canon, Nyanaponik Thera writes:

> *"When an untaught worldling is touched by a painful (bodily) feeling, he worries and grieves, he laments, beats his breast, weeps and is distraught. He thus experiences two kinds of feelings, a bodily and a mental feeling. It is as if a man were pierced by a dart and, following the first piercing, he is hit by a second dart."*[59]

The first dart is the direct pain we experience throughout our lives – that which is inescapable. So long as we are human, none of us are immune to this type of pain. When a loved one dies, when illness arises, or when tragedy strikes, we each experience some type of pain or distress. While the above translation notes that this is

---

[59] https://www.accesstoinsight.org/tipitaka/sn/sn36/sn36.006.nypo.html

bodily, it might contain some degree of emotion as well. In fact, the two are intertwined; when a loved one dies, we embody the emotion deep within our physical body.

Now, after the first dart is thrown by life, what often happens is that we ourselves toss a second dart. These are our reactions to the first dart. They are the mental maneuvers we add on to the direct experience of pain. This is our unnecessary suffering.

To help clarify this, here are a couple of examples:

1. You are out for a walk on a sunny day before the weather turns bad unexpectedly. Dark clouds move through the sky and, leaving no time for you to seek shelter, rain begins tumbling towards the earth. You are soaked from head to toe, boots full of rainwater, and you are a 40-minute walk from home.

   The first dart might be the physical discomfort of your body during the walk home. The second dart would be any spiraling thought streams along the lines of: "This beautiful day is now ruined!" or "Nothing ever goes as it 'should' for me."

2. Your partner tells you they've been offered a temporary job three hours from home and that they are considering taking it for the summer. They will have to live away during weekdays for the next three months.

   The first dart is the drop in your stomach or the physical contraction you observe in the body. The second dart would be thoughts along the lines of: "I'll be so lonely; this will be unbearable," or "How dare you consider leaving me for this much time. You mustn't be as committed to our relationship as I am."

Whatever the case may be, the important point to note is that the first dart is what life throws; the second is what we toss next as an unconscious reaction to the situation.

## The Effect of Secondary Reactions

First darts are indeed painful. Recognition of our second dart reactions is not to deny ourselves the pain experienced when life challenges us. However, our reactions to these raw and unavoidable experiences of pain cause a chain of secondary effects that impede our embodiment of well-being in many ways. And, they hold us back from moving through any challenging feelings with grace and ease.

In his book *Buddha's Brain: The Practical Neuroscience of Happiness, Love, and Wisdom*, Dr. Rick Hanson explores how our secondary reactions to the first darts of life are deeply embedded within the physical body. They trigger a cascade of internal responses that powerfully impact our physical and mental experience of wellness.[60] Some of what we know about the effect of secondary darts, as highlighted by Hanson, include:

- **The amygdala (the brain's fear center) switches on** – This stimulates secretion of norepinephrine, which prepares both the brain and the physical body for action.

- **The nervous and endocrine systems are triggered** – The sympathetic nervous system (fight or flight response) turns on, as does the hypothalamic-pituitary-adrenal axis (HPA axis). Cortisol, along with other hormones, are secreted.

- **Cortisol secretion fuels the stress response** – Cortisol, the body's primary stress hormone, continues to stimulate the amygdala while suppressing activity in the hippocampus.[61] The hippocampus (a curved formation in the brain associated with learning, memory, and emotion) would typically help to reduce amygdala functioning.

---

[60] Hanson, Rick. *Buddha's Brain: The Practical Neuroscience Of Happiness, Love, And Wisdom*. Readhowyouwant.com, 2011, pp. 56-72.
[61] https://www.futurehealth.org/articles/The-First-and-Second-Dart-by-Rick-Hanson-PH-D-100610-242.html

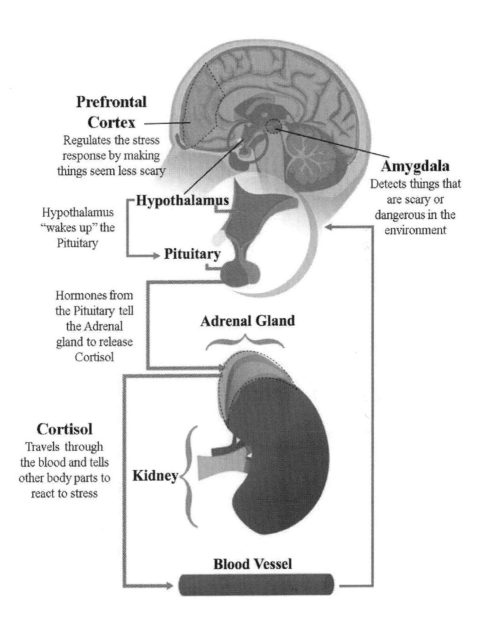

(Image from: https://kids.frontiersin.org/article/10.3389/frym.2017.00071)

- **Reactions and emotions intensify while executive control is reduced** – The prefrontal cortex, the part of the brain responsible for planning, decision making, and moderating behavior, loses control – which means *we* lose control. Without realizing it, we are caught in the spiral created by the second dart.

All of this has a wide range of implications on both body and mind. The fallout of our second darts (and the chronic stress they create) can cause:

- Gastrointestinal issues such as ulcers, colitis, irritable bowel, poor nutrient absorption, diarrhea, or constipation

- Reproductive issues such as erectile dysfunction, reduced libido, and infertility

- Cardiovascular challenges such as increased risk of heart attack, stroke, hypertension, and atherosclerosis[62]

- Energy depletion and chronic fatigue due to weakened adrenal glands

- Immune system challenges such as slower healing and increased risk of illness

- Mental health issues such as increased tendency towards anxiety and depression

## Minding the First Dart

So what can we do about this? We can begin by mindfully tuning into the first dart and by observing our tendencies to launch those second darts. By drawing curious, patient, and compassionate awareness to our tendency to spiral, we are invited back into the raw experience of the first dart. When something challenging arises (physical or emotional), we can compassionately inquire:

---

[62] https://www.ncbi.nlm.nih.gov/pmc/articles/PMC6460614/

*What does this feel like in the body before the mind adds additional layers to the experience?*

Another great analogy we might consider is that of the two wolves within us. Both wolves are ravenous and grow stronger according to the amount of energy we feed them. The first wolf is the wolf of loving kindness and compassion; the second is of jealousy, anger, and hatred.

Through our thoughts, our emotions, and our actions, we fuel either one of these two wolves. While we all have both wolves within us, what differs amongst us is the strength of each. If you've been habitually feeding the second wolf for some time, be patient with yourself as you undo that tendency. By remaining patient, compassionate, and curious towards your inner experience, you support yourself in transitioning into more nourishing thoughts and behaviors.

Overtime, one wolf will rule. Which one will it be?

## Exercises for Observing Thoughts and Feelings

First Dart-Second Dart Reflection

Take your time to consider an encounter or experience that was challenging for you. Start with a situation that, if ranked on a scale from 1 to 10 of difficulty, would be around a 4. If it feels comfortable to dive deeper after this first exercise, progress with something more challenging.

As you mindfully reflect upon this experience, answer the following questions with patience, curiosity, and compassion:

| What happened? | |
|---|---|
| What did I experience? | |
| What did my thoughts have to say? | |
| What was my direct sensory experience of the situation? | |

## Mindfulness Meditation for Emotions

When challenging thoughts or feelings arise, we can practice a self-guided mindfulness meditation during the experience. In order to do this:

1. Find a comfortable seated or lying down position – whatever is most accessible for you in the present moment.

2. Take a few moments to ground yourself through the natural flow of your breath, opening and softening with each respective inhalation and exhalation.

3. Scan the body first, noting any direct physical sensations that might be present. Without judgment or assessment, notice any tingling, tightness, contraction, or movement might be present within you. Breathe into these sensations.

4. Then, draw your attention to the mind, noting what stories might be associated with the experience. Inquire:

   *What beliefs am I holding about this experience?*

   *What stories are recurring? What patterns can be observed?*

   *Can I become a witness to this dialogue rather than becoming immersed in it?*

5. After a few minutes of compassionate inquiry, return your attention to the breath. Then, come back to the direct sensations of the physical body. When you are ready, slowly open your eyes.

## Coming Together Reflection

When we are in conflict with another or struggling to see eye to eye, we can use our awareness of the Ladder of Conclusion to deepen our curiosity of the situation. We might (along with the other party) explore the following steps:

1. **Pause.** Take some time to sit with what has been exchanged. Go to the root of the feeling – what needs might be at the root of both your own words and the others?

2. **Consider what assumptions are being made.** Where have you narrowed your lens and made an assumption or conclusion that might not represent the full picture?

3. **Ask for clarification.** If you are struggling to identify with the views of another, ask for more information. You might inquire about how they arrived at particular conclusions, what needs are most important to them, or what their biggest concern is that they feel is not being addressed.

4. **Listen mindfully.** After asking for clarification, let your ears be entirely open to what the other party has to say. Be mindful of your inner tendency to defend, deny, or respond, listening instead to gain understanding.

5. **Mind your pace and tone.** We can facilitate understanding by doing our best to convey our message in a way that won't instigate the other party's stress response. Take your time to formulate your words, embracing silence where needed.

### Debriefing with the Ladder of Conclusion

We can also debrief after a difficult interaction or conversation by considering and answer the following questions:

| What was said? | |
|---|---|
| What did it mean to me? | |
| What assumptions did I make? | |

| | |
|---|---|
| What did I think or believe then? | |
| What am I now beginning to feel or see in a new way? | |

## Summing Up

One of my favorite quotes from Buddha says *"Nothing can harm you as much as your own thoughts unguarded."* It was true in his time 2500+ years ago and it is true now.

After having studied this phenomenon of thoughts from various angles – mindfulness, neurobiology, cognitive sciences, psychology and even philosophy, I have come to a personal conclusion in my life, an abstraction of which says *overthinking is perhaps the biggest cause of stress, anxiety and unhappiness in general.* And I have developed a personal practice where if I begin so see my mind filling up with too many thoughts, I purposefully decide to take some time to do some nourishing activities like meditation, walking in the park, reading something wholesome - just as a gentle reminder that there are other things in life that that can bring me immediate sense of peace and joy, so why persist with this "thoughting" as I like to call it.

# ENDNOTE:

## The Road Ahead: Climbing Mt. Neverest

Now that you're familiar with the core techniques and most fundamental applications of mindfulness, the real journey begins. You're equipped with the basic tools that you will require to grow both horizontally and vertically, but how will you integrate them into your life? This is one of the most common questions: How do we embody what we've learned?

The techniques we've explored are easy enough to understand but require commitment and discipline to practice. So the challenge is to patiently devote the time and energy required to master them. The value of these practices is not in understanding them intellectually or in holding an intention to practice; the true value of these techniques arises when we devote ourselves to them. This requires discipline and commitment as they do not root themselves in the framework of our being overnight.

Mastering these techniques then does indeed take time, and yet if we understand that mindfulness is a journey rather than a fixed destination, we might find ourselves more patient with the process. Taking the time each day to explore mindfulness through formal practice helps us to embody this way of being more integrally.

The truth of the matter is that mindfulness is not something we 'do'; it is something we become. For instance, we don't 'do' mindful language; rather, we communicate mindfully with ourselves and those we interact with. In the same way, we don't 'do' mindfulness of emotions; instead, we develop the skills overtime to be mindful of the waves that move through us.

In this way, mindfulness is a path we are invited to walk – to take a journey upon. We can facilitate this movement by letting go of any urgency to 'get there'. Often, we hold preconceived notions of what it would look like to arrive at a 'place' of being perfectly mindful in all situations, at all times. By cultivating care and compassion for ourselves regardless of where we are and what our present capacity to be mindful is, we support ourselves in taking whatever our own next step might be. Then, we take the next, and then the next, and so on.

Undoubtedly, the path is not always an easy one. When we are cut off in traffic, when our boss or co-worker yells at us, or when things just don't seem to be 'going our way', it can be difficult to remain mindful of the present moment. That's okay. We each have different areas to learn and to grow in; none of us need to be perfect at this.

And so this is the journey along the face of Mt. Neverest. It is a journey with no end; one that we must stick with in order to reap its benefits. The further you venture, the greater the views become – and yet unlike Everest, this is a mountain with no peak. When you set aside the possibility of arriving at a fixed destination – at some precipice – you might ask yourself: Can I open myself up to enjoying the ride?

As you move along this journey of living mindfully, consider that comparison is not only futile but unhelpful. Each one of us is on our own path, and that path cannot be compared to another. Since we each have different challenges, histories, and inner processes to work with, there is no sense in comparing yourself to where someone else might be on their path. It is like comparing a banana to an apple; yes, they are within the same category of things, but they are both unique and miraculous in their own right.

If you do feel called to make a comparison, let that be only to a previous version of yourself. Which direction are you heading in? Are your thoughts and actions becoming increasingly mindful or less aware? Avoid comparing yourself to a future you. Indeed, the you of the future will likely be more aware of yourself and the world around you than you are now, but focus instead on where you are now and where you've come from.

Finally, I invite you to set aside any absolute goals and outcomes for achieving a specific state of feeling. Often, we equate mindfulness to being absent of feelings or emotions we deem to be 'negative', though this is a misunderstanding about what mindfulness really is. Commit only to your continued evolution and let your practice take care of the rest. Breathe deeply and trust that, with your commitment, all will unfold in due time.

# SECTION 3

I Am Not the Body, I Have a Body:
Nurturing the Inner Self

What does it mean to nurture our innermost selves?

That question is where all journeys of healing should begin. But it's a question that requires us to have a somewhat ontological question of *Who am I?* When I say 'I', do I mean the body or emotions or thoughts and feelings, or all of it? And how do I access all levels of myself and ensure my well-being?

Is well-being about reducing stress, getting rid of depression, and effectively managing diagnoses and psychopathology? Or, could there be something more to it? Could welcoming in positive energy be just as important as reducing the negative? These are some of the questions we will explore in this section.

Ancient traditions have long understood that in addition to enhancing our ability to navigate the difficulties of life, mindfulness and meditation can enrich and broaden our lives beyond crisis management and goal pursuits. These modalities can deepen our understanding of who we are and guide us towards finding a sense of peace and purpose within this world. Through practice, we can enhance positive qualities and inner experiences such as abundance, gratitude, compassion, and joy.

In order to enhance our understanding about who we really are and how these modalities create an inner sense of expansion and deep nourishment, it is worth taking a look at two different (though not contradictory) approaches: the secular and the ancient. By diving deeper into both realms, we broaden our understanding of who we are as a whole and begin to see more clearly how these practices can radically enhance our lives.

**Journey from Ancient to Secular: Lost Wisdom vs. the Scientific Approach**

Growing up in India, I originally related to meditation as a spiritual practice, which is probably understandable as my initial exposure was mostly to Vedic and Brahminic traditions, but I could not have been more limited in my view. For as soon as I traveled the world studying different cultures, traditions and ancient wisdom, I began to realize that meditation predates religions for sure and almost all ancient cultures seem to have their own version of it. The practices differed widely but a deep dive brought to me the realization that one of the goals of a meditative tradition was to pass down ancient wisdom about life itself, from one generation to another and I realized this additional attribute-goal of meditation.

Later in life when I studied biomedical signals, cognitive sciences etc., I began to see how science has focused on more physiologically measurable effects of meditation. So after well over a decade of study and practice, I was still left with a question of *"What is meditation and what is its purpose?"* Now I am not sure anymore that there is a fixed answer to that, I am more intrigued by the question of; *"What is possible with meditation?"* And this section is written with that thought in mind.

## Many Approaches, Many Benefits

In ancient traditions, whether that be Vedic, Mesoamerican, Egyptian or otherwise, the boundary between spiritual beliefs and the culture's meditation traditions was thin. Though not always the case today, meditation was understood to be a spiritual activity; a way of connecting with some higher form of awareness or power. Through practice, meditation was believed to help humans access realms that were beyond our mind-body vessel and beyond the immediate macrocosm. This has not been entirely lost today, but these beliefs do not stand at the forefront of most modern practitioner's understanding of these practices.

Today, meditation practice for many is largely secular, meaning it is not associated with any particular spiritual or religious tradition, Non-secular practices exist as well of course and provide their own flavor of richness to the spectrum. Most modern modalities and teachings focus on principles and virtues that most anyone can connect with regardless of their beliefs and practices around spirituality and religions. Some such practices include cultivating presence, focus, and compassion – *hard to say no to, right?*

Alongside the shift towards meditation practices absent of spiritual associations, science has taken a keen interest in what secular teachings have to offer. Standardized secular programs, such as Mindfulness-Based Stress Reduction (MBSR) and Mindfulness Based Cognitive Therapy (MBCT), have provided an opportunity for the basic practices of mindfulness and meditation to be explored through a scientific lens. The applications of these findings are far-reaching, playing a crucial role in better understanding how we can treat mental health issues, addiction, chronic pain, neurocognitive diseases, and various other health conditions.

However, even though there are many great benefits of these secular teachings and programs as they stand, the ancient wisdom of spiritual traditions should not be totally overlooked. Whether we are consciously aware of it or not, secular teachings have their roots in these ancient wisdoms, which is why they are worth exploring even just to deepen the understanding of the foundations of where moderns practice come from. For example, what would MBSR be without the rich Buddhist tradition it emerges from? It's possible that opening ourselves to the spiritual underpinnings of these practices might expand our understanding of *who we are* and even further deepen our *personal practice.*

In this section, we will examine these somewhat complementary lenses or approaches to mindfulness and meditation. From delving into subtle energy systems to exploring the six main pillars of esoteric meditations to taking a deep dive into new findings in brain science, we will explore both the secular (scientific) and the ancient with openness and curiosity.

However, before we get there, we can consider that one of meditation's primary goals according to many spiritual beliefs is around man finding harmony within the macrocosm. And that takes many forms and expressions, depending on the tradition. For example, in the Buddhist tradition it could be summarized as end to suffering and nirvana, whereas in some other eastern traditions it could imply experiencing oneness, or having timeless knowledge of creation revealed to you. That being said, the common theme that lies at the core of these traditions is essentially accessing a deeper meaning of who we are and why we are here – *a sense of meaning and purpose.*

Nowadays, this focus has largely been lost in the secular tradition. What the scientific community and many practitioners are interested in is how we can reduce things like stress, anxiety, and depression, or improve memory and delay the onset of Alzheimer's, etc. In this way, it would probably be fair to say that the secular approach is more focused on managing disorders or psychopathology than on deepening an ontological enquiry.

But what if we broadened our lens? What if we also welcomed in the pursuit of finding harmony, balance, joy, and purpose? These two approaches (over generalized as reducing the negative and promoting the positive) do not come at the expense of one another. Rather, we can invite *both* into our consideration, turning towards the ancient wisdom of spiritual traditions to perhaps broaden what we understand these practices to be all about.

We can hold onto and explore ancient wisdom without challenging our own spiritual beliefs. As we investigate some of these more subtle understandings about who we are and what meditation can offer us, we might find that certain teachings or esoteric practices speak to us in a way that exclusively secular teachings have not. When approaching these ancient understandings, we can consider them to be timeless wisdom rather than dogmatic teachings. This approach naturally helps us to retain a sense of curiosity and openness.

Within this, we can embrace the scientific approach as well. Again, science is not contradictory to spirituality; it is complementary. Only until modern times have we been able to shine a scientific lens on these less-than scientific practices, and as technologies develop, there is no doubt they will shed more light on what is behind these seemingly simple teachings and exercises.

We must keep in mind, however, that the benefits of mindfulness and meditation are not only evidenced by what science can measure. And, we need not wait until science can 'prove' the efficacy of these teachings in order to reap their benefits.

The impact of mindfulness and meditation on our overall well-being extends beyond what is measurable. Simply because we have yet to find the tools to fully explain how these practices can amplify one's life in unexpected ways does not imply that the benefits are not there. In all likelihood, overtime, science will continue narrowing the gap between these understandings, bringing to light a new sort of dialogue with consciousness.

So as we move deeper into our personal practice, we can open our hearts and minds to the possibility that ancient wisdom need not be dogmatic or exclusively religious or spiritual. The secular path does not need to discard wisdom traditions but can invite these long lost teachings back into practice with openness and curiosity.

To deepen our understanding about the importance and power of both the ancient and scientific understandings, we will explore:

- **Who Am I? A 'Subtle' Perspective**

  This chapter will take a deep dive into the question, "Who am I?" Most of us can sense that we are more than skin and bone, but how can we begin to understand what exists beyond our physicality? We will explore the different layers of the human being beyond our 'hardware', as well as the 13-point chakra system that can be tuned into to help nurture the subtle aspects of our consciousness.

- **The Six Pillars of Esoteric Meditations**

  To better understand what makes an esoteric meditation different from a modern-secular mindfulness practice, we can break it down into six primary components. Some of these components overlap with secular teachings, but the later pillars take our practice a step further by invoking spiritual principles. By combining these six pillars with our understanding of the subtle systems within the body, we can learn to direct the flow of energy within us and create an overall energy field that we call consciousness, that is in alignment with our goals, vision, and mission.

- **Ontology of Advanced Meditations**

Meditation is a boundaryless practice in many ways. Most traditions believe that the same foundational practices, when engaged with diligence over time, can lead to awakening that enables transcending the mundane experience of life to a *supramundane* experience that also allow for manifesting of advanced faculties and higher intelligences. Some of these meditations require techniques that are founded in advanced invocations, visualizations and energy alchemy that are beyond the scope of this book. However, we will very briefly visit some core technique pegs in this chapter.

- **Meditation, Mindfulness, and Brain Science**

The final chapter of this section will take a closer look at the brain, diving into recent findings about this powerful organ. We will consider the brain to be a bridge between the subtle and physical aspects of our body and how through our conscious effort, we can direct and reprogram the brain in ways that inspire and uplift us.

As you delve into these chapters, remember to keep a curious mind and open heart. None of what is presented to you here must be adopted in order for these practices to be effective. Simply consider that there are numerous lenses through which to view mindfulness and meditation – and perhaps it is when we find harmony between the two that we can maximize our awareness of who we are and how we can best nurture our innermost selves.

# CHAPTER 9

Who Am I? A 'Subtle' Perspective

To deepen our understanding of where meditation can take us, we might ask the question: *Who am I?* It is not an easy question to answer without deep inquiry; yet when we look towards more 'subtle' understandings of the body, we quickly come to realize that we are, indeed, more than meets the eye.

Mindfulness practices and modalities such as MBSR, progressive body scans, and the five aggregates, are largely focused on this physical aspect of our being and tend to see the physical body as a door to the subtle aspect of our being, like thoughts and emotions. Since what happens in our physiology indeed has a powerful impact on our state of well-being, these practices and approaches are of great value. However, if we yearn to further our progression along the vertical axis, we must engage beyond the physical. This is where awakening to our subtle body comes into play.

Before we dive into the notion of the subtle body, it can be helpful to understand that there are two main approaches here: the bottom-up approach and the top-down approach.

The first approach that we've explored in detail thus far is the bottom-up approach. This means working with the physical aspect of our being and working upwards or broadening from there. This is the technique that mindfulness practices like MBSR employ. They work with the body by engaging the physiological constructs like the nervous system, lowering cortisol, and influencing other biomarkers that bring the body into a state of relaxation.

On the other hand, the top-down approach is employed by esoteric traditions and associated meditations. These practices engage the energetic body, which trickles down to impact our emotions, thoughts, vitality and therefore our body too. It is a technique of cleansing our energy systems, which stimulates the physical body in a corresponding and complementary way.

Neither the bottom-up nor top-down approach is better than the other; they are simply different processes that create different results or same results through different pathways. In some cases, such as where the physical body is more engaged, the bottom-up approach is better suited. This includes addressing eating habits, cultivating stronger relationships, and easing physical tension. Where the top-down approach is more effective is in curating consciousness and healing on an auric level. It is the approach that leads to spiritual unfoldment, increased awareness of the subtle body, heightened intuition, and the ability to self-heal.

For those that are open or ready to ascend along the vertical axis, a variety of esoteric practices are available. First, however, we must gain a better understanding of what the subtle body is and what these lesser-understood energy systems look like.

## You Are Not the Body; You Have a Body

The most rational part of ourselves we can identify with is the body; it is tangible, observable, and concrete. When we look in the mirror, we see the thing we call 'me', which reaffirms the belief that we are what we can see and touch. However, who we really are is not the body. We might have a body, but we are not defined by it. Most of us can sense intuitively that there is more to our own being than what we can observe or feel in a tangible sense.

Beyond this limited construct of the human self exists the subtle bioplasmic field that envelops it. Also called the *aura*, the subtle energy body is made up of invisible energy bands (or auric fields[63]). Held within our aura are thoughts and feelings, and so through

---

[63] Dale, C. (2013). *The Subtle Body Practice Manual: A Comprehensive Guide to Energy Healing*. Sounds True.

esoteric meditation, we can begin to shift these energy signatures in a way that is more sustainable than through working with the physical body alone.

Metaphorically speaking, it is often understood that emotions belong to the heart and thoughts belong to the brain. However, neither thoughts nor emotions exist literally or tangibly in the physical body. They are stored in the more subtle aspect of our being, which is why esoteric approaches to healing are so effective in dealing with the things that mindfulness practice cannot seem to permeate in a lasting way.

The subtle bioplasmic field can be broken down into three layers:

## 1. Etheric layer

The etheric layer (or the etheric body) is what is the vitality layer of the aura or a store of energy for health and vitality. The denser this aura is, typically, the higher the level of vitality is. The function of the etheric layer is also to be the interface between the physical body and the subtler layer emotions (also called the Astral Layer).

Alice Bailey, an influential thinker and founding theosophist, calls the etheric body, 'the symbol of the soul'. As Bailey writes, it links the purely physical body with the astral or emotional body and is connected to every part of the body. Its function of store house of vitality is best illustrated as the battery of the cell phone.

## 2. Astral layer

The astral body is the next layer beyond the etheric body. This is the layer that houses more subtle desires and is the place where we store our emotions – both positive and negative. The denser and cleaner this layer of the aura is, the more emotionally balanced we become.

Esoteric literature says this layer of the aura is where the soul begins to identify with the astral form over the physical form of our being.[ii] In the cell phone analogy, it is part of the communications software that enables connection to the spiritual realm.

### 3. Mental layer

Lastly, the third layer is the mental body – this the realm of our thoughts and most processes related with thinking and perception. This layer is where our logical mind and abstract mind arise.

According to esoteric literature, in this layer of the auric field, consciousness transfers out of the head or brain and into the mind.[64] This is also in alignment with software that makes connection with the spiritual aspect of being possible.

These three auric fields together comprise the subtle body. Through esoteric meditations, we can energize, cleanse and harmonize these layers. As a result, our integrated consciousness expands and we begin to tap into abilities such as clarity of intuition, ability to impact lives beyond our own (through transmitting positive energy), and self-healing.

Now, our auric field is just one aspect or understanding of subtle energy that is associated with the human body. The chakra system is another energetic system of our being that we can tap into through meditation in order to more fully understand how our consciousness arises. First, however, we must understand what this system is so that we can effectively work with these energy centers in the body.

---

[64] https://www.lucistrust.org/online_books/the_light_the_soul/book_ii_the_steps_union_part4

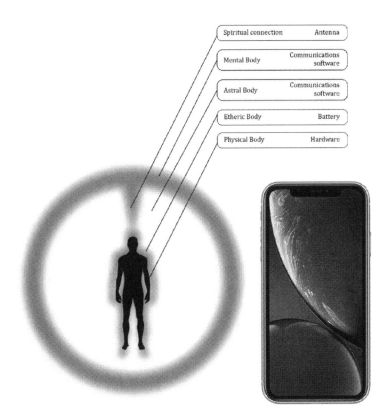

| | |
|---|---|
| Spiritual connection | Antenna |
| Mental Body | Communications software |
| Astral Body | Communications software |
| Etheric Body | Battery |
| Physical Body | Hardware |

## The 13-Chakra System

Whether you are familiar with the notion of chakras or not, the 13-chakra system may be entirely new to you. Most commonly, the 7-chakra system is discussed and worked with in modern day energy work and it is drawn from the Indian Yogic system. While well known and ancient in its own right, in some ways it is a less than complete description of the human energy body and chakra system.

A more complete system explores the 13 chakras, with the special function of including some chakras at the back of the body (*which have over time been lost in yoga in my personal opinion*). The 13-chakra system has been used by many ancient systems, including the Kabbalah, and modern healing systems (*like Pranic*

Healing developed by Master Choa Kok Sui and BEWell Science Energy Medicine modality developed by Master Del Pe). One of my mentors, an amazing healer, first introduced me to the 13 chakras and also how to integrate them effectively with my meditations and energy alchemy.

But, before we begin this exploration and any meditation upon these points, we first need to understand what chakras are. In her book *Eastern Body, Western Mind*, Anodea Judith explains:

> *"A chakra is a center of organization that receives, assimilates, and expresses life force energy."*[65]

From a Sanskrit word that can be understood to mean 'wheel', chakras are energetic orbs in the body that spin along major energy channels and impact the functioning and well-being of corresponding organs and glands. Problems arise when energy flow to or from a chakra is inhibited, which leads to either a deficiency or excess in those regions. Master Choa Kok Sui describes chakras as gates through which prana (or life force energy) can flow either into or out of.[66] To elaborate on prana, Yogi Ramacharaka describes this energy as:

> *"... the Force by which all activity is carried on in the body – by which all bodily movements are possible – by which all functioning is done – by which all signs of life manifest themselves."*[67]

As we discussed above, there is a diversity of information surrounding how many chakras there are in the body: some systems say 7, others say 13, and I have personally trained with teachers where I was able to clairsciently and clairvoyantly validate more than that also. Over time, I have an increasingly less-fixed view of the 'number of chakras', rather focusing my attention on how to integrate them into effective practice of meditation and

---

[65] Anodea, J. (2004). *Eastern Body, Western Mind* (p. 4). Celestial Arts.
[66] Sui, C. (2006). *The Origin of Modern Pranic Healing and Arhatic Yoga.* Institute for Inner Studies Publishing Foundation, Inc.
[67] Lansdowne, Z. (1986). *The Chakras & Esoteric Healing.* Weiser Books.

self healing. This line of thought becomes even more important when we consider the fact that most important/major chakras are actually commons across systems. I am however providing a brief overview of the some of the major chakras, details about them (or other chakras) are outside the scope of this book:

1.  The Base Chakra – The energy center located at the base of the spine that controls and brings life force to the blood, the adrenal glands, the skeletal system, and the muscular system. This is also the center of regulation of abundance energy, practical instincts and ability to materialize goals.

2.  The Sex Chakra – Located in the pubic region, this chakra influences the sexual and urinary organs (excluding the kidneys). It is also the anchor of sexual energy and has the capacity to impact creativity. As they say, "creativity and procreativity are linked."

3.  The Navel Chakra (and back of the Navel Chakra) – This energy center is composed of both a front and back chakra. Located on the navel, this energy point influences the appendix and large intestines. It also regulates instincts, agility, sense of timing and also acts a store for vitality energy and stamina.

4.  The Solar Plexus Chakra (and the 5. Back Solar Plexus Chakra) – This energy center is composed of both a front and back chakra. The front is located between the ribs and the back solar plexus chakra is behind it. These are connected to the pancreas, the liver, and the stomach. It is the clearing house of emotions and passion (drive, emotional commitment, desire, etc.)

5.  The Spleen Chakra – This is located on the left side of the abdomen and controls/regulates the functioning of the Spleen. This energy center is important for regulation for vitality and also for release of toxins from the body.

6. The Heart Chakra ( and 8. Back of the Heart) – Another energy center with both a front and back component, these chakras are located on either side of the heart. They are connected to the lungs, the heart, and the thymus gland. This energy center regulates love, kindness, compassion, emotional intelligence, generosity, etc.

7. The Throat Chakra – Located in the throat region, this chakra influences our critical thinking, planning and organizing ability. Our mental faculties and perception are also governed by this energy center. Physiologically, this chakra also regulates and brings energy to the thyroid glands.

8. The Ajna Chakra – This energy point is located between the eyebrows and is connected with the functioning of the pituitary and endocrine glands. This chakra influences our abstract mind, mental will, one-pointed focus and also philosophical aptitude. Important to note that this is sometimes wrongly referred to as $3^{rd}$ Eye, which is a completely different energetic construct.

9. The Forehead Chakra – In the center of the forehead up from the Ajna chakra, this energy center is connected to the nervous system functioning and the pineal gland. All psychic faculties are regulated by this energy center, and also regulation of pain and pleasure, and memory.

10. The Crown Chakra – Located at the crown of the head, it is connected to the brain and the pineal gland. The qualities of intuitiveness, inclusiveness, spiritual guidance from within and dispassion are governed by this energy center. This can well be seen as the anchor for the soul energy in our body.

11. The Soul Star Chakra / Egoic center – This chakra is located outside of the body, 12 inches about the head, it is believed to mediate between the Soul and the incarnated personality (the human body).

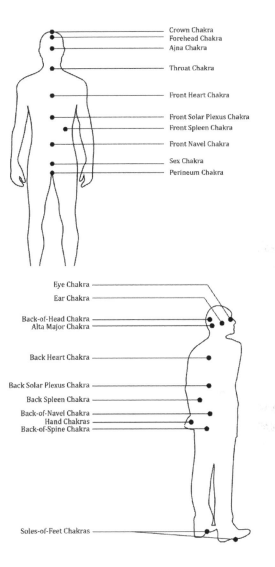

Crown Chakra
Forehead Chakra
Ajna Chakra

Throat Chakra

Front Heart Chakra

Front Solar Plexus Chakra
Front Spleen Chakra

Front Navel Chakra

Sex Chakra
Perineum Chakra

Eye Chakra
Ear Chakra

Back-of-Head Chakra
Alta Major Chakra

Back Heart Chakra

Back Solar Plexus Chakra
Back Spleen Chakra
Back-of-Navel Chakra
Hand Chakras
Back-of-Spine Chakra

Soles-of-Feet Chakras

The diagrams above outline the placements of the chakras in this system that correspond with locations in the physical body. As we become familiar with where they are located, it becomes easier to harness their energy through meditation.

It should be noted that this system is not the only energy model available to us. For instance, Traditional Chinese Medicine (TCM) outlines a network of meridians (energy channels) that circulate life force known as 'qi' through the body. Nadi Yoga also outlines patterns of energy flow through three main channels known as nadis. These weave along the length of the spine through the 7 major energy points in the body. Also, these systems have a lot of inter-relatedness or correspondences. Just to give you an example, the Heart Chakra Corresponds to CV17 acupuncture, and back Heart Chakra to GV11. Similarly, Solar Plexus front and back correspond to CV15 and GV 9, the Ajna is M-HN3, etc. The simple point is that Chakras, Energy Meridian, Acupuncture points all have internal correlation.

So it's important to get the larger point that who we are is much more than a 'physical body' and for meditation, self healing and energy alchemy, the subtle energy anatomy may be much more important to understand than the physical anatomy.

## Subtle Energy Systems and Science

What does science have to say about these subtle energy systems? Though there is much still to be understood by modern day science in this realm, research has been conducted that validates the presence of these energetic fields. Dating back to 1963, researchers at Syracuse University reported the first measurements of the magnetic field emanating from the human heart.[68] This was in the same decade that sensitive magnetometers called SQUIDs (Superconducting Quantum Interference Devices) were being used to map extremely subtle biomagnetic fields of the human body.[69]

A few decades later, Dr. John Zimmerman used the SQUID magnetometer to measure a biomagnetic field emanating from the hands of a therapeutic touch practitioner.[70] Similar results

---

[68] https://www.sciencedirect.com/science/article/abs/pii/S1360859297800137
[69] https://link.springer.com/chapter/10.1007/978-1-4613-0581-1_6
[70] https://www.ncbi.nlm.nih.gov/pmc/articles/PMC4147026/

were also observed by a research team measuring the biomagnetics stemming from the palms of those who emit external qi.[71]

Another technological modality that uses energy principles is that of bioresonance. Bioresonance therapy measures the frequencies coming from a patient's body and uses their own electromagnetic waves to restore optimal balance. This non-invasive, energy-based therapy has been shown to be effective in smoking cessation[72], activating non-specific protective mechanisms in those with rheumatoid arthritis[73], and reducing allergy symptoms.[74]

All of these findings are continuing to evolve as technologies and scientific methods further develop. As our understanding of quantum physics grows, so too do the possibilities for using energy systems in healing and well-being. Though the mechanisms of energy healing are largely beyond what the conventional mindset can currently comprehend, technology is fast evolving. And, as one paper by Christina L. Ross, PhD., expresses:

> *"To both understand and treat the entire human being, current practices in Western medicine must expand concepts of healing to incorporate physics of the HEF [human energy field] into modern medical practice."*[75]

The evidence for the subtle body can fill many volumes and I have chosen only very few easy reads to cite here. My personal view is that as science advances, it will begin to eventually catch up with the subtle body understanding that has existed in the ancient systems for thousands of years.

## The Role of the Subtle Body in Healing, Meditation, and the Expansion of Consciousness

---

[71] https://pubmed.ncbi.nlm.nih.gov/1353653/
[72] https://www.karger.com/article/FullText/365742
[73] https://link.springer.com/article/10.1023/A:1021599216581
[74] https://benthamopen.com/FULLTEXT/TOEPIJ-8-1
[75] https://www.ncbi.nlm.nih.gov/pmc/articles/PMC6396053/

As emerging science is continuing to reveal, the subtle body indeed has a role to play in healing. As research continues, it is expected that the implications of energy medicine and devices that influence energy equivalent of physical organs (i.e. bioresonance devices) will continue to evolve. The applications are ultimately unlimited.

When it comes to emotional and behavioral challenges such as anger, fear, guilt, grief, anxiety, and the fall outs of these, working with our energy body is an important factor in long-term healing. Since emotions and thoughts are stored in our subtle energy body, the etheric, astral, and mental layers must be cleared in order to experience deep peace of mind and compassion in heart.

A holistic intervention to healing would likely incorporate both a bottom-up and a top-down approach for optimal results. We can work on both a physical and an energetic level at the same time in order to provide immediate results (i.e. through stimulating the parasympathetic nervous system or physical organs in different ways) alongside larger shifts in our aura (through esoteric or energetic principles).

Furthermore, through meditation we can create certain responses in the body by stimulating specific energy centers. For instance, a loving kindness meditation becomes more profound when we focus on the heart and the crown chakras (connected respectively to compassion and universal acceptance). Likewise, if we struggle with focus and attention, we can tap into the throat and ajna chakras to empower our practice.

The more we engage our subtle energy system through meditation, the more we cultivate a profound experience of well-being while at the same time healing any imbalance. This creates less of a need for us to engage in the physical body since the impact of a balanced, radiant aura is long lasting and pervasive across all aspects of our lives.

Energetic principles and understandings can further empower our meditation practice by facilitating an expansion of consciousness.

It might feel unusual or even lackluster at first if we are unfamiliar with these subtle systems, but as we continue to practice and open ourselves to what is invisible to the naked eye, we unlock a world of understanding and possibility for ourselves. This facilitates our growth along the vertical axis, enriching this life in the deepest of ways.

## Why are we discussing this anyway

This subject is vast and in part esoteric, I have purposefully decided not to delve into this with too much detail. I did, however, want to cover the basics to essentially communicate the following key points :

- As Human beings are just that; "a being" not just a "body". Another way of saying it is; "we have a body, we are not a body."

- Vitality, thoughts, emotions are energetic substances that reside in a subtle layer of the bioplasmic field called "aura" that envelops our physical body.

- The knowledge of energy centers/chakras can help us deepen our meditations and also cultivate virtues associated with them.

- Meditations for self healing specially related with emotional, mental issues are especially more powerful when we can use our knowledge of subtle energy.

- Not everything about how our consciousness works is understood by science but it's catching up – mostly validating and confirming what ancient systems already know.

In subsequent chapters and meditations we will use the knowledge of the chakras without explicitly referring to them directly, but when we do, you will know what the intent is.

## If you don't like raw egg yolk, eat chocolate

Here is a true story that seems like fiction. You don't have to believe it – sometimes when I think of what transpired, I find it hard to believe too. But the wisdom from it is clear and I hope that stays with you.

Early in my training as a meditator and energy medicine (healing science) student, I had the opportunity to travel through South Africa with my mentor. He was actively engaged in working with HIV positive communities, especially orphans, and with amazing results. One of our local contacts organized a training program for us in Cape Town and we decided to travel there for a few days. On one of the days, after a particularly grueling schedule which included 12 hours of teaching and missing lunch, etc. we finally managed to get away to have a couple of hours to enjoy some fresh air and to have some food.

By the time we arrived at the closest restaurant – a small eatery, they were out of everything vegetarian but on being prodded, agreed to cook some eggs for us. One of our colleagues explained the order to the waiter while I excused myself to go to the restroom. I have often wondered how my French colleague explained the order to the waiter, but for some strange reasons that I still cannot fathom, the waiter returned with a large bowl full of barely cooked - almost liquid egg yolk with chopped onions in it. By this time, to say I was hungry is an understatement and so is saying that I was livid at seeing this bowl of egg-gruel, if you can call it that.

Long story short, I began to protest, only to be firmly told that the kitchen was now closed and this is all we could get, with the waiter insisting that this is exactly what my colleague ordered. This angered me even further and just as I was probably about to make a scene and get thrown out of the eatery, my mentor intervened and said, "Relax; let's see what we can do." I sat back down.

Then my mentor asked me if I was willing to let go of my previous memory of what the liquid egg tastes like, and he asked me this in real earnest. I thought this was some kind of a test and that he wanted to see if I can/could overcome my taste buds. I confidently (faking it) replied that I most certainly could. He responded by saying, *"OK then, we don't have an issue."* He then made a gesture as if he was blessing or energizing the food for a few moments and then asked me to taste it.

Very gingerly I took a little bit of it in my spoon and while completely bracing myself for a horrible taste, I sampled it. To my utter amazement and shock, the liquid egg tasted like chocolate. Not quite exactly like a chocolate but chocolatey enough!

I was stunned and turned to my mentor and asked him how this was possible. He responded by saying that taste is a feeling and feeling is energy, food is also energy – just grosser than a feeling. As long as you know how to transmute the energy with alchemy, no taste or feeling is ever fixed. You can always make your mind 'unconditioned'.

My mind was therefore tasting transmuted energy and the egg was tasting like chocolate. By this time, I had lost complete interest in food and being in total or utter amazement, I was trying to make meaning of this experience, including pinching myself to see if I was sleeping. After a few awkward silent seconds, I asked if he had transmuted the egg energy to taste like chocolate or influenced my mind to process that taste of egg like chocolate. He smiled at me as he replied; "It doesn't, matter does it? What should matter to you is that you can also learn this energy alchemy!"

Needless to say, I continued to study with this mentor for years – one of the most amazing periods of my life – and I learnt a lot of cool energy stuff from him, including pushing people to fall by throwing energy balls at them or rotating a tin foil with energy of thought, etc. This did fundamentally shift my understanding of energy as an abstract spiritual concept to something really tangible that, through meditation and other esoteric techniques, we can learn to master and channel.

When I share this story, I am often asked if I ever got to the level of expertise in my training; to be able to transmute the taste of egg to chocolate. Well, if you ever see me relishing broccoli soup then the answer is yes... and if you see me suffer through it, then the answer is no!

On a more serious note, I will close by saying that mastering the science of energy is mastering of lived experience. And meditations certainly become so much richer, deeper and profoundly moving when we can include energy alchemy within them. This is precisely the reason why I decided to include this chapter in the book.

**Suggested ayam<sup>(TM)</sup> Practice:**

Mediation : Calm, Sleeep Well, Focus, Abundance

# CHAPTER 10

The Six Pillars of Esoteric Meditations

This chapter is what I call a micro chapter, which to me means I am attempting to explain here some concepts only conceptually 😊, without delving deeply into them or offering practices to develop the skills. This chapter provides you the background context for some of the practices of meditations we will engage in towards the end of the book. For those who are using my online meditations or the *AYAM app* this will provide more explanation and grounding in the "why" of the *ayam meditations*!

## What is so Esoteric about Meditations

The word Esoteric has traditionally referred to an obscure knowledge (some would call it 'secret') that is available or revealed to a very small number of people. In the context of meditations, what this means is *more advanced* techniques of meditation that were mostly available to senior students of meditation teachers. These techniques essentially build upon basic training in a wide range of subjects including breathwork, creative visualization, mantric knowledge etc. For centuries, these teachings were only shared with the "initiated", however, in the modern context, we can use some of the same techniques in a more practical and everyday context to deepen and enrich our meditative experience.

Esoteric meditations are something like a string of pearls. Composed of individual beads (or microelements), it is the combination of these singular components that leads to the full piece of work. Each microelement needs to be substantially mastered in order for us to be able to self-guide these kinds of meditations, and so breaking them down into their individual components can give us a better idea of what makes an esoteric meditation what it is.

More familiar to most of us than esoteric meditation are traditional MBSR/MBCT or Vipassana sitting practices. In these more common mindfulness and meditation techniques, focus or awareness tends to be held on any number of the five aggregates (as we explored in chapter two and three). For instance, in mindfulness meditation, we might increase our awareness of the breath, the body, our emotions, or the mental patterns we experience. These play a role in esoteric meditation, and yet the focus of these more unconventional practices is really to help us ascend along the vertical axis. Through the application of energy principles, affirmations, and visualization, our practice deepens (or heightens) beyond traditional mindfulness techniques.

By stringing together each individual micro-practice (the basics of some of which are explored in MBSR/MBCT and other mindfulness teachings also), it becomes possible to use meditation to fulfill a particular intent. Though not rigid, esoteric meditation is systematic, providing us with a guide to move step by step towards an expanded state of awareness.

## The Six Pillars

Each of the six pillars represent a type of practice that functions as an ingredient in esoteric meditation. We can imagine the coming together of these using the pearl necklace analogy, each practice being a single pearl that gets woven together with the others to make something remarkable. Alternatively, we might consider meditation to be like baking bread. Anyone who has baked knows that the process is something like magic. When the ingredients are mixed in just the right way, something profound happens: alchemy occurs.

## Preparation

Before we jump into any practice however, it is important that we prepare ourselves as best we can. Often there are elements of our environment (such as outside noise) that are beyond our control, but we can support ourselves in going deeper by making a few preparations where we can before settling into the practice.

First, we will want to prepare our physical space to be as conducive to the practice as possible. This might include ensuring our phone is on silent, moving into the quietest room of the house, or telling those we live with that we will need some alone time for the next short while. If something is nagging for our attention (such as the dog needing to go outside), it is best to take care of that first. This will help the mind to settle more effortlessly into the meditation.

As we then settle into our seated position, it is important to ensure our posture is as conducive to focus and awareness as possible. The spine should be straight though the shoulders relaxed. For some, this is attainable while seated on the floor. Others will be most comfortable on a meditation bench or in a chair. It does not matter where you are seated; simply ensure that the spine is straight and the rest of your body can relax with ease.

Next, you'll want to attend to the state of your internal environment. What is your intent for the practice? What feelings or thoughts have been with you today? By noticing what is here and what our intention is for practicing, we begin to make that connection with the more subtle aspects of our being.

Now, while noting our intention is beneficial, it is equally important to let go of the intent and to trust the process. One of my Buddhist teachers one told me, *"let the meditation come to you...."* Holding onto our intention too tightly can intervene with the natural flow of insight and energy. Be aware of what you're here for, soften your grip on it, and then settle into the breath to help you anchor in the here and now.

## 1. Breath Awareness

The first pillar of esoteric meditation is the breath. Mindfulness of breath naturally increases our awareness of the innate flow of this life force through our being, helping to ground us deeply into the present moment through simple observation. However, we can take this awareness a step further by understanding that it has multiple uses. The breath can be held, directed, left to flow freely, or used in combination with hand gestures and energy points. Each of these uses has a different purpose in cultivating specific types of energy.

Depending upon our intent, we will apply these basic breath techniques differently. For instance, a meditation for compassion will use the breath in a different way than one for abundance. Using the breath in intentional ways can help to cleanse and align both mind and body and stimulate specific types of energy. The following are four basic types of breaths we can explore that (amongst many others) are used in esoteric meditation according to our purpose.

### Purification Breath

The purification breath is used to clear the astral and mental aura, including negative or difficult emotions such as anxiety and anger. If our environment is toxic, whether physically, mentally, or emotionally, using the breath for purification purposes is one way to bring us into greater energetic balance. This technique works directly with the subtle body.

### Balancing Breath

The balancing breath works to bring harmony to our inner state, including by regulating the nervous system. As we've explored, the sympathetic and parasympathetic nervous systems work differently to one another – the sympathetic side is responsible for the fight-flight-freeze response and the parasympathetic for our feelings of restfulness and well-being. This breath brings us internal homeostasis, similar to the effects of the yogic *anulom vilom* breathing technique (or alternate nostril breathing).

## Energizing Breath

To alleviate feelings of depletion and fatigue, the energizing breath helps to simulate the energy body in a way that increases vitality. This is crucial if we want to move deeper into our esoteric practice because in order to experience an expansion of consciousness, we need to first address energy depletion. Since chronic fatigue is a struggle for many, this type of breath is a necessary step towards elevating consciousness.

## Calming or Centering Breath

Lastly, the calming or centering breath is designed to help bring about increased feelings of equanimity. It naturally guides us into greater inner alignment from where we are less likely to be swayed by moods. Moving into following pillars is most effective when we come to them from a place of being grounded and centered within.

All of the 4 above types of breath have specific structures to follow, including hand positions, how long you hold the breath before exhaling, which energy centers you focus on, etc. Detailed discussion of them is beyond the scope of the book but the meditations that are provided in the last section provide detailed instructions on how to engage in these type of breaths for specific meditations and we also have an e-course that goes into greater detail about the ontology and mechanics of these breaths for those who may be interested in learning more.

## 2. Focus (or Concentration)

Focus, or concentration, is another micro-discipline that has an energizing effect on mind and body. Concentration meditation involves focusing our attention on a single object, or fixed point of reference or an energy center within your subtle body. Meaning thereby that depending upon the practice and the expected outcome, this object can be internal or external. Where it relates to the subtle energy body, focus may be held on a single energy center of a combination of them within ourselves.

Through focused meditation alone, sometimes we might come to experience *satori*[76], the Japanese Buddhist term for the inner, intuitive, and unexplainable experience of Enlightenment. But usually Focus (or one pointed focus as referred to in Vipassana) is practiced in combination with other techniques for esoteric meditations.

Focus technique, when combined with energy centers/alchemy, has an activating or energizing effect on that energy center, triggering a causal chain or related energetic and physiological responses.

### 1. Awareness (diffused or open)

The third pillar of esoteric meditation is awareness, in which our attention is open or diffused. If we consider the martial arts terms 'hard eye' and 'soft eye', open awareness takes the soft eye approach as it includes 360-degree awareness; our entire environment is sensed and perceived. 'Hard eye', on the other hand, is when our attention is on a specific target, correlating with the practice of focused meditation.

Open awareness simply means that nothing is left out of our awareness; all perceptions and senses are witnessed openly. This practice is different from the experience of oneness. To '*be one*' is an intentional act of observing everything around and within us '*as one*'. Open awareness meditation might include glimmers of perceived oneness, but this is not to be used as the boundary of our experience or the goal itself. Allow whatever recognitions and perceptions that naturally flow to arise and remain open to whatever else may come. This is one of the more difficult aspects of meditation to master for people who have been originally trained in other traditions that rely on one-pointed focus. And ironically, I have found that children learn this foundation very quickly.

---

[76] https://www.britannica.com/topic/Satori

During deep states of open awareness, you can experience a sense of boundarylessness where perception barriers of literally where you begin and end, what separates you from the external environment, simply disappear. There is much more that can be said about this subject but is outside the scope of the book.

## 2. Visualization

The fourth pillar is that of visualization, more recently popularized by the book Secret; this is a technique that is thousands of years old and common across practically all meditation systems. Fundamentally, visualization is about creating an energy matrix in alignment with our intent. The visions we create during this process create an energetic reality that exists not only in the visual cortex of the brain but also in our 'consciousness', which is the ground of everything we experience in life in the first place. So visualizations produce a specific energetic effect on the body that creates an energy field of possibility within which our desired outcome is available and more likely. In this way, visualization is not simply about manifesting a particular outcome; it is about preparing the soil for new possibilities and outcomes to arise naturally. As they say, 'your intention always fulfills itself'.

You may like to note that visualization is not the same as imagination. Imagination might be one type of visualization, but visualization has many subsets. In esoteric meditation, visualization is a more conscious process that is directed by our intent. When we visualize with intent, we set a particular energy in motion, which will have a reciprocal effect on the body and mind and the fabric of reality in turn.

## 3. Affirmations

The fifth pillar of esoteric meditations is affirmation practice. Affirmations empower our intentions, helping to establish them more integrally into the neural networks of the brain. This is the fifth pearl we add to the strand as affirmations have the greatest impact on our mind and energy field when we are in an aligned and clear state of being. The intention becomes embedded into our aura, from where it ripples out into all aspects of our lives.

Mantras (such as *om mani padme hum*, or, *I am that I am*) and positive affirmations (such as, *I speak with courage and compassion*) are two different forms of affirmations. Upon repetition of your chosen affirmation, the energy of the words are integrated into who you will become. They shape the filter through which you view life, creating a ripple effect on what is to come.

Emerging research of psychoneuroimmunology (PNI) is also confirming the fact that not only do beliefs become biology but that what we think, tell and affirm to ourselves can have a profound and lasting effect on our health and well-being. I guess medicine is finally catching up with what meditation teachers have known for thousands of years!

### 4. Hand positions or Mudras

The word *Mudra*, originally from Sanskrit, means 'seals of energy', and we could also call them 'energy switches'. The most common of the mudras is the Anjali mudra, in which you bring the palms of your hand together in front of the heart with your finger pointing upwards.

So mudras are mostly hand gestures with symbolic meaning that are used in conjunction with breath and meditation for circulation of life force or prana in specific ways.

The use of mudras with meditations is not limited only to Indic systems but is common across most ancient cultures with meditative practices. Using different mudras, we can direct the chi/prana/energy to have specific effects on our body, like bringing on tranquility, increasing vitality, radiate blessing to sentient beings, etc. Some of the more advanced meditations in the *ayam collection* use mudras to make the practice richer and deeper.

## Building Upon the Scaffolding

These pillars create a framework for a systematic and impactful meditation. They are the scaffolding required for us to ascend along the vertical axis and expand our consciousness. When we master each pillar individually, we create a strong foundation for our esoteric practice and can then weave the five components effortlessly into any self-guided practice.

To fulfill the specific intents we bring to our meditation practice, we can combine these foundational practices with awareness of the subtle energy system within us and specific hand gestures, or mudras, to direct the flow of energy in effective ways. Specific visualizations can also empower our practice by helping to create an energy field in alignment with whatever our overarching mission, vision, and goals might be.

In the next chapter, we will explore specific practices to help cultivate our mastery of these techniques. We will also consider how awareness of energy systems and hand gestures can elevate our practice and contribute to an expansion of our consciousness.

The meta goal of the chapter has also been to introduce you to the idea that with practice, you can craft a deep meditative experience without trying too hard. I am sharing below a true (may be) story of a meditator who had the experience of getting into a high state of meditation just serendipitously!

## Story of a meditator and a mysterious well

A busy corporate executive, Zach had been thinking of going to a Vipassana retreat: a traditional Buddhist practice of 'insight meditation' where the meditator lives in total silence for 10 days except for some discourses and very brief consultations with the teacher – but nothing would fit his schedule. He really longed for the tranquility and peace his peers had described to him that they had found on completion of such a retreat. One of them had gone on to wax eloquently about the teachings and experience of Samadhi in this tradition, leaving him even more inspired to participate. While Zach had had a well grounded daily meditation practice for years, somehow things were just not falling into place yet for this retreat.

Finally, he decided that even if he couldn't go to the silent retreat, he would take some time off to go for a shorter vacation to rest and recharge. Being fond of Europe, he ended up in Lisbon. While on a walking tour of the city art, he met a young couple that had just come back from Sintra (another city) who strongly recommended to him that he should visit. With a weekend at his disposal, he took a morning train and on arrival at Sintra, he felt as if he knew the city instinctively; almost as if he had lived there in the past. He found his way to the famous well of Sintra at the Quinta da Regaleira, which was reportedly used for mystical initiation rituals by the freemasons.

On arriving there, Zach felt a strange feeling of light-headedness and decided to sit down by the staircase. As soon as he did so, he found his eyes closing and almost as if on cue, riveted his attention on his breath. It was almost as if the energy of the place was drawing him to meditate. Within a few minutes, he was blissfully anchored in a state of deep relaxation. As his breath deepened and slowed down, he gently slipped into a deeply meditative state, experiencing the sense of inner calm and peace. Only a few moments would have passed before everything suddenly became still for him, inside and outside – absolute peace and tranquility – an experience where he felt that he ceased to exist as a separate being, but just as an eternal breath. However, this experience lasted only for a couple breaths, before he felt himself being shaken by the shoulder. Opening his eyes, he found a group of young Brazilian travelers trying to 'wake him up', telling him in heavily accented English; "...*the gates are closing soon, you should leave now!*"

A surprised Zach looked at his watch, knowing that he had arrived at the staircase around 10 am and it certainly could not be later than 10:30. After all, he had only been in breath meditation for 5-10 minutes, only to notice his cellphone showing 6:10 pm and a quick look around confirmed to him that dusk was setting in. But how could that be? How come 8 hours had passed in a matter of a few breaths?

Not knowing what to believe and in a bit of stupefied state, Zach walked back to the train station and returned to his hotel. That night, Zach slept well, literally drifting away the moment his head hit the pillow. Up early the next morning, showered and ready at 5 am, he sat down for his routine meditation. As he formed the intent for meditation of attaining thoughtlessness, it finally came flooding back to him what one of his teachers had told him years ago: *in samadhi there is no sense of past or future, not that time stands still but the present moment is eternity itself.* For a moment, he considered the idea that he had experienced the state of *samadhi* in that mystical place and time had just flown by without him noticing it, or maybe he had just fallen asleep. He considered these thoughts briefly and then let both them go, clinging no more to the need for an explanation. Bringing his attention gently back to his breath, he continued his meditation, working towards a state of pure consciousness or thoughtlessness.

Zach remains a life long meditator and is now a meditation teacher.


**Suggested ayam**[TM] **practice:**

Meditations: Joy, Focus, Love and Compassion

Programs : Deepening Your practice, Meet Your Beautiful Sefl

# CHAPTER 11

The Ontology of Advanced Meditations

Since I called the last chapter a "micro chapter", I have no choice but to call this a "nano chapter".

As this is going to be even a smaller chapter. I almost considered wrapping it into the last chapter too, but decided to keep it separate for two reasons. Firstly, because I am addressing here techniques that may seem like "far out" for many readers whose current practice is anchored in the Buddhist tradition of MBSR/MBCT. At the same time, they will seem very familiar to those who have practiced the esoteric or indigenous traditions or energy healing sciences, even though they may not know how they fit within the larger scientific-secular context.

Additionally, some of these practices are actually included in specific ayam™ meditations, especially *Goodwill, Gratitude, Self Healing and Forgiveness*, so demystifying them will be helpful.

Let me begin by introducing the significance of the two terms from the title "ontology" and "advanced". *Ontology* can be simply described as the study of the nature of being and reality. It's an important theme in the Metaphysics branch of Philosophy. Now metaphysics itself is quite interesting in the sense that ancient and Greek philosophers and thinkers thought of it as *the science of being, reality, causality, etc.* but in the modern context, it essentially refers to the study of what cannot be reached through objective studies of material reality. This then brings us to ask what such things could be. Let me share some themes with you to give you an idea: '*transcendence, being, existence in its individual and communal dimensions, causality, relations, analogy, purpose*', etc. Now not everything in Metaphysics is esoteric – this study also includes

Big Bang Cosmology, Physical Cosmology, Plasma Cosmology, etc. In fact, there is a whole rapidly growing field of 'Philosophy of Physics' and in most leading universities you will notice leading Physicists with such titles. So the larger point I am making is that Metaphysics is a blend of art, science, wisdom and spiritual themes and Ontology is part of its expression that comes close to being able to describe a way of being or an experience that is not strictly 'material or physical'.

Phew, that had to be confusing and if you didn't quite understand it, it's fine – you really don't need to make sense of it to understand the rest of the chapter or experience these meditations.

Now, moving to the other word, 'advanced' – what does that even mean? Advanced essentially means something that is deeper, more complex that something else. Most ayam meditations are pretty advanced in their own way, however I chose this word to describe meditation that uses some technique with a metaphysical/esoteric ontology or in easy speak, principles of energy or transcendence of some kind.

There are a few core techniques I will discuss in the next page or so. The idea is not to make you a subject matter expert or to that extent even provide detailed explanation of *how they work*. Rather, the idea is to simply explain the intent of *"why we do what we do."*

So here are some of those techniques:

## White Light Showers

In a couple of meditations we visualize and intend that we are immersed in a brilliant white light shower. The intent here is to use the rejuvenating energy that is available from our 13$^{th}$ energy center (egoic center) and intentionally bring it to different parts of our body (including the subtle body). This serves the purpose of a "resetting" and "rejuvenating" effect being triggered in our bioenergetics and their physical counterparts (organs). On the surface, this may seem like a simply spiritual or metaphysical exercise, which it is. But it's also not much different in guiding principles than the Body scan technique of mindfulness, except for the fact that we are not only using the "spotlight" of attention, but we are also engaging our "subtle energy" and instructing it more specifically with an intent. In transpersonal psychology, the work related with the energetic shifts that our guided intent produces is beginning to get empirically documented. In advanced experiments of quantum physics also, there is beginning to be more empirical exploration of how our "intent" can affect the state of matter. So my personal feeling is that until science catches up, it's OK to think of this as a metaphysical exercise, but it works fantastically, regardless!

## Being the Sun; Radiating energy to points of light

Much of what I have to say about this is more or less a repeat of the previous paragraph. I will briefly add two points. The phenomenon in quantum physics of quantum entanglement, superposition and downward causation make it abundantly clear that the relationship between mind and matter is beginning to be more clearly understood. It is possible to see how information can be exchanged between objects that are physically separated and a change of state in one can immediately effect the change in state of the other.

The techniques above essentially use the same principals to convey the "intent" by way of a visualization with other people that we tend to visualize as points of light. The key here is that "intent" is also just information. Energy follows thought and intent is just that – 'a thought'. So another way to say it is that energy and information are two forms of the same building block of consciousness. In simple speak, if you wish people well, they get the "vibes" and they feel it. That's all there is to this! We are essentially wishing people well or other forms of wholesome thoughts and just using the visualization to empower the communication more richly and effectively.

There are many other techniques that we have not included in ayam meditations, like *invocation, evocation, power of sounds/chants, science of colors and alchemy, etc.* Some of you who attend my live events may stumble upon them. The only thing you need to do is to follow it as guided, your mind will know "how". And if you attend some of my workshops, you will find the detailed information on how each of these techniques work. With the facilitators I train, we go deep into this bridge between science and spirituality – equations and all 😊. But the purpose of this chapter was simply to demystify a little bit the two techniques you will encounter. Hopefully, this has familiarized the meditations for those of you who are curious about it.

For others, I have one of my favorite quotes (a little paraphrased) here:

What is mind?... It doesn't matter!

What is matter?... Never mind!

– *"Punch" Humor Magazine, London*

**Suggested ayam⁽ᵀᴹ⁾ Practices:**

Meditations: Self Healing, Forgiveness

Eseentials: Gratitude, Goodwill

# CHAPTER 12
Meditation, Mindfulness, and Brain Science

This chapter could not be more different from the chapter that precedes it. We spent much of this section of the book looking into subtler aspects of who we are and how to engage that subtle body in meditation. Now in this chapter, we will return back to the physiological body and undertake a very short exploration of what I find is the most fascinating aspect of the human body. The big B...– the brain! No discussion of meditation and mindfulness is complete without exploring how the pivotal organ, *the brain*, functions. Phenomenon like thoughts, feeling, creativity, imagination, visualization, etc. are often all studied by scientists with brain activity as the access door. Except for the study of HRV (heart rate variability), no other phenomenon has been more co-mingled with research on meditation and mindfulness than brain physiology, neuro chemistry, neural activity and brain waves.

In this chapter, we will take a very brief look at some of the initial research, dipping our toe carefully, just to establish the hypothesis that meditation and mindfulness do have measurable effects on various leading indicators of brain and behavioral health. This is not meant to be even a primer, rather just a taster for more medically or scientifically included readers to find a trail they can follow to take a deeper dive.

### Getting started

Throughout the majority of this exploration of how mindfulness and meditation can enhance the quality of our lives, we have thus far largely honed in on the macro physiological functions that help to explain the mechanisms at play. As we know, both mindfulness and meditation have an impact on helping to ease the sympathetic nervous system during times of stress, which can reduce our experience of anxiety, being overwhelmed and fatigue, and increase our emotional resilience.

However, while these mechanisms are an important factor to consider when exploring how these practices impact the body, mind, and our overall wellness, there is much more to the enhancement of well-being than these specific mechanisms. We humans are complex beings and so is the way we experience the world. The difference in our perception of and reaction to the events in our lives is based on more than just nervous system functioning. To dive deeper, we can take a look at the neural happenings within the brain.

This journey into what goes on in the brain is as complex as our neurocircuitry is - an entangled web of actions, reactions, and interactions. Much has been uncovered and learned about this organ's intricacy, and yet there is still much to be revealed. Science is continuing to develop, but thanks to some of the more recent advancements in the field, we are beginning to better understand just how mindfulness and meditation influence this incredible command center. Among other mechanisms, mindfulness and meditation work via the brain to influence our sense of well-being by shifting neural functioning and wiring. Hormones and neurotransmitters, too, play a role.

We will examine some of the recent clinical findings in this regard to gain a clearer understanding of how these modalities lead to the observable psychological and physiological benefits they have been found to offer. In addition, we can fuel our understanding of this vastly powerful organ by considering that the brain is more than just a driver of our physiology – the brain is a bridge between the subtle and physical body. Understanding how mindfulness and meditation influence the brain can therefore deepen our understanding of how these practices lead to long lasting effects when practiced habitually.

Within this field, there is much noise regarding meditation and brain science. Terms such as 'brain hacking' suggest that by following a few easy tips and tricks, it is possible to unleash almost superhuman powers. While many of the suggestions and practices offered contain some degree of truth, fast results are not long lasting. The most sustainable and enduring brain modifications come only through sustained practice. Neurocircuitry does not shift overnight.

So what does recent science even say? How do we impact the structure, functioning, and circuitry of our brain to boost our positive experiences? As we dive into the most recent findings related to neuroimaging, neurochemistry, and neurocircuitry, you will begin to gain a clearer picture of how the brain functions and in what ways it is indeed possible to shift what goes on within the confines of the head.

## Neuroimaging: The Brain on Meditation

The world of neuroimaging is not a new one, relatively speaking. Neuroimaging techniques have been around since the late 1800s[77] when it first became possible to measure blood flow in various parts of the brain. Of course, since then, the tools and techniques used to understand this organ and all the systems connected to it have flourished considerably. Now, there are numerous different methods for assessing what is going on within our skull.

Conducted during a brain scan, neuroimaging can be structural or functional in nature and includes:

- Computerized tomography or computerized axial tomography (CT or CAT)

- Magnetic resonance imaging (MRI)

- Positron emission tomography (PET)

- Regional cerebral blood flow (rCBF)

- Functional magnetic resonance imaging (fMRI)

---

[77] https://academic.oup.com/brain/article/137/2/621/280970

These technologies (along with other emergent tools) provide us with a more nuanced understanding of how the brain works. When it comes to mindfulness and meditation, much research is being conducted in the field to better assess how these ancient techniques can be understood beneath a modern, scientific lens. Since the brain is an incredibly intricate organ, it can help to break down this command center into its various regions to better understand the mechanisms at play.

## Prefrontal Cortex

Firstly, we can take a look at the prefrontal cortex (PFC). This part of the brain is the cerebral cortex that covers the front part of the frontal lobe. Science has discovered that it plays a role in decision-making, emotional regulation, executive functions, and pain processing[78]. As with most regions of the brain, it can be further divided into subcomponents, such as the dorsomedial prefrontal cortex (dmPFC) and the anterior medial prefrontal cortex (amPFC).

Some of the specific findings connecting mindfulness and meditation practice to the prefrontal cortex are outlined:

- One study found that in one focal region of the Brodmann area in the cerebral cortex, the average cortical thickness of 40-50-year-old meditation participants (those with extensive insight meditation experience) was similar to the average thickness of 20-30-year-old meditators and the control group. This finding suggests that regular meditation practice may be beneficial in slowing the rate of neural degeneration in this region within the brain.[79]

- Another study found that three months of meditation practice led to increased connectivity between the dmPFC and the rostral anterior cingulate cortex (rACC, which causes an immediate (and sustained) increase in resilience.[80]

---

[78] https://pubmed.ncbi.nlm.nih.gov/29876878/
[79] https://www.ncbi.nlm.nih.gov/pmc/articles/PMC1361002/
[80] https://www.frontiersin.org/articles/10.3389/fnhum.2019.00101/full

- It has also been found that 8 weeks of mindfulness-oriented focused attention meditation training increased activation in the dorsolateral prefrontal cortex, an area of the brain involved with holding and monitoring one's focus of attention.[81]

## Insula Region

Another part of the brain that deserves much consideration is the insula. This is one of the least understood regions and it is a structure found deep within, sitting between the frontal and temporal lobes. The insula is said to be involved in processing emotion, arousal, awareness of one's bodily states, and other executive functions.[82]

Some of the research that shows the influence of mindfulness and meditation on this region of the brain is as follows:

- Studies have found that disorders that involve a lack of emotional awareness and regulation show a deficiency of interoceptive awareness, largely within the insula cortex. It has been found that mindfulness increases interoception as well as insula connection strength.[83] Interoception is the sense that allows us to feel and understand what is happening within the body.

- Another study found that in those who were long-term meditation practitioners, the strength of anterior insula activation was negatively associated with trait compassion when mindfulness meditation was practiced immediately before observing the social pain of another. This suggests that mindfulness meditation may provide an adaptive mechanism for coping with distress while also increasing compassionate behavior.[84]

---

[81] https://www.sciencedirect.com/science/article/abs/pii/S0278262615300439
[82] https://www.sciencedirect.com/science/article/pii/S0074774216301131
[83] https://www.nature.com/articles/s41598-018-26268-w/?sf192114460=1
[84] https://onlinelibrary.wiley.com/doi/full/10.1002/hbm.23646

## Amygdala

One part of the brain that has gathered a lot of attention for its role in contributing to our experience of fear and anxiety is the amygdala. This small structure rests inside the anterior-inferior region of the medial temporal lobe. It has been found that quite a number of neurons in the amygdala respond to unpleasant stimuli but very few to pleasant ones.[85] Getting to know how it operates and how mindfulness and meditation influence it's functioning can help us to better understand the efficacy of these practices.

Highlights of some of the scientific findings related to the amygdala, as it is influenced by mindfulness and meditation, are noted:

- Results of one study found that breath awareness decreased amygdala activation and increased amygdala-prefrontal integration. Through this pathway, it is suggested that attention to the breath can help to regulate one's emotions.[86]

- One body of research found that participation in a 3-day intensive mindfulness meditation training intervention (in comparison to a 3-day relaxation training without mindfulness) reduced right amygdala resting state functional activity.[87]

- Another study makes a further case for participating in an intensive meditation retreat. Lower amygdala reactivity to negative pictures was observed in connection to hours of retreat practice.[88]

- Additionally, not only has mindfulness and meditation been shown to influence the functional activity of the amygdala, but it is also suggested that meditation can help to decrease the overall volume of this fear-processing structure.[89]

---

[85] https://www.sciencedirect.com/science/article/pii/B978012374512500013X
[86] https://www.sciencedirect.com/science/article/abs/pii/S1053811916002469
[87] https://academic.oup.com/scan/article/10/12/1758/2502572
[88] https://www.sciencedirect.com/science/article/abs/pii/S1053811918306256
[89] https://link.springer.com/content/pdf/10.1007/s11682-018-9826-z.pdf

## The Hippocampus

Another important structure within the brain (though indeed, they are all important) is the hippocampus. This structure is most commonly associated with memory. It takes the shape of a horseshoe and rests adjacent to the amygdala.[90] This part of the brain also plays a role in regulating neuroendocrine functions and emotional behavior, as well as depression and anxiety.[xiii]

Some of the findings that connect the hippocampus to mindfulness and meditation are listed here:

- In one study that looked at the impact of MBSR on those with mild cognitive impairment, reduced bilateral hippocampal volume atrophy was observed as compared with controls.[91] This is significant because reduced hippocampal volume is a core feature of Alzheimer's disease.[92]

- Another study involving the hippocampus found that mindfulness training can protect against proactive interference, which is when previously relevant information impedes one's ability to retain new information. The study also found that this was specifically related to hippocampal volume increase.[93]

## Additional Findings

In addition to the above findings, mindfulness and meditation have been found to have a significant impact on the constitution of matter in various regions of the brain – that is, on the presence of gray matter. Gray and white matter are two components of the brain and spinal cord, the former of which is central to the healthy functioning of sensory and muscular activity. Furthermore, many neurodegenerative diseases are associated with gray matter atrophy.

---

[90] https://www.sciencedirect.com/science/article/pii/B9780123739513001125
[91] https://www.sciencedirect.com/science/article/abs/pii/S0304394013009026
[92] https://www.thelancet.com/journals/laneur/article/PIIS1474-4422%2817%2930343-5/fulltext
[93] https://link.springer.com/article/10.1007/s11682-018-9858-4

One review of numerous studies conducted to assess the impact of meditation on gray matter discovered that in various regions of the brain, meditation interventions resulted in significant increases in gray matter volume.[94] Thus, it can be said that meditation plays an important role in reducing the risk of neurodegenerative disease and some of the complications of aging.

The work being conducted in this field is still emerging. New technologies are being continually developed and expanded upon, which is enabling scientists to gain a closer look and deeper insight into what really happens in the brain when we practice mindfulness and meditation. As our tools for neuroimaging further develop, so too will our understanding of the precise mechanisms at play here.

## Neurochemistry: The Lasting Effects of Meditation on the Brain

In addition to the functional and structural components of the brain, there is also an ever-important chemical component to this organ. Neurotransmitters and hormones, two different types of chemicals that send messages throughout the body, are both influenced through mindfulness and meditation practice. As the secretion of these various chemical messengers shifts (largely stemming from their origins in the brain), so too does our experience of the world around and within us.

Our exploration of the influence that mindfulness and meditation have on hormones and neurotransmitters has largely looked at the stress response thus far. This is because it is one of the most widely understood links between meditation and/or mindfulness and well-being. Yet while the adrenals (the two glands often focused on in regards to the stress response) are indeed directly responsible for the secretion of cortisol, the brain is intimately interwoven with and primary in the cascade of events in this response. When we encounter a stressful situation, the hypothalamic-pituitary-adrenal (HPA) axis is activated, which signifies that the brain has much to do with our stress response.

---

[94] https://content.iospress.com/articles/journal-of-alzheimers-disease/jad160899

When the HPA axis is activated, neuropeptides are released in the brain, which manage the activity of various structures in this control system, including the amygdala. When we encounter a stressful situation, the amygdala releases a cocktail of neurotransmitters, such as noradrenaline, glutamate, and serotonin.[95]

The hypothalamus, too, plays an important function. In fact, this is where the HPA-focused stress response begins. It is within this part of the brain that corticotropin-releasing hormone is secreted, which binds to receptors on the anterior pituitary gland. Adrenocorticotropic hormone is released as a result, which binds to the adrenal cortex and causes the secretion of cortisol.[96]

The secretion of hormones and neurotransmitters via the brain is what impacts the functioning of our other bodily systems. We cannot understand the impact that mindfulness and meditation have on, say the nervous system or the cardiovascular system, without considering the brain's central role. Since the amygdala, the hippocampus, and the pituitary gland are primary drivers of our chemical composition (i.e. cortisol secretion, dopamine levels), it stands to reason that the ripple effect of mindfulness and meditation's benefits start from the top.

Now, the exact mechanisms for how mindfulness and meditation reduce the secretion of cortisol in the first place is not clear; much more research is needed to understand how these modalities interact with this system. And yet regardless, it is important to note that the adrenals on their own are not the sole determinants of the stress response. The chemical cascade begins in the brain, whether that be negative or positive.

## Feel-Good Hormones

While it is important to consider the stress response and the need for it to be regulated in order to improve well-being, it is not

---

[95] https://www.intechopen.com/books/the-amygdala-where-emotions-shape-perception-learning-and-memories/the-key-role-of-the-amygdala-in-stress
[96] https://www.integrativepro.com/Resources/Integrative-Blog/2016/The-HPA-Axis

only through mitigating crises that meditation provides benefit. Meditation and mindfulness practice are certainly beneficial when we are faced with anxiety, depression, fatigue, and any other challenging condition and yet, the human experience is about more than problem solving. It is about maximizing joy, gratitude, compassion, and vitality.

Research in the field of positive psychology has begun to investigate the impact of mindfulness and meditation on our feel-good hormones. A selection of these findings are revealed below:

- Serotonin levels have been found to be higher amongst Transcendental Meditation practitioners. Not only was it discovered in one study that prior to meditation, the TM practitioners exhibited higher amounts of serotonin levels in their urine than control groups; they also measured for higher levels than the control *prior* to meditation.[97] This suggests that sustained practice can increase our resting states of this hormone, not just boost them when we practice.

- One study examined the impact of Arigato-Zin (Gratitude Zen) meditation on oxytocin levels. Oxytocin is sometimes referred to as the 'love hormone', one that is produced by the hypothalamus. It plays a key role in our ability to develop social attachments. The study found that salivary levels of oxytocin were significantly increased after Arigato-Zen practice.[98]

- Another study looking at this hormone found that mindfulness practice, too, can help to increase salivary oxytocin.[99] Additional research supports the idea that this important hormone helps to develop the emotional and cognitive aspects of empathy,[100] which have a huge impact on one's relationships with others.

---

[97] https://www.ncbi.nlm.nih.gov/pmc/articles/PMC4769029/
[98] http://96.126.98.199/index.php/ijnr/article/view/2209
[99] https://onlinelibrary.wiley.com/doi/abs/10.1002/smi.2942
[100] https://www.sciencedirect.com/science/article/abs/pii/S016503271200016X

- Dopamine, often referred to as the *feel-good* hormone, has also been found to increase through mindfulness and meditation practice – specifically Yoga Nidra.[101]

- Additionally, meditation (in this study, Transcendental Meditation) has been found to increase plasma melatonin levels.[102] The hormone we often refer to as the 'sleep hormone', this chemical messenger is necessary to ensure we get an adequate night of rest. Not only does this have a positive impact on our sleeping hours; as we know, the quality of our sleep has a huge impact on our embodiment of well-being during the day to follow.

## Shaping Brainwaves

In addition to the way that these modalities impact hormone and neurotransmitter levels, we can also consider the impact that they have on brain waves. Based on the current state and activities of the brain, this organ will emit a specific frequency or electrical pulse. When we are sleeping, for instance, the brain emits a very different frequency compared to when we are immersed in contemplative work or critical thinking.

When it comes to brain activity, the primary frequencies we experience are:

- Delta – Greatest amplitude, slowest frequency; associated with deep, dreamless sleep states

- Theta – Occurs most often during sleep; associated with memory, intuition, and sensory withdrawal

- Alpha – Occurs during quiet thoughts and certain phases of meditation; associated with feelings of ease, relaxation, and presence

---

[101] https://www.sciencedirect.com/science/article/abs/pii/S0926641001001069
102 https://www.sciencedirect.com/science/article/abs/pii/S0301051100000351

- Beta – The forerunner of our waking state, this is a fast frequency with low amplitude; associated with problem solving, decision making, and overall mental activity

- Gamma – The highest frequency of our brain waves; associated with peak concentration, being 'in the zone', compassion, gratitude, and high cognition

These various states of brain activity are not levels we enter into consciously; they are the natural result of our present moment state of being. That being said, through mindfulness and meditation practice, we are indeed able to shift between frequencies. Studies have looked at the differences of brainwave states amongst meditators. Some of the findings are noted:

- One study found that practitioners of one of three different meditation traditions (Vipassana, Himalayan Yoga, and Isha Shoonya) all exhibited higher gamma amplitude than control subjects during meditation.[103] Again, these are the frequencies associated with heightened concentration, compassion, high cognitive functioning, and being in the flow, all experiences worthy of cultivation if we long to live vibrantly and fully attuned to our lives.

- Another study found that compared to relaxation (in this study, closing one's eyes and simply sitting in a state of rest), meditation had a greater impact on the cultivation of theta and alpha brainwaves in various regions of the brain.[104]

- Furthermore, a revelatory study looking at the practice of long-term Buddhist practitioners revealed that it is possible to self-induce high-amplitude gamma waves as a result of mental training. Not only that, but it was also found that the ratio of gamma-band activity to slower activity was higher in the resting state amongst these practitioners as compared with the control group. This

[103] https://journals.plos.org/plosone/article?id=10.1371/journal.pone.0170647
[104] https://www.liebertpub.com/doi/abs/10.1089/acm.2009.0113

suggests to us that mental training can help to establish both short-term and long-term neural changes.[105]

On that final note, it is indeed becoming clear that mindfulness and meditation practice go beyond our present-moment experience of peace and tranquility. Thanks to the ever-expanding field of neuroplasticity, it is becoming clearer than ever that the brain can change in lasting ways. Just as our brains take shape during our earliest formative years, it is indeed possible to harness this power of transformation in adulthood to shape our brains in wise, loving, and joyful ways.

## Our Role in Shaping the Brain

Given what we've uncovered about the impact that these practices can have on the structure, functioning, and networking of the brain, what is our role in shaping this delicate and powerful organ? As we deepen our understanding of neuroplasticity, we come to realize that we can have a huge impact as to if and how the brain will shift.

The first thing we must remember is that sustainable, long-lasting change takes time. We cannot expect the brain, which developed through a slow and subtle magic of its own, to shift after a few practices. Through continual practice, however, we can play our part in affirming neural networks that are in alignment with our highest values.

Since the brain contains a negativity bias (that is, the tendency to give more weight to negative experiences than positive ones), it requires an active effort on our part to internalize positive occurrences, as Dr. Rick Hanson explains in his book, *Buddha's Brain*.[106] Since we more easily remember and internalize the hurts and pains we've experienced, mindfulness is a prerequisite for leveling out the playing field. By focusing on the good that occurs in our lives (such as through gratitude practice, whether formal or informal), we begin to rewire the brain to see, to believe in, and to perceive more goodness.

---

[105] https://www.ncbi.nlm.nih.gov/pmc/articles/PMC526201/
[106] Hanson, Rick. *Buddha's Brain: The Practical Neuroscience Of Happiness, Love, And Wisdom*. Readhowyouwant.com, 2011, pp. 74-77.

Literally, what occurs in the brain is a rewiring. New associations are made between the world around us and the one within, associations that root themselves in the networks that underlie our thinking and feeling processes. For instance, if we hold the belief that we are unlucky and that things never go our way, this is not just an abstract thought with no roots. This belief, along with all the others we hold, is carved into our neural wiring.

As we start to open ourselves to the positive alternative of this story – for instance, to a belief that good things happen to us and that life is providing us exactly what we need – we begin to develop new patterns of thought that develop stronger neural roots overtime. Again, this is not a once-and-done type of endeavor. For meaningful and lasting results, we must commit to cultivating the good as the rule, not the exception.

Ways that we can step up to our role as the co-creator of a new brain include:

- Practicing gratitude each morning and night. Note what you have to be thankful for either within the confines of your mind, in a journal, or expressed to a loved one.

- Exploring meditation practices that focus on cultivating positive virtues, such as abundance, joy, compassion, and goodwill.

- Remaining open to positive data points. As we know, our personal biases impact the data we select; practice being receptive to positive notes.

- Grounding ourselves in the breath and body when we experience difficult emotions. This will soften the stream of thoughts that fuel any limiting or negative stories.

- Bringing to mind positive emotions when negative ones are present. As Hanson notes, these will serve as an antidote to the negative feelings.[xxviii]

- Cultivating the virtues of love, kindness, and compassion. Whether in a conversation with another person or wrapped up in the narratives within your mind, where is it possible to soften judgment and invite more love into our lives?

Beyond these specific examples we can point to for cultivating the good, any consistent mindfulness and meditation practice will help to shape the brain. As we know, sustained practice helps to increase hippocampal volume, the area associated with our memory. General practice also helps to improve emotional regulation, granting us heightened clarity over our experience. A commitment to practice will also help to slow the brain's aging by boosting grey matter and reducing the risk of neurodegenerative disease. So long as we are bringing curiosity, compassion, and patience to our practice, we will facilitate the process of undoing the old and cultivating a beautiful 'new'.

## The Brain vs. The Mind: Who Are We?

It goes without saying, after reading all of this but likely before, that what happens within the brain is crucial to our well-being. The brain directs the way we perceive the world around us and helps us to navigate the world as best as we can. By tending to the care and nourishment of the brain through mindfulness and meditation, we become more resilient, more focused, more loving, and more present in our lives.

In addition, however, it is worth noting that the brain is not the same as the mind and that the brain is not indicative of the entire human experience. Indeed, it is a crucial piece of the life puzzle; a good life is not possible without a healthy brain. Yet we are more than just the functioning of our brain. We also have a mind – a mind which constitutes more subtle aspects of our being that contribute to the wholeness of our experience.

We can consider that the brain is the host of our mind; it is the part of our being that receives data and runs it through our physiology in different ways. When we encounter a threat, for instance, the brain takes in the information presented to it, which sparks a cascade of responses to help protect us from danger. Meaning, however, is made in the mind. It is within the mind that we process our more subtle experiences and where our awareness of intertwining thoughts and emotions take place.

As we explored in chapter 8, there are different layers to our being or our auric field. The brain is an integral and crucial part of the physical body, but beyond it we have additional bodies. Within that broader understanding of our energetic being lives the mind. We might also understand it by considering that the brain is a bridge between our more subtle energy bodies and the part of ourselves that we can see and feel in a tangible way. But indeed, we are more than our hardware.

Beyond the brain rests the mystical phenomenon called consciousness; a concept and experience that has probed the hearts and minds of spiritualists, seekers, philosophers, and the like for centuries. What does it mean to be conscious of our experience and aware of the phenomenon of life itself? These are big questions that lie beyond the scope of this chapter, but what it invites us to sink into is the knowledge that we are infinitely more than biochemical processes. We are made of energetic fields, just like the world that surrounds us, and through the tool that is the brain, we can awaken ourselves to our highest values and deeper layers of who we really are.

# SUMMING UP

## Why You Need Not Believe or Use Any of This

Of everything you've taken in from this section, there is nothing you need to believe in. Whether or not you resonate with the concept of the subtle body, the mudras, esoteric meditations, or even neuroplasticity will not change what you can hope to experience through practice.

The more spiritual or esoteric teachings outlined in these chapters (along with others you might learn about with greater depth elsewhere) will resonate with each one of us in unique ways. This is because each of us hold pre-existing belief systems and unique past experiences. When we learn about new models, beliefs, and philosophies, this newly absorbed information will be processed in different ways – and this is entirely acceptable.

For some, concepts like the chakra system and the power of mudras may be intriguing at most. For others, these understandings will complement existing beliefs systems and provide a framework for diving deeper. For others still, these teachings will contradict existing programs and belief systems and therefore not resonate. It does not matter what the impact of these teachings is for you.

Because regardless of how these teachings resonate with each one of us, there is no 'right' or 'wrong' lens through which we must view the power of mindfulness and meditation. What matters is that we remain committed to the practice, irrespective of why we think it works. Belief does not give these modalities their power to expand and transform.

To elaborate on this, we might consider what it takes to drive a car. Is it necessary to know, with the expertise of an auto mechanic, how the car gets your from point A to point B? In other words, do we need to know how a car functions in order to effectively drive it?

Knowing how a car works might help you to get more value out of it and optimize its performance, but these insights aren't necessary to get you to where you wish to go. Likewise, we might use this analogy on physical exercise. Is it necessary to understand the scientific underpinnings of weight loss and muscle strengthening in order to reap the benefits of a workout? Though such knowledge might help us to maximize the effects of our efforts, we will get what we need out of the session regardless of our expertise.

Meditation is much the same. You can follow guided practices without believing in the explanations for how it works and without learning specific details beyond what is required for you to move through each practice. So long as we approach each session with a willingness to follow what is presented to us, we will receive the benefits we require.

In chapter 4, we explored the hygiene of learning: how to prepare the mind and what to bring with us into each section. Non-judgment, patience, the beginner's mind, your personal experience, and self-compassion were all on that list. Belief was not. Though belief can help us to feel more connected with what we are practicing, it is not a prerequisite.

The ancient wisdom included in this section has solely been provided for those who would like to gain a broader or deeper understanding about the 'how'. For those whom these teachings resonate with, having this framework can certainly help to deepen one's practice. When we have a more nuanced understanding about anything, it can propel our exploration of that thing in unique and unexpected ways.

That being said, it is important to note that this is not the same as saying that those who do not believe in any or all of these teachings will have a less enriching experience. Quite simply, when we are inspired by some new piece of knowledge of concept, this inspiration guides us to journey deeper into what draws us. It might enhance our mental understanding of what is happening during practice, but it does little to the felt, embodied results of time spent in meditation.

A pilot of an aircraft, its crew members, and its passengers all arrive at the same place when the journey is complete. Meditation is no different. The view you have of your travels will be different according to what window (or lens) you're looking through but ultimately, the real magic is in the aircraft itself.

As you move further into your own practice, hold onto what inspires you. If that is the chakra system or particular mudras, that is wonderful. If what inspires you is neuroplasticity, the quiet peace you experience while watching your breath, or the focus you cultivate through practice, that is equally exceptional.

It is often said that the best mindfulness or meditation practice is the one that works for each of us. Likewise, the best belief system to hold is that which brings us a sense of curiosity, commitment, and inspiration. Let what ignites you be your guiding light as you sink into the benefits of practice – regardless of what your beliefs might be.

# SECTION 4

Living a Mindful Life

The ways in which mindfulness and meditation can impact our lives are infinite and far reaching – as they were destined to be. They are not just teachings designed to enhance our ability to sit quietly on a mat to steal a moment, but to profoundly impact how we move through and engage with the life around us. In other words, mindfulness and meditation are not just about 'I', the individuals – they are about *us*, the full, dynamic web of life.

The most complete embodiment of these practices occurs when we are able to apply these teachings and wisdom to all facets of our lives – to our relationships with others, to our interactions in the workplace, to our own personal health and well-being, and to our work as leaders. As mindfulness becomes integrated into the fullness of living, it finds its home.

In this section, we will explore how we can positively nurture our interactions in everyday life using these principles and techniques. In doing so, we deepen our lived experience of and truest embodiment of these practices, positively impacting the lives of all those who cross our path, as well as our own.

# CHAPTER 13
Mindful Togetherness

In this chapter my mother intent is to provide just a bit of context and trigger a mindful inquiry. By no means am I qualified or intending to offer any relationship therapy advice, but I am certainly interested in expanding your awareness about how you are feeling about any of the points I bring up that resonate with you.

This subject is vast and deep, and impossible to cover in volume – let alone a few pages. Therefore, I have carefully curated some conversations and cases drawn from my own experience in life and of those I have worked with to create real life scenarios where a mindful enquiry has been a powerful access to create more harmony, balance, love and peace. My intent is not, and I hope it shines through clearly, to arrive at any answers, but to just invite you to experience exactly what comes up for you as you engage in this enquiry.

Throughout my life, I have had a rainbow of relationship experience – lots of ups and downs, and even in the most beautiful relationships I have shared, there have been moments when I have felt vulnerable and hurt. Early on I did work with some self healing meditations and forgiveness to move past them and it has worked magically, but later in life I have concluded that imbibing the lesson that life was trying to give me is at least as important as *how I feel*. So when I was designing the *ayam collection* of meditations, I promised myself if there happens to be a book around it, I will devote some space in it to trigger some mindful enquiries to make room for expanding awareness and insights to arise, so here is that chapter!

## What is Togetherness?

In our modern way of relating, there is much confusion about what it means to be together. We might share a home with someone or an office, but does that mean we are authentically in union with another? As we dive deeper into our mindfulness exploration, we come to realize that mindfulness is not an individual practice. When fully embodied and expressed, it radiates through our dynamic life and all the relationships we foster.

Togetherness is not a mixture of two things; it is not about the physical space we share. Though it takes place in space, togetherness is an alchemy – an alchemy of dreams, of thoughts, of aspirations, of emotions, and of everything else that rises and falls throughout our lives. It is a subtle, dynamic dance, with qualities and needs that are constantly in motion. You might consider togetherness to be a piece of art or music, trailing off into an indefinite, undefined future. The notes, tones, and colors ebb and flow by some uncontrollable force.

*alchemy (n.) – a power or process that changes or transforms something in a mysterious or impressive way*[107]

Relationships begin with a foundation – some shared bond or experience that establishes the base layer of togetherness. However, what frequently occurs in our relationships is that we never alchemize that foundation. We overlook or lose sight of the dance of dreams, emotions, thoughts, feelings, and beliefs that express the aliveness of our relationship.

When that happens – when we miss the opportunity to honor the alchemy of our relationship – we deny the natural process of nature and of life. The only thing constant in life is change, and when we resist that deeper truth, our relationships falter. Our failure to alchemize leads to judgment and resistance overtime. We struggle to see those we are in relationship with as dynamic beings, resisting their natural flow (and often, our own as well).

[107] https://www.merriam-webster.com/dictionary/alchemy

*"The only thing that is constant is change."*
*Heraclitus*

When judgment and resistance are given space to flourish, they, in turn, result in resignation, cynicism, and often indifference. The result is neither a state of being happy nor sad; rather, we end up in a state of submission. Without the tools or skills required to navigate the challenges of the relationship, we resign to indifference and a feeling of 'giving up'. This is not where we experience the vitality of togetherness; on the contrary, it drains the vital force of our being.

In addition to this movement from shared bond to resistance to resignation, many modern day relationships involve a high degree of attachment: attachment to a person or object, an outcome, a belief, or a vision. Often, we hold many attachments, many of which inhibit the flow within our relationships.

Now, there is often some resistance to the notion that we should be without attachment in our relationships. However, we might ask ourselves: what is really on the opposite side of attachment? Is it indifference, and denial of human needs and emotions? Or is the opposite of attachment a state of flow and acceptance? When we consider that non-attachment does not mean we are without needs or without commitment, the idea of softening our attachments can be welcomed with greater ease.

And since attachment can often lead to suffering, exploring where (and how) we are attached – and softening where possible – creates space for more love, lightness, and vitality to flow through our togetherness. This is the case for friends, co-workers, partners, and family members. When our relationships are given space to breathe – to flow in accordance with their unique and mysterious rhythm – contentment and peace are the result.

Arriving at this state of openness and full acceptance can take time as we become mindful of our habits, tendencies, and hardwired mental constructs or biases. It does not mean that every moment will feel joyful; however, with honest and reflective mindful inquiry, we begin to find peace in the alchemy of our relationships – through both the 'good' times and the 'bad'.

---

### Mindful Pause

Take a moment to reflect upon the following questions, remaining curious, compassionate, and non-judgmental towards your experience:

*Can you recall a time you have resisted change within a relationship?*

*What was moving through you during this moment of resistance?*

*How does it feel to consider softening any attachments you hold?*

*How does it feel to consider embracing flow and unconditional acceptance?*

---

## Mindfully Navigating Our Relationships

Learning to navigate our relationships in authentic and thoughtful ways begins with mindfulness. Each of us holds our own personal biases and beliefs that fuel our decision-making and reinforce our limited views of the world (as we explored through the Ladder of Conclusion). Mindfulness requires us to witness our own inner experience with non-judgment and non-attachment so that we might open to life with greater curiosity and acceptance.

While many of us might think (or have thought) that what our relationship needs is for our partner, colleague, or loved one to change their ways or to see things differently, mindfully navigating our relationships must begin within. It requires us to take responsibility for what we ourselves are bringing into togetherness.

Mindful inquiry into the nature, needs, joys, and challenges of our relationships can involve any number of questions. You might consider:

*What is the shared bond?*

*What am I contributing to this union or shared space?*

*Does this relationship provide care and nourishment?*

*Does it provide opportunity for growth and fulfilment?*

*Are there sources of anguish, confusion, grief, or any other difficult emotion?*

This inquiry is not about finding someone or something to blame or finding a problem that needs fixing. It is exclusively to help us witness our togetherness from all angles – without needing to draw quick conclusions about what we find.

When we reach that final question – *are there any sources of anguish, confusion, grief, or any other difficult emotion?* – we are invited to turn towards our experience wholeheartedly. Without suppressing, denying, or attempting to fix the experience, can we simply be with whatever emotions are present for us?

**Mindful Pause**

If you are experiencing any relationship challenges at present, take a moment to sit in mindful awareness of any emotions or feelings that are present within you now. Noting where the mind might attempt to overlay your experience with thoughts and beliefs, see if you can simply acknowledge this emotion – exactly as it is in its raw form. Ground through the breath if this becomes unsettling.

One of the keys here is to avoid problem solving. Without our conscious recognition of the tendency, the mind tends to jump into high gear when we encounter what we deem to be a relationship 'problem'. However, mindfulness calls us into 'being' rather than into 'doing'. Rather than 'fixing' whatever it is we deem to be a problem, can we open ourselves to a new way of being with this experience? And, to a new way of being together with another?

The goal is not to achieve an answer or definite outcome (as outcomes are like anything else and subject to change); instead, the goal is to achieve a state of flow. Once we acknowledge or recognize what is present (also recognizing that this experience is happening where we are and not where our partner or the situation is), we can then open ourselves up to acceptance.

Again, acceptance does not mean that we do not have preferences as to what might happen. It simply asks us to move beyond our preferences of outcome and into a greater embrace of what is actually occurring within and around us. For instance, we might prefer that our adult child settles in the city where we live; however, when they move to another country for work or love, can we still find a sense of acceptance despite our hopes?

Acceptance is about integrating reality into our experience. It invites us to let things be – without contortion. Despite whatever pain or mental anguish an experience creates, can we find the peace beneath, within, and all around it?

Mindfulness not only invites us into a greater state of flow: it helps us to achieve it. Through non-judgmental, compassionate witnessing of events as they unfold, our reactions naturally start to soften to the world around us. This doesn't mean life will be perfect as things will continue to occur in life that cause pain or difficulty (so long as we are human). But what we can be sure of is that whatever unfolds will do so naturally.

> *"Let go of the battle. Breathe quietly and let it be. Let your body relax and your heart soften. Open to whatever you experience without fighting."*
> Jack Kornfield

Furthermore, navigating our relationships is not only about how we witness and open to acceptance of challenges; it's about the care and attention we grant ourselves and the other in all moments.

First, we must honor our need for self-care, regardless of the relationships we are also nurturing. It is very difficult to authentically care for another when we are not doing so for ourselves. Whether we have children, a partner, or a demanding career, taking the time to care for ourselves – in whatever shape and form that comes in – restores our energy so that we may be of service to others as well.

Furthermore, mindfully managing our relationships is not just a reactive measure in challenging times. During lighthearted conversation around the dinner table or while out running errands, can we grant the same care and attention to those we are with through mindful presence and communication? What we practice in times of ease goes a long way in helping us to peacefully navigate the challenges that may later arise.

## The Requirements of Different Relationships

At the root of each of us exists the same needs, the same capacity for the range of human emotion, and the same deepest yearnings. We all want to be heard, loved, and cared for, and so in a sense, there is no difference between the needs of a 5 year old child and a 70 year old grandparent. The same care, kindness, and compassion can be applied throughout all of our experiences of togetherness.

At the same time, different relationships undoubtedly require different things – and at different times. For instance, what a parent-child relationship requires when the child is 5 versus 35 is likely quite different. Similarly, the way we navigate differences of opinion with our children versus our partner will require appropriate language and a tailored response.

Let's have a look at some of the areas in which we might explore mindful togetherness. Read through the examples and reflect upon where you might explore these subtle approaches and techniques in your own life.

## Mindful Partnership

Partnership is a relationship of two. Whether that's an intimate pair, two friends, or a set of co-workers, partnership is a prime opportunity for us to deepen our understanding of what it means to be in a mindful relationship. Rather than trying to navigate the needs, dreams, emotions, and thoughts of numerous people, we can focus on the unique dynamic between just ourselves and another. In this section, we will exclude parent-child relationships, looking at those further on.

We will start with a reflection exercise. As you move through this, be mindful of whatever arises, holding your inner experience with compassion and curiosity. There are no 'right' or 'wrong' thoughts you can have – there is simply your experience.

1. Consider a relationship you have with one other person. This might be a partner, spouse, sibling, friend, or co-worker. What is the shared bond you have with this person?

2. Now, expand your awareness of this relationship to consider on a more visceral level what *your* experience of this shared bond is like. What emotions or feelings arise when you think about your relationship with this person? Reflect for one minute.

3. Expand a little further now to consider what additional emotions, feelings, and beliefs arise with this person in mind. Our relationships are hardly defined by one type of emotion; they are far more layered than that. Without judgment, consider: what else is present in this experience of togetherness?

4. Now, where things get a bit difficult is where there is conflict or difference of opinion. Without judgment or assessment, can you call to mind a disagreement you might have with this person? What is one thing you view or experience differently?

5. Consider: Is there space within the relationship for different views, beliefs, or feelings to co-exist? What about uncertainty, confusion, or lack of resolution? First, inquire with the mind. Then, inquire with the heart. Notice the difference.

Mindful partnership invites us deeper into the mystery of human relationships and of life itself. It encourages us to be present with whatever our experience of relationship is – whether happy, sad, 'good', or 'bad'.

Of course, this mindful witnessing of our relationship dynamics *does not* suggest that we should remain physically present in abusive or harmful relationships. In fact, it promotes the opposite. As we practice mindfulness, we begin naturally to gravitate towards the heart – to a place of love. Since love begins within – urging us to take care of ourselves – mindful relating might steer us away from relationships that do not promote inspired growth, love, and nourishment.

Often, however, there is room for both to grow in our relationships – room for both sides of a partnership to become more present, more loving, and more supportive of the natural alchemy of relationship.

Now, let's look at two examples to illustrate how this mindful way of relating might play out in various scenarios.

### Example 1 – Olivia (36) and Michael (35), couple, unmarried

*Olivia and Michael have been dating for almost 7 years. Their relationship feels strong, more or less, aside from where the question of marriage arises. Michael has always been 'against' the idea of marriage and, until recently, Olivia was, too. However, Olivia has started longing for a symbolic way of expressing their commitment to one another. Olivia has begun to question Michael's commitment to her due to his refusal to discuss the idea further, and Michael has become frustrated with Olivia's change in tone on the topic and her persistence in exploring the idea.*

Take a moment to consider:

What assumptions could Olivia be making? What thoughts may have led her to the conclusion that Michael is not committed to their partnership? What might she not be accepting about Michael? Where could she become more curious?

Likewise, consider what assumptions Michael has made. What beliefs and thoughts could be present for him? What might he not be accepting about Olivia? How might he try softening his beliefs and inquiring more thoughtfully with Olivia's ideas?

While there could be any number of thoughts and beliefs present for Michael and Olivia, a few things worth taking a closer look at include:

- Olivia's belief that marriage equates to commitment – could there be an opposing belief to this that Michael holds?

- Michael's resistance to the change in Olivia – could her change be accepted here (without assumption of what accepting this change means)?

- Olivia's concerns about Michael's commitment – could there be something else going on in their relationship?

- Michael's unwillingness to discuss the subject – could conversation be encouraged rather than avoided?

These are just a sample of directions you might take this in if you wanted to inquire a bit further – and if you were, of course, either Olivia or Michael. Like your own personal inquiry, this is not in an effort to discover the 'right' or 'wrong' side of any situation. It is simply to help bridge the perceived gaps that divide us.

## Example 2 – Lily and Louise, friends, early 50s

*Lily and Louise have been close friends for 20 years. Both separated from the respective father of their children, they were each other's closest companion as they raised their kids side by side. However, Lily recently began dating again. And, four months into her relationship with a man named Pete, she's decided to move in with him. Louise says Lily's changed, disapproving of her friend's new lifestyle. Lily and Pete are behaving in a way that Louise would call 'reckless', moving too fast too soon. Lily has withdrawn from Louise because she feels they're no longer 'on the same page'.*

Take a moment to consider:

What might Lily be feeling or experiencing in her relationship with Pete? What emotions, thoughts, or beliefs might underlie her feeling that Louise and herself are 'on different pages'? What might Lily not be understanding about her friend Louise at this time?

Likewise, what array of emotions is Louise likely experiencing? What thoughts, beliefs, and assumptions could she be making about Lily and Pete's relationship? What is she not seeing or understanding about Lily's experience?

Again, there are any number of ways we might dive into this if we were either Lily or Louise. Ideas or curiosities worth exploring further could include:

- Lily's emotions and feelings being in this new relationship – could this be explored more intently?

- Louise's emotions and feelings about the change in her relationship with Lily – could this be discussed with courage and care?

- Lily's withdrawal from Louise – could there be another way of engaging with Louise?

- Louise's resistance to Lily's change – could this change be simultaneously celebrated and grieved?

When we remain curious and compassionate towards the experience of both halves of a partnership, we soften any tendency towards judgment and resistance. Again, this does not mean we lose our personal preferences entirely; it simply enables us to see where mutual growth and understanding are possible. This mindful way of being opens us up to a deeper embrace of things as they are – of people as they are.

### The Windy Paths Of Togetherness

One thing that has always interested me in working with couples is inviting them to restate what brought them together in the first place – where the genesis of "us" took place. Many times, couples have a hard time recalling that. At other times, when the couple recalls it, there is a barrage of emotions that come with it. This exercise does not automatically heal or strengthen the relationship, but it does give them some common space to experience from where they can trace their own journey, even if it in many cases has gone in different directions.

I often remind the couples that just as "coupling" is a creative exercise where we work on creating a shared future together, it's also possible to "uncouple" mindfully, while supporting each other. Of course, this isn't possible in all circumstances, especially when one person is moving faster than the other, and it does not have to be the same for both partners. However, the "gentle reminder" to be mindful of one's actions, words and being empathetic to the other does create more space to deal with what is so. As my mentor use to say, " ...some pain in any separation is inevitable, but lasting suffering can be consciously avoided".

Mindful togetherness therefore is as much about "mindfulness" as it is about the collective consciousness of "together" or "us". Not to replace our own individual sense of space or freedom but to be mindful of what exists or has been created together. Finding compassion and respect for that does allow one to work with more space.

All the practices of mindfulness that we have discussed thus far lay but a foundation for them to bring into our life as we engage in our relationships that are closest to us, especially when it feels difficult to be able to do so.

## Mindful Parenting

In many ways, mindful parenting is no different than mindfully relating in any other way. However, when we're communicating and experiencing life with a child, the way we do so is a bit different than when we are with a friend or partner. Depending upon the age of the child, unique opportunities and challenges exist.

Children have a unique ability to see the world without preconceptions – though at the same time, they are without the wisdom and experience of their caregivers. When we're mindful of the way we're engaging with our children, these differences provide opportunity for awe and for growth. But, if we don't have the mindful resources or insights at hand, parenting can leave us depleted.

When children are still young, we as adults are in the leading role. We have a better ability – or responsibility at the very least – to witness our emotions and to then respond rather than react. Children don't have the same capacity to filter information before responding. What they feel is made clear before they develop the capacity to sit with their thoughts.

As children get older, our relationship to them changes – a shift that continues until the parents are elderly and the once young children are now adults with their own kids. This movement through the life span perfectly reflects the innate presence of 'change' throughout all of life.

We will begin this exploration with another reflection exercise. If you do not have children, you can either read through in any case or else skip to the paragraph that follows this inquiry. Again, reflect mindfully upon the following questions. Try to refrain from judgment as new insights or information arises.

1. Draw to mind your relationship with your child (just one if you have multiple). How would you describe the bond you have with this individual? How does this bond feel within your body? Notice the difference.

2. Consider the range of emotions or feelings you have in regards to your relationship with your child. Spend a few minutes here letting whatever rises be present. Note both light and heavy feelings, mindfully observing it all without becoming caught up in any particular emotion.

3. Now, reflect upon the role and responsibilities you have as a parent. Can you simultaneously hold both the effortlessness and the difficulties that arise with this role? Can you honor

the experience without judging it as right or wrong, good or bad?

4. Inquire about what it feels like to be a parent – first with the body, then with the mind, and lastly with the heart. Notice the differences.

Now, let's consider for a moment that parenting is not just a topic of consideration for those that have children. Many others have made the choice not to have children or have not been able to, both of which reflect that consideration has been made about what parenting means for them in their own lives.

Whether we have children or not, our lives are influenced in any case. Both the presence and absence of children brings its own challenges and opportunities, neither of which is better or worse.

Let's explore this in our first example to help us gain a better sense of what it means to parent (or not parent) mindfully.

**Example 1 – Anika (46), in a partnership, without children**

*Anika has been in a long term partnership with Sam for 15 years. The two were unable to have children naturally; and, after plenty of discussions, they decided against seeking treatment to support fertility. Both felt complete in their lives without children. Ten years since that decision was made, Anika wonders if she missed out on an opportunity. What if they had tried alternative methods? What if they had adopted? She is content with her life as it is but more than frequently wonders 'what if'.*

Take a moment to consider what it would mean for Anika to mindfully accept her experience. Without problem solving or 'fixing' her present difficulties with the decision they once made, she might consider:

• What is the experience of not having kids?

• What *else* is the experience of not having kids?

- In what other ways do I embody the 'mother' role?

- Can I find peace in my place, holding both the challenges and opportunities of not being a parent at the same time?

### Example 2 – Mateo (40), Alice (38), and Ellie (4), parents and child

*Mateo and Alice welcomed their daughter Ellie into the world 4 years ago. Since then, their own relationship has shifted as they've taken on new roles as mom and dad. In recent months, they've been more stressed than usual as Ellie is showing signs of having a developmental coordination disorder known as dyspraxia. Worried about what this will mean for both Ellie and for them as parents – paired with looming financial concerns – they are feeling the weight of parenting now more than ever.*

Take a moment to reflect on how Mateo and Alice might mindfully ease into the discomfort they are experiencing. Without avoiding, denying, or suppressing the feelings that are present, one might inquire:

- What does Ellie's potential disorder (to be confirmed or ruled out in time) mean for Mateo and Alice as parents? As individuals?

- What does this potential diagnosis *not mean* for them? In other words, what might fear be indicating that is not indeed a sure fact?

- What do each Mateo and Alice need for self-care and support during this time?

- What does – and what will – all of this mean for Ellie? What does she require?

By asking ourselves provocative questions – even if the answers lead us into the unknown or into some challenging emotion – we start to uncover the full range of our human experience. In doing this, we tend to realize that nothing is too unbearable to face – and that when we look directly at our experience, some wisdom, insight, or opportunity awaits.

## Navigating Relationship Transitions

Each of us is familiar with the truth that relationships change, though we don't always like to think about it. From break-ups and make-ups to divorces and bereavement, the nature of life means that our relationships are not permanent. So long as we are human, we cannot escape the inevitable.

Some transitions are painful, some are bittersweet, and some are welcomed with open arms. Examples of relationship transitions include (but are certainly not limited to):

- Coming into parenthood
- Adult children leaving home
- Separation and divorce
- Losing touch with friends
- Parents becoming elderly
- Children caretaking their elderly parents
- Gaining a new boss or group of colleagues
- Taking on a new role in the home or at work
- Mental or physical illness of self or loved one
- Death of a loved one

Less obvious are the subtle shifts that occur overtime, such as the changing dynamics between a couple as both individuals grow. We can't always put our finger on what the transition is, but things do tend to change with time.

All transitions – whether easy, difficult, or bittersweet – require our compassionate attention to fully integrate the experience. This involves witnessing and honoring our emotions, holding and nurturing any pain or difficulty, and noting our own resistance to change itself.

When we practice this, it's important to note that relationship transitions are not a result of failure or achievement. Their presence does not signify that something is wrong – they are simply life happenings. Transitions welcome the next stage of life, which brings new opportunities and challenges and requires that we embrace a new reality. They invite us to practice acceptance – even when what we are experiencing is not what we desired.

Let's look at an example to explore this:

### Example 1 – Erik (45) and Josefine (47)

*Erik and Josefine have had a solid relationship for many years. The two have shared many interests and values, making for a relatively seamless eight years together. Over the past year, however, Josefine has begun studying and practicing bhakti yoga with utmost commitment. In fact, it has consumed much of her free time. Her and Erik still get along, but something has shifted. Erik feels uncomfortable with chanting and with spirituality in general, though he's not sure why this is the case for him. Josefine has begun to question their relationship. She wonders: Do we have enough in common anymore for this to be a mutually enhancing relationship?*

Before drawing conclusions on the outlook of their relationship, Erik and Josefine might mindfully explore what's happening within themselves and within the other. On their own and also together, they might inquire into:

- Erik's discomfort with hearing Josefine chanting – can that be compassionately explored for greater understanding?

- Josefine's fear that they don't have enough in common anymore – is this based exclusively on her new practice or is there something else at play?

- Their willingness to learn more about the other – after eight years together, are they still curious to learn more and to evolve together?

- Their commitment to their relationship – what is the shared bond they have?

- Their attachment to how things 'were' – can they find peace and contentment with how things are now?

Again, these are just examples of some of the directions that this inquiry might take. However, if both are willing to explore what is present – before jumping to conclusions – they will come to a more grounded understanding of how each views the future. Do they move forward together or go their separate ways? Only life will tell.

## Mindful Togetherness Exercises

Embodying mindful togetherness is an art. As such, it is not something that can be easily outlined with clear guidelines. Like any art form, it takes practice to arrive at mastery – and even then, there is always more to learn.

With that said, there are a few practices we can keep in mind that will help us to arrive at a more intimate way of being in a relationship. Some tools you might consider include:

## Letter Writing

Mindful communication, as we explored earlier, is one of the cornerstones of mindful togetherness. At best, we are able to communicate clearly, compassionately, and consciously while speaking; however, sometimes we need to take small and slow steps to get there.

Where we have difficulty mindfully expressing our thoughts, feelings, and needs, we might explore letter writing to help us say what we need to say. Taking the time to journal and then write a letter where appropriate can help us to formulate what it is we wish to say in the clearest, most compassionate way possible.

## Breath Awareness

Coming back to the breath is another useful tool to help anchor us in the present moment. When we are authentically anchored within the present, acceptance comes more gracefully. Away from the racing mind, the breath reminds us that here we are – that all is alright.

Other meditation practices can also support us in opening up to the present moment with unconditional acceptance. The right one for any of us is the one that works; there is no rule book.

## Self-Care

Though a solitary act, self-care allows us to be present with and available for those we have relationships with. Self-care looks different for each of us, but it might include things like meditation, nature, writing, art, music, movement, or anything else that brings us into balance.

## Metta Meditation

The Buddhist metta meditation (or loving kindness meditation) is another invaluable tool we can use to reconnect us to our shared humanity. The practice entails drawing various people to mind in sequence – oneself, a loved one, an acquaintance, someone with whom we have difficulty – and then the entire world. Holding each of these entities in our awareness, we repeat a set of loving kindness phrases like:

*May you be well.*

*May you be loved.*

*May you be safe.*

*May you be at peace.*

The practice helps us to reconnect with the loving center that is within all of us. From here, we might uncover a more peaceful way of navigating the entangled web of relationships.

Finally, as a footnote, I want to say that self-care and well-being are inseparably intertwined with each other. Well-being cannot arise or be sustained without self-care; and self-care becomes richer, deeper and more profound when undertaken with the intent of improving well-being. Only if we can care for ourselves and our well-being will we have the empowerment and space to take care of the ones that we love. But we must always start at home!

## Epilogue

Early on in my life I went through a series of very difficult times in a number of my relationships and it crushed my world with guilt. *How could I be teaching mindful togetherness and still struggle with my most basic emotions?* Intellectually, I knew that both are not mutually exclusive but for a while, I did feel like a fake. Till one day, I realized that my practice of mindfulness has got nothing to do with "what happened" but everything to with "how I am responding to it". This shifted my focus from thinking of it as a tool to make life/ relationships perfect to making more space for "letting be".

I would be lying if I said no pangs from these experiences are left, but it's true that this realization has made a sea change in my life – literally more breathing room, more compassion and unconditional acceptance has become available.

Two of my mentors I worked and trained with closely for a long time had very rocky relationships in their personal lives, including with partners and children. Often, people around them would "judge" them for it and one day, when sitting with one of them, I asked, "`What is the lesson here?" And my mentor responded, "Patience – it's always the final lesson of personal growth."

I did not understand this then, but I understand it much more now. Patience is sometimes the difference between automatically reacting and consciously responding and that space in between my friends is what mindfulness helps to expand.

**Suggested ayam<sup>(TM)</sup> Practice:**

Programs: Overcoming Crises; ayam for life (available Live only)

Meditations: Self Healing, Forgiveness, Love and Compassion

# CHAPTER 14

Mindfulness at the Workplace

This is from a decade ago: I was relatively new to Texas and was in the process of setting up an office. I had only one team member (I will call her Casey) working with me in the small borrowed camp office we set up. I was traveling a lot those days between our global locations and was hardly ever in town, so the main responsibility of finding a location for our long-term office, designing and furnishing it, fell upon Casey and she did a terrific job.

One day, I came back from a trip and found that my room in the office was beautifully furnished – I had planned on assembling some of my stuff over the next weekend, but finding it all done and ready to use was a pleasant surprise. I took a leisurely walk through the rest of the office and realized that Casey had probably spent much of last week getting everything in place – from break room to library and conference room – all of it. Excited and happy, I walked into her office to thank her for going out of her way to take care of it all. She responded in her characteristically sweet Texan way, saying, *"You are very welcome… I enjoyed doing it as the office is like a second home to me."* Her simple answer caught me by a surprise; I had never had someone describe their office like that to me. And it triggered a chain of thoughts that had me realize that for most of the last 5 years, I had spent 40% more time in my office than I did at my home – where I literally only went only to sleep! ☺

This phenomenon is however not limited only to workaholic people. I guess most of us who have a corporate job that includes a commute in a big city can identify that we spend 12-14hrs everyday either at work or commuting back and forth from it. In many cultures, most of our social interaction also comes from the workplace and our friendships later in life also emerge from networks we build in the work environment. So Casey was actually very right in calling the office a "second home", though many of us may not feel like that but the number of hours we spend may qualify it as so.

Assuming this hypothesis is true, how much of our life is influenced by it? How many of us bring our "work persona" home or vice versa? Can we ever really separate our work and home life?

For most of us, the answer may be No! But in either case, it's probably a great idea to begin to explore how our experience at work may be transformed by intentionally integrating mindfulness practices.

Over the years, I have worked with several companies, including the ones I helped found, to create a culture of mindfulness and it has almost universally led to reduced stress, increased productivity, employee engagement and rising levels of job satisfaction. Recently, the ayam team put together the best practices from that and created a set of 10 week curriculums by the name of *ayam for leaders* and *ayam for work*. While a detailed discussion of them is well outside the scope of the book, I will very briefly explore the theme in the sections that follow and hopefully some of these techniques will benefit you. All of you are of course welcome to our 10 week program, which I personally believe can be a truly life-altering experience!

## Modern Workplace context

In most modern day societies, there appears to be a perceived split between our lives 'over there' and our lives 'over here'. This split, which appears to separate our work lives from our home lives, leads to the need for what we call 'work-life balance'. And while the need to balance any two aspects of our being is certainly important, it would seem that the emphasis on this particular split is growing stronger as our work lives become more stressful.

There are plenty of statistics that shed light on the atmosphere of our workplaces. Some recent studies have resulted in the following findings:

- 94% of respondents in one survey of US and UK workers indicated feeling some level of stress at the workplace. Over half rated the stress they experience as moderate to unsustainably high.[108]

- In another study, 'work' ranked second in a list of common stressors (60% of respondents indicated it was a very or somewhat significant source of stress for them). 'Money' was found to be the leading cause of stress.[109]

- Furthermore, another study revealed how employees believe stress impacts them in the workplace. The findings showed:

  o 41% reported that stress made them less productive

  o 33% reported that stress made them less engaged

  o 14% said that stress increased their absenteeism[110]

These are just some of the numbers that indicate how stressful our work lives have become. However, we can also turn to our direct experience for confirmation of this:

*How do you feel being in your place of work?*

*How does workplace stress impact your well-being and your ability to contribute meaningfully to your company?*

*How does workplace stress impact your life at home?*

*How have you observed the effect of workplace stress on colleagues and loved ones?*

---

[108] https://www.wrike.com/blog/stress-epidemic-report-announcement/
[109] https://www.apa.org/news/press/releases/stress/2014/stress-report.pdf
[110] https://www.coloniallife.com/about/newsroom/2019/march/stressed-workers-costing-employers-billions

As we've learned, mindfulness plays an important role in helping to broaden our perspective and in managing the body's innate stress response. As we learn to respond mindfully to our environment (rather than to habitually react to it), we become more resilient to the world around us – and more attuned to the work we're doing and the people we are doing it with.

We've briefly explored in previous chapters how mindfulness plays a significant role in workplace well-being. In chapter 6, we looked at how mindful communication in particular can increase trust and transparency, improve work relationships, and lead to fewer conflicts and misunderstandings (among many other benefits). Let's take a closer look at how mindfulness as a way of being – communication included – can help to foster health and harmony within organizations and their individual constituents.

## Stimulating Creativity and Innovation

Within a rapidly evolving world, creativity and innovation are needed more than ever. As a collective, we are facing new challenges that require us to take unprecedented, inventive approaches. A lack of creativity and innovation within the workplace makes it hard to keep up with the times – and, when these qualities are not valued and celebrated, employees hold back on their full, creative potential (whether consciously or unconsciously).

There are a few different barriers to creativity in the workplace. A study by Microsoft[111] unveiled three primary obstacles to working creatively:

- Uninspiring workplaces

- Stressful work atmosphere

- Lack of appropriate spaces to focus

---

[111] https://news.microsoft.com/en-gb/2017/07/27/british-companies-risk-creativity-crisis-micro-soft-surface-research-reveals/

These, along with other factors (such as fatigue, lack of relevant training, poor work environment) are contributing to what is being called a 'creativity crisis'. This has a range of negative effects on both employee and organizational well-being. When creativity is not supported, employees are left uninspired, opportunities and challenges are not harnessed, and the business loses its forward-thinking edge.

To harness the power of creativity and innovation, mindfulness can indeed be of benefit. Studies have revealed that the mindfulness skill of observation helps to promote creative thinking through supporting a broad attentional focus and through increasing flexibility of thought.[112] Another study looked at the effect of breath awareness meditation on creative problem solving. After meditating, participants showed a 40% improvement in solving a creative problem upon the second trial.[113]

Furthermore, mindfulness helps to promote the open listening and empathy required for people to feel safe and supported in sharing their ideas. Creativity and innovation are group processes – and in organizations where individual success is weighed greater than collective learning and growth, the flow of ideas gets thinner. Compassionate communication and open dialogue (both a part of mindfulness practice) help to soften fears and judgments that arise during the creative process.

Mindful awareness also helps an organization to compassionately and effectively navigate changes in the world and one's customer base. By remaining open to that fundamental life force of change, we become better able to creatively respond to the curveballs life throws.

Now, while we might clearly sense and understand that creativity is essential to a thriving workplace, the challenge comes with the

---

[112] https://www.researchgate.net/publication/282354120_Mind_Full_of_Ideas_A_Meta-Analysis_of_the_Mindfulness-Creativity_Link
[113] https://www.researchgate.net/profile/Ravi_Kudesia/publication/265846802_Mindfulness_and_Creativity_in_the_Workplace/links/58a92c9b4585150402f8db6b/Mindfulness-and-Creativity-in-the-Workplace.pdf

'how'. How do we mindfully encourage creativity and innovation at the workplace?

As with all of mindfulness practice, we can take both an individual and a group approach to encouraging innovation. In other words, when it comes to stimulating creativity, we can look at ways of both supporting ourselves in our personal creative process and also consider ways of encouraging the team to think outside of the box.

For example, let's say you are a chemist for a well-established skincare brand. Up until relatively recently, little attention has been given to the sustainability factor of the company's products. However, as the population becomes more concerned with the impact of consumption on the environment, customers are growing increasingly interested in eco-friendly skincare products. Numerous of your ingredients are now being called into question.

Mindfulness begins with our relationship to what arises in our environment. In this example, individual mindful engagement with the challenge at hand would involve:

- Curiously considering the needs of the customer base and of the environment

- Being open to new suggestions and new possibilities for skincare formulas

- Gaining additional insights and information from other departments and experts

- Noticing where there is inner resistance to change

- Taking pause to contemplate rather than jumping to conclusions

- Collaborating with others, remaining open to the insights of colleagues

As the leader of the team of chemists (or of other departments within the company), mindfulness in the name of encouraging creativity would include the above but also:

- Embracing the change in customer demand as opportunity – and conveying this to the team

- Remaining transparent about the needs and concerns of the company as production shifts

- Practicing patience and open-mindedness

- Encouraging mindful discussion and welcoming new ideas from the team

As a team leader, some specific exercises you might facilitate during an opportunity like this include:

1.  Mindful Brainstorm Session

    When a challenge arises that calls for creativity and innovation, taking time to brainstorm without barriers is a powerful practice for encouraging flow. Within a boardroom, before anyone shares their ideas for how to move forward, all minds could be invited to jot down images or ideas they have for steps forward. Taking this time to contemplate before speaking offers everyone a chance to mindfully consider the possibilities. It also encourages those who identify as being introverted to explore their inner terrain for possible solutions.

    After 10 to 15 minutes, all individuals in the boardroom could be invited to share. The team leader would write down all ideas on a large board so that all possibilities, all viewpoints, and all ideas can be considered collectively. No possibility is overlooked.

2. Mindfulness Meditation – Breath Awareness

As previously mentioned, meditation (with focus held on the breath) has been shown to facilitate creative problem solving. One of the theories for why this is the case is that during focused meditation, we detach ourselves from previous attempts – or in other words, from previous ideas about how things 'work'. When we come back to the challenge at hand, the mind is less attached to accustomed ways of viewing things. This provides space for new solutions to arise.

As a team leader (or even as an individual exploring this on one's own), a 10 to 15 minute meditation session focused on the breath can help to soften assumptions and make space for something new to arise.

As an employer, you will also likely want to consider the other factors that inhibit creativity. Can the workplace and its vision be made more meaningful and more inspiring? Can reducing stress levels throughout the organization be a proactive measure rather than a reactive one? Can space be dedicated to brainstorming and to contemplating? Whatever we can do to support the innate creative potential we each hold within us will go a long way in the well-being of the employee and of the organization as a whole.

**Dealing with Performance Pressure**

The pressure we feel to perform as per clearly defined goals set by the organization can leave us feeling great levels of stress and anxiety. To some degree, goals and visions for success are a necessity; they motivate us and keep us moving forward. Yet all too often, the degree of pressure we feel beneath these goals has the opposite effect that we might hope for.

The graph below represents the Inverted-U Theory, a theory developed in 1908 by psychologists Robert Yerkes and John

Dodson.[114] The diagram of an upside down 'U' outlines the relationship between pressure and performance. What it suggests is that when pressure is too low, we feel unchallenged and uninspired to move forward. When pressure is too high, the result is high stress, anxiety, and unhappiness.

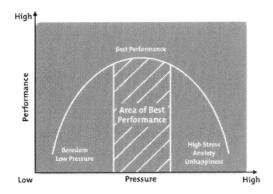

From:https://onlinelibrary.wiley.com/doi/10.1002/cne.920180503

Somewhere in the middle is the sweet spot – the degree of pressure that leaves us inspired and motivated while at the same time happy and at ease. This is what we might be looking for to keep employees both engaged and relaxed.

There are plenty of reasons why the pressure we experience at work often falls outside of this middle zone. However, much of it is the result of less than mindful interactions between and within employees of all levels. Some examples include:

- Trickle down pressure through multiple organizational levels (i.e. if the message sent from the top prioritizes performance over well-being)

- An environment of high competition (i.e. employees subconsciously and frequently compare themselves to their colleagues)

---

[114] https://onlinelibrary.wiley.com/doi/10.1002/cne.920180503

- Expectations set by the organization's leaders are too high (or too low)

- Curiosity, learning, and joy are not valued sufficiently

- Repercussions for not meeting goals and expectations are high (i.e. falling into disfavor, risk of losing job)

- Lack of meaningful dialogue around visions, hopes, and plans for the company (as well as when things don't go as planned)

- Lack of self-awareness – how are we communicating our organizations needs and fears?

In addition to these external factors, there are internal reasons for feeling high or low levels of motivation and ease at the workplace. An individual's propensity for feelings of anxiety, their personality, and other personal factors play into how they will experience the pressures that arise in the workplace.

Mindfulness helps to balance performance pressure by encouraging mindful engagement across all levels within an organization. First, when organization leaders are able to engage mindfully with their subordinates, they send out a compassionate, supportive, energetic ripple that affects each level beneath. This means communicating with patience, warmth, and compassion – and rooting any challenging conversations in the heart before communicating.

Leaders of all levels can ground themselves in this compassionate energy before discussing goals, offering feedback, and making changes within the organization. By connecting to this energy, we are reminded that all employees within the company have the same needs, hopes, and fears that we do.

Employees and leaders at every level might also enhance mindful awareness of how they are perceived by others. We each transmit energy that either supports or detracts from mindful relating within the workplace; keeping this in mind encourages an environment of warmth, openness, and respect.

Furthermore, mindfulness practices help us to come back to what is important, relieving stress and anxiety when pressure rises to an unmotivating degree. Since mindful breathing, for instance, helps to mitigate the body's stress response, practicing a simple breathing meditation during times of peak performance pressure helps to ground us back into the present moment. From here, we are better able to assess our options:

*Do we need to have a compassionate conversation with our boss?*

*Do we need some time off, more support, or clarification of a task?*

*Would a mindful meeting help everyone to release a bit of anxiety?*

*Are daily mindfulness meditations enough to keep us feeling at ease?*

*Is what we need simply to come back to the breath from time to time?*

Let's explore an example. Consider you are the owner of a typically busy restaurant in your city's entertainment district. Over the past few months, sales have been declining due to lower average bill prices and fewer customers in general. Your employees (both front and back-of-house staff) have been with you for longer than industry average. Lately, the restaurant's reviews have been less than favorable. Now, you worry your staff are growing complacent and aren't tending to guests as one would hope. How might you mindfully navigate this situation to motivate and support your employees in a compassionate way? You could overlook the root issues by pushing your employees to upsell dinner items and encourage wine pairings; however, you want to get to the underlying cause of the decline.

Some of the considerations and conversations you might explore include:

- Holding a team meeting to share the restaurants performance numbers

- Non-judgmentally (and without making assumptions) sharing some of the reviews that have come in over the past few months (withholding names from this group setting)

- Having one-on-one meetings where necessary, remaining compassionate and curious about the experience of individual employees (i.e. meeting with those who have received negative reviews)

- Asking employees: What do you think our customers are missing? What might we do to ensure guests have a great experience?

- Mindfully examining assumptions about and biases towards certain employees (recall the Ladder of Conclusion)

- Grounding through the breath or through body awareness before any of these discussions or team meetings

Employees, upon hearing of the latest numbers, could mindfully explore their own experience:

- What do I intuitively sense customers might be missing during their visits here? Where are the areas of improvement (both personally, interpersonally, and within the organization)?

- Where has my head and heart been recently? Have I been practicing compassion with customers and co-workers?

- How can I be of greater support to those I work with?

- How can I more effectively manage stress when it arises in the workplace?

- Calling to mind one particular guest interaction that led to a negative review (whether connected to oneself or a co-worker):

  o Can I soften my inclination to pick a side? Can I become more curious about the guest's experience?

Can I become curious about my own role and experience (or of the roles and experiences of those involved)?

Specific exercises that could be explored in this scenario include:

1.  Breathing Breaks

    'Smoke breaks' are common 'time-outs' within the restaurant industry and throughout other workplaces. They offer employees a chance to step back from customer needs and to ease any tension in mind or body. We can use this practice of taking five minute breaks, but instead of turning towards any addictive pattern, we might instead explore the power of the breath to center ourselves.

    The above scenario might benefit from enacting a long-term plan to offer employees five minute breathing breaks while on shift. All employees could be offered a 30-minute to 1-hour workshop that teaches them how to mindfully meditate using the breath and what the benefits of such a practice are. The result would be employees who are better equipped to manage job stress when it arises.

2.  Compassionate Self-Inquiry

    Taking the time to reflect upon the way we react when under stress and the way we engage with others (whether co-worker or customers) offers us invaluable insights about where we can grow. In this example, the pressure to perform is about offering customers a positive experience that makes them want to come back.

    The restaurant owner might invite all employees to partake in a compassionate meeting focused on learning rather than judgment. During this meeting, a mindfulness meditation would be led to ground each employee into the present moment and to soften any resistance to openness. Then, the meditation would deepen into a compassionate reflection of some past experience:

I.   Can you recall a time when you reacted to a stressful situation in a way that you might now see as ungrounded?

II.  Without judgment – and without clinging to being 'right' – can you sense the emotions that led you to react this way?

III. Can you visualize a more compassionate way of responding to the situation in question? What does it feel like in your body to do so?

Upon completion of the meditation, sharing would be encouraged to offer each employee the chance to learn from one another's experiences and insights.

## Building Resilience, Vitality, and Focus

How many of us go to work and come back home feeling centered and energized? Probably, not many. Most workplaces are not yet designed to offer employees the tools required to remain energized, resilient, and focused throughout the day. And since most of us spend 8 hours at work each day on average, consciously taking steps to ground and re-energize ourselves is of utmost importance.

Our modern times have brought a certain ease to our workdays. Technological advances have meant increased automation and more time saved. However, at the same time, many of us are feeling more distracted and fatigued than we did before. Why is this?

Getting to the root cause of fatigue, distraction, anxiety, or whatever else may be weighing us down at work requires personal inquiry. We each have unique reasons for feeling tired and less than fully alive at the workplace. However, there are some common workplace and lifestyle factors that play into our energetic depletion. Some of those include:

- Little movement or physical exercise in modern workplaces, sitting all day

- Many hours spent looking at screens (a combination of personal devices and work screens)

- Lack of inspiring, meaningful social engagement at the workplace

- Lack of natural lighting, time to relax and recharge during the day

- Unnourishing food habits and addiction to stimulating substances that create fluctuating energy levels (i.e. caffeine, sugar)

- Workplace stress creating hormonal imbalance and sleep challenges that exacerbate fatigue

- Lack of resources to support mental health and well-being

Building resiliency, vitality, and focus comes down to prioritizing what brings us peace and harmony in both our personal lives and within the workplace. Since our lifestyle and workplace habits are largely habitual, mindfulness is required to help us better understand what is depleting us so that we might compassionately make nourishing adjustments.

For example, as we become more mindful of the time spent in front of our devices, we start to notice the effect this has on our posture, on our eyes, on our strength and flexibility, and on any other measures of physical well-being that stand out in our awareness. We become more conscious of the body's needs to stretch, to bend, and to exert itself in some way.

The same thing goes for our eating and drinking habits. Mindful awareness gets us more attuned to our body's cycles. We might start by noticing the highs and lows of our caffeine consumption or how our breakfast choices makes us feel. This growing awareness inspires and encourages us to take vitality into our own hands as it prompts us to make choices that fuel us.

Furthermore, we become more mindful of our emotional and mental reactions to the world around us. We start to note our own biases towards co-workers, any resistance or fear we hold in relation to our bosses, and any unsupportive thought patterns that keep us feeling less than energized. We begin noticing how stress impacts our well-being, and we start learning tools for self-support.

Mindfulness practice also encourages us to become more focused while at work. Through breath and body awareness, we cultivate the skill of presence. It becomes easier to witness and soften unsupportive thought patterns and to hone in on the task before us. Numerous studies support this, exhibiting how even brief meditation sessions improve attention.[115] [116]

Consider an example now. Draw to mind an image of an employee (of any workplace or industry) who is drained at the end of each day, unfocused while at work, sleeping poorly most nights, and 'on edge' throughout the majority of their days. He or she feels a growing complacency not just for work, but for life in general, lacking the energy to make changes that would bring greater peace and contentment. What might he or she do?

Each of us will likely have different ideas about this person based on our own assumptions, biases, and beliefs (again, the Ladder of Conclusion can be referred to in order to better understand our thought processes). However, some of the mindful inquiries we might make if we were the person in question could include:

---

[115] https://www.ncbi.nlm.nih.gov/pmc/articles/PMC6088366/
[116] https://www.tandfonline.com/doi/abs/10.1080/13674679908406332

- What does my mind need right now? What does my heart long for? What does my body require?

- What habits are standing in the way of full focus and vitality for me? Can I hold these in mindful awareness without judgment and without condemnation?

- What is one thing I can nourish myself with in this present moment? Consider anything that brings you deeper into your body (i.e. breath awareness, body awareness, mindful movement, open awareness).

- What small step towards greater well-being can I make a priority?

- Where can I get support? What kind of support might I need (personal or professional)?

If we are the leader of an organization, noticing that any of our employees are struggling in this way, we might explore:

- Compassionate group or one-on-one meetings to mindfully brainstorm ways of improving mental and emotional well-being, supporting employees

- At-work mindfulness sessions for employees (i.e. half or full-day workshops, breathing breaks, yoga, tai chi, nutrition classes, etc.)

- Activities to encourage social connection (i.e. an extra 15 minute break during the day, increased collaboration between departments)

- Space and equipment conducive of physical and mental well-being (i.e. meditation benches, standing work desks, yoga mats, meditation room)

Specific exercises we could explore in relation to building resiliency, vitality, and focus include:

1.  Mindful Lunch Breaks

    Mindful eating (as we explored previously) involves awareness of our food, the journey it took to arrive on our plates, our mind and body, and the way the food feels as it fills us. Mindful lunch breaks could be organized as a single workshop for all employees, or it could be explored as an individual practice.

    When our days at work are busy or less than inspiring, we might feel the urge to eat as fast as possible. While this is an understandable tendency many of us are familiar with, meal times are ideally a time of slowing down – of reflecting, of being present, and of honoring this break from exertion.

2.  Mindful Movement Breaks

    Inviting movement into the workplace is once again something that can be organized as a group activity or individually. This might include general stretching, yoga, tai chi, or any other form of movement that requires mindful presence. We might also explore simple mindful awareness of the body, closing our eyes and noting which areas are calling for activation, stretch, or release. Then, in whatever space is available to us, we can practice honoring this call from within.

## Teamwork and Collaboration

One of the biggest challenges of cultivating mindfulness at the workplace is where we are called to collaborate. This is not just the case in work life however; it happens everywhere. Due to our attachment to our own personal views, beliefs, and opinions, working with others who hold contradicting viewpoints to ourselves poses us difficulty. However, through mindful awareness, we might start to see this challenge as an opportunity instead.

Mindful collaboration requires mindful social engagement. It invites us to cultivate deeper awareness of both ourselves and of others. When it comes to ourselves, mindfulness asks us to witness and hold (without judgment or self-righteousness) our beliefs, our opinions, and our conclusions. Through mindful awareness, it is possible to hold opinions without being closed to others; this is part of what we are called to do here.

When working with others, we are also invited to be mindful of our own energy. How are we being perceived by those we are collaborating with? While mindfulness is not about changing who we are at our core, it does include awareness of our own appearance and energy. For instance, what tone are we giving off through our voice or through our eyes? Is this tone or energy adding to togetherness or fueling judgment and dismissiveness?

Mindfulness of others invites us to recognize that each of us holds different views, beliefs, and opinions for different reasons – and that none of us are fundamentally more 'right' than another. We simply come to the field with different experiences to contribute. This doesn't mean we can't eventually make our way to a 'best' decision at any moment (in fact, life requires that we are able to). It simply means we hold off on our judgments and aim to take all information into consideration without judgment or resistance.

In this way, mindfulness improves our ability to think creatively and to arrive at unique answers and conclusions. Ten minds approaching a challenge or opportunity results in ten unique ideas for ways forward. Somewhere amongst all of these ideas rests the bits and pieces that together create the path best suited for the present moment.

Furthermore, as we practice mindfulness in team settings, we bring everyone's views and opinions into the light. In this way, we witness the feelings, needs, and experiences of all at the table, building a sense of collaboration and unity. In addition, it helps to mitigate interpersonal conflict and provides tools for addressing challenges that do arise.

Mindfulness does not lead to perfection; it does not lead to everyone agreeing on all fronts. It does, however, help us to see one another as a human being just like ourselves. It helps us to value the unique contributions of others so that we might all learn and grow. It helps us to see our differences as blessings and as our strength as a team.

Let's consider an example. Imagine a small team of product developers are gathering in a meeting room to discuss which of their proposals will be taken to the next stage of development. Sam, Julia, and Nabil have each put an idea forward for consideration. The product line? Prepared foods, canned and frozen. Sam tends to lean towards recipes that can use locally grown products (organic where possible). Julia caters first and foremost to the customer. Nabil prioritizes the company's bottom line. Can they come up with a single product that fits all of their needs?

Some of the ways they might move forward with this include:

- Taking a moment to mindfully ground themselves into the meeting (perhaps using breath awareness or a loving kindness meditation)

- Courageously sharing their product ideas, including what their biggest concerns are and why they believe those concerns are important

- Compassionately and non-judgmentally listening to the ideas of their colleagues, listening to understand rather than listening to respond

- Considering if there is a way they might meet the needs of everyone involved – the organization, the employees, the customers, and the environment as a whole

- Witnessing and softening any barriers they might hold to new ideas

- Coming back to the breath if tensions begin to rise

- Taking pause before offering thoughts and feedback

Some specific exercises they might explore during this meeting include:

1. Silent Grounding Meditation

   At the start of this meeting, all three employees might take a moment to sit in silent awareness for 3 to 5 minutes to ground any fears, tensions, anxieties, or expectations that might be arising. Through simple breath awareness, they would be guided back into the body (whether self-guided or through a recording) to help ease any emotions or feelings that might interfere with compassionate, confident, and calm expression.

2. Echoing What's Been Said

   A great practice for deepening our understanding of others is to echo what has been said. For instance, after Sam finishes her presentation of 'Savoury Lentil Mushroom Burgers', the others might repeat something back like:

   *"From what I've gathered based on what you've said, this product could be made from 90% locally grown products (within a 200 km radius). It's environmental footprint would be low, which is important given the impact of transportation on the environment. Now, I sense that the environmental impact of our new products is important to you. Am I correct in assuming that this is of top concern for you right now?"*

From here, clarifying questions could be asked – all from a compassionate, curious, and open-minded heart. The same would be done for the other presenters.

## Mindful Culture and Employee Performance

There are perhaps no other two words in the OD jargon that are so over(mis)used and less understood than Culture and Performance.

Too many books have been written on this subject already and I am certainly not going to add to that literature by taking a deep dive into these in the book end of this chapter, but simply giving a shout out to some enquiries that could drive you to your own insights.

Every organization is not only made up of people, processes and infrastructure but also another very important ontological construct that I like to call *"network of conversations"*. I was first introduced to this term by one of my executive coaches (a former Microsoft executive – great guy) but in a different context. The more I thought through that and made my own experiment while working with a wide variety of leadership teams, I came to the conclusion that there does exist a *"living, breathing ontological element"* which is simply a sum total of all that people continuously discuss at their workplace.

The building blocks of it can include simple conversations around policy, procedures, the boss, compensation etc. but overtime they do develop a more "flavorful" context that includes simplicisms – *What makes people successful here? What gets rewarded? How do people engage with each other? What is OK to say or do in a meeting? How do we treat our customers or partners? etc., etc.* These conversations may be sourced from the vision and values but have a life of their own and often will ring more true to the culture than formal statements that hang on the walls.

What is interesting is that in many cases this "network of conversation" may be completely undistinguished from the leadership consciousness – almost like that "white" in the white board, where literally you focus on other colors to write... and white is relegated to the background, unacknowledged. I remember talking to a communications head of a multibillion dollar global organization about it and she got back to me after a couple of weeks pretty surprised, saying that she discovered that the most consuming conversation within that company had been about *"restructuring"*. It was something that they did every year and surprisingly enough, was never a theme in their communications calendar, although it was the one "all consuming" conversation that their whole team engaged in for the better part of the year!

Ultimately, it's the "network of conversation" that creates the lived experience for people at the workplace – after all, this is what occupies their mind space for most of their workday.

These networks of conversations however can be carefully curated to reinforce values and principle and also demonstrate organizational commitment to employee success. Just as naturally these conversations will include compensation and politics, equally naturally, you can seek to include conversations around well-being, self-care, collaborative approach and mindfulness as well.

This is perhaps the fastest way to bring a cultural focus of integrating mindfulness at the workplace by quite literally creating a "buzz" around it. Inviting people to sample, immerse and integrate these practices.

In my personal practice, I have approached this in many different ways, ranging from leadership retreats, formal mindfulness programs, making digital resources available and having group work, etc. There is clearly no one-size-fits-all approach to success here and every organization will need to experiment to draw their own lessons and learnings. But it's a conversation that is worth every leader's attention.

**Suggested ayam(TM) Practice:**

*Programs: ayam for work (avaliable live only); Overcoming Crises*

*Meditations: Focus, Abundance, Calm*

*Essentials: Vitality, Peace and Calm, Breath Awareness*

# CHAPTER 15

Working Through Health Challenges

There is an old Arabic proverb that goes something like: *"One who has health has hope, one who has hope can do almost anything"*. I first came across this when I was in my early 20s and like a lot of young people, I felt I was bullet proof and it was going to last forever. Life of course, in its richness of experience, has shown me how fragile it can be and how intentionally we need to take care of ourselves. Earlier in my career working with medically non-responding diseases, I had a series of experiences where I saw the hopelessness and resignation in the eyes of people that were dealing with some of these. When I would practice or teach them meditation, a lot of them would remark that the greatest benefit they felt was a sense of "relief of burden" for the few precious minutes of meditation and after it. Some of them later reported to me that while their disease was still as aggressive as before, "being with it" had become easier for them as they deepened their meditation.

While profound on its own, it was an early anecdotal brush with how mindfulness and meditation can be an empowering tool to navigate the most complex health challenges. Since then, I have studied and worked with subjects on how people with different forms of health challenges including chronic pain, brain and behavioral health disorders, mood disorders, traumas, auto-immune conditions, etc. can benefit from this expression of self-care and well-being. I am now a true believer that while mindfulness and meditation are great practices for not only destressing, increasing joy and vitality but also creating "more space" around the health conditions that we are dealing with and how it's impacting us in other areas of life and those around us. In this section, I am sharing some starter practices that we can adopt and I hope to eventually write a whole book around this subject with fellow researchers who have been working in this area.

## Where are we now

As mindfulness and meditation become more common in modern day societies, the perceived divide between mind and body begins to lessen. No longer do we believe that the mind and the body are distinct from one another. Rather, it has become clear that the well-being of one seemingly 'separate' aspect of ourselves impacts the well-being of the 'other'.

Due to this inextricable connection between mind and body, mindfulness and meditation can be used as effective health interventions for a wide variety of health challenges. By addressing our relationship to the inner world of thoughts and to our sensory experience, we influence the functioning of the rest of the inner world. Our hormones, our blood pressure, our breathing, our brain functioning, and countless other internal measures of health begin to shift.

Furthermore, not only do these interventions play a direct role in shaping our physiology, but they also influence the relationship we have to the more nuanced aspects of health challenges. Pain, chronic illness, and difficult diagnoses, for instance, can each be addressed through mindful insight and awareness. Where we cannot change the physical makeup of the body through thought alone, we can focus more intently on shifting our relationship to whatever is moving through us.

It is important to note that regardless of what type of health challenge we are faced with, mindfulness practices are not the only intervention we should employ. The root of our health concerns are often quite complex and are best supported with a multi-faceted healing approach. Nutrition, movement, medications, and therapies all have their place, depending upon who we are and what we are battling. Let mindfulness inform, direct, and facilitate your journey towards greater health and vitality.

## Supporting Brain and Behavioural Health

One of the most prominent areas of mindfulness interest and research is the domain of brain and behavioral health. For centuries, meditation practitioners have understood the effect of such practices on inner peace and contentment, but it took some time for modern science to catch up. So what does the science say about the capacity for mindfulness to support our mental well-being?

Before diving into it, you will want to familiarize yourself with two common acronyms: MBSR and MBCT. MBSR stands for 'mindfulness-based stress reduction' and MBCT for mindfulness-based cognitive therapy. These two terms are significant because they reflect standardized mindfulness approaches that have been the foundation of many scientific studies. MBSR is a program developed by Jon Kabat-Zinn in the 1970s. MBCT was developed some time after as a way of integrating cognitive-behavioral therapy with the techniques of Zinn's program.[117]

MBSR is an 8-week intensive stress reduction program that helps individuals to manage a wide range of health challenges, from mental well-being and chronic illness to the experience of pain.[118] Since it is a standardized method, it is easily implemented into scientific studies.

Scientific research into the measured impact of these methods include:

- In a meta-analysis that included eighteen randomized controlled trials and 2,042 participants, MBSR was found to have moderate effects in reducing depression in young

---

[117] https://www.ncbi.nlm.nih.gov/pmc/articles/PMC2834575/

[118] https://www.institute-for-mindfulness.org/offer/mbsr/what-is-mbsr

people.[119] Those aged 12 to 25 years were included in the study.

- Another study found that MBSR helps to improve depressive symptoms regardless of religious affiliation, sense of spirituality, degree of mindfulness experience prior to MBSR training, sex, or age.[120]

- One MBSR study found specific changes in brain functioning that contribute to reduction in anxiety and depression symptoms: reduced amygdala activity and increased activity in areas of the brain involved with attentional deployment. This study also observed reduced emotional reactivity and increased emotion regulation.[121]

- An MBCT meta-analysis found that during a 1 year follow-up, MBCT reduced patient relapse by 40% (among those with three or more previous episodes of depression).[122]

- MBCT was also found to have resulted in an increase in mindfulness and self-compassion and a decrease in rumination, anxiety, depression, and stress among participants.[123]

In addition, another well-known form of meditation has been observed for its effects on mental health: that is, Transcendental Meditation (TM). A form of meditation developed by Maharishi Mahesh Yogi, TM involves the use of mantras to help one focus during practice. It, too, has been studied in a scientific context. One such study found that it helped to decrease blood pressure in conjunction with decreasing psychological distress.[124]

In another study of 40 secondary school teachers and support staff working at a therapeutic school for those with behavioral

---

[119] https://www.ncbi.nlm.nih.gov/pmc/articles/PMC6021542/
[120] https://www.ncbi.nlm.nih.gov/pmc/articles/PMC4365440/
[121] https://www.ncbi.nlm.nih.gov/pmc/articles/PMC4203918/
[122] https://www.ncbi.nlm.nih.gov/pmc/articles/PMC5030069/
[123] https://www.frontiersin.org/articles/10.3389/fpsyg.2019.01099/full
[124] https://academic.oup.com/ajh/article/22/12/1326/182024

difficulties, TM was found to reduce perceived stress, depression, and overall teacher burnout.[125]

There are countless mechanisms that can help to explain how these techniques support healthy brain functioning. In addition to shifting functionality in various parts of the brain, these practices help to transform and enlighten the relationship we have with our thoughts. As we start to perceive our experiences in a new light, we find ourselves better equipped to deal with life's stressors and challenges.

Many mindfulness practices can help you to develop this more empowering relationship with your inner world. A few techniques you might consider exploring include:

**Mindfulness of Your Emotions**

When you feel a surge of some kind of challenging feeling or emotion, consider coming into a quiet and safe space where you can rest comfortably for a few moments. Sitting upright or lying down (whatever is accessible for you), close your eyes as you move through the following practice:

1. Begin by taking a few slow and steady breaths to ground yourself. Notice the sensation of each inward and outward movement.

2. Then, turn your attention towards the physical body to begin your exploration of the emotion or feeling. Where is this emotion located within the body? Can you be present with this physical manifestation of the emotion?

3. Some people might sense a tightness in the throat, a heaviness in the chest, a pit in the stomach, or any other visceral sensation. Sit with this feeling as you breathe into it.

---

[125] https://www.ncbi.nlm.nih.gov/pmc/articles/PMC3951026/

4. See if the experience dissolves on its own – without pushing anything away. Be absolutely present with whatever is here and whatever shifts. Then, see if you can observe some distance between yourself and the emotion that is present. Can you watch the emotion while witnessing yourself as the observer of it?

5. Resist the urge to 'figure it out'; let insights arise in their own time as you compassionately and curiously open yourself to whatever moves through you. Continue to use the breath and the body to ground yourself until you are ready to end the session.

## Gratitude Practice

This practice is not to be used as a way of denying or avoiding our innermost emotions; however, we can begin retraining the mind to view the world more positively by practicing gratitude. When you are feeling somewhat neutral or even a little bit 'down', you might take out a journal or sheet of paper to practice:

1. On the left hand side of the page in front of you, write the numbers 1 through 10.

2. Spend the next few minutes (or as long as it takes) to write something you are grateful for next to each of these numbers. It does not matter what you note; simply see if you might attune yourself with greater awareness to the blessings that live within and around you.

## Focused Belly Breathing

Where stress and anxiety are prevalent, deep belly breathing is a useful practice. This can be practiced at any moment during the day – when we wake up with a pit in the stomach, during stressful or rushed movements through the day, or in those minutes before we fall to sleep. Belly breathing helps to move us into 'rest and digest' mode and out of our 'fight or flight' response, easing the body's stress response (as explored in chapter 4). To practice:

1. Come to a seated or lying down position, placing one or both hands on your belly.

2. Take a few natural breaths to begin, noting what parts of the body the breath engages. Is movement primarily in the belly or in the chest?

3. Now, see if you can shift the breath so that the bulk of the movement observed alongside each breath is in the belly. Take ten deep belly breaths here with the eyes closed and shoulders softened.

4. Let your breath come back to its natural pace and then note what may have shifted in the mind. Open your eyes when you feel finished.

## Navigating Chronic Health Conditions

Mitigating the effects of chronic health conditions is another way that mindfulness can be of great benefit to well-being. Where one's health challenge is treatable but not curable (such as multiple sclerosis, diabetes, and HIV), mindfulness interventions may be of benefit as an adjunct to any other necessary treatments.[126]

Various studies have been conducted with chronic health conditions in mind. Results have found mindfulness to be of benefit for the following health challenges (note that this is not the full extent of chronic health conditions that mindfulness can support):

Multiple Sclerosis

Though research in regards to the effect of mindfulness-based interventions on multiple sclerosis (MS) is in its early stages,

---

[126] https://www.ncbi.nlm.nih.gov/pmc/articles/PMC3336928/

studies suggest that such interventions might influence the course of this disease through various brain-to-immune system pathways.[127] Furthermore, since various regions of the brain that control cognitive functioning are impacted by MS, there is hope that mindfulness interventions may prove to be of benefit through additional mechanisms over time. More studies are required to fully understand the role of mindfulness in MS as this is a new field of research.

Diabetes

One study that was conducted to assess the impact of MBSR on patients with type 2 diabetes found a decrease in anxiety, depression, and psychological distress in patients of the pilot study. Furthermore, a reduction in A1C (a blood test for those with diabetes) of 0.5% was noted, as was reduced mean arterial pressure of 6mmHg.[128]

Human Immunodeficiency Virus (HIV) & Acquired Immune Deficiency Syndrome (AIDS)

Over recent years, research has also looked at the impact of mindfulness on HIV and AIDS. Some of the findings suggest that mindfulness interventions may lead to fewer symptoms related to antiretroviral therapies at follow-ups, improved psychological outcomes, and an increase in NK cell activity (NK cells help to fight off viral infections).[129]

In addition to these, there is research to suggest that mindfulness may be of benefit in decreasing irritable bowel syndrome (IBS) symptoms, reducing cardiac symptoms in those with chronic heart failure, and managing the distress that comes with chronic pain.[130]

---

[127] https://www.ncbi.nlm.nih.gov/pmc/articles/PMC5972188/
[128] https://spectrum.diabetesjournals.org/content/22/4/226
[129] https://www.ncbi.nlm.nih.gov/pmc/articles/PMC3671698/
[130] https://www.ncbi.nlm.nih.gov/pmc/articles/PMC3671698/

All of these condition-specific details aside, mindfulness and meditation help to shift our relationship to ourselves and to our experience. When diagnosed with a chronic condition, it is understandable for the mind to sink into worry, fear, grief, anger, or any other number of challenging emotions. Through its influence on our mental and emotional state, mindfulness can lead to a greater capacity for acceptance, patience, self-compassion, and self-efficacy as we navigate our condition.

## Pain versus Suffering

In Chapter 7, we explored the difference between pain and suffering; that is to say, between the Buddhist metaphor of the first dart and the second dart. Pain – the first dart – is an inevitable part of life. When we are unwell, pain often arises to let us know that something is not functioning as it 'should' be. The pain we experience can be anywhere from subtle to severe, having a varying influence on our lives.

Suffering is what we add to the pain. It is the narrative we add to the direct experience of pain – one that exacerbates the challenge of our experience. When it comes to illness, suffering is fueled by words and beliefs including (but not limited to):

- "This shouldn't be happening to me."

- "I hate this!"

- "This/that is to blame."

- "This will never end."

- "What if this doesn't improve? What if this leads to x, y, or z?"

When we are not mindfully aware of the thoughts we add to our experience of pain, our inner dialogue fuels the flames of our discomfort. A pattern develops that is hard to get out of – that is, until we tune back into the direct, raw experience of the present moment.

When it comes to pain that arises due to illness, mindfulness can help us to be more present, attuned to, and compassionate towards our experience of pain. It can interrupt our mental spiraling that leads to secondary darts, leaving us to rest with the pain itself.

Numerous studies have explored this scientifically, carefully looking at how mindfulness can be of benefit in cases of chronic pain. It has been found to improve symptoms related to a range of painful disorders, such as irritable bowel syndrome, chronic lower back pain, pelvis pain, migraines, and fibromyalgia.[131] MBSR is the most common mindfulness intervention to appear in these studies as, again, it is highly standardized.

There are various explanations for why pain (or our perception of pain) changes when we meditate – explanations that guide us towards the brain. One study used functional magnetic resonance imaging and a thermal pain paradigm to explore the difference in pain experienced between Zen practitioners and a control group. The study revealed that Zen practitioners had reduced activity in the prefrontal cortex, amygdala, and hippocampus, areas related to emotion, executive functioning, and evaluation. Paired with that, sensory processing regions of the brain were activated to a larger degree in meditators.[132]

Research also suggests that mindfulness plays a role in the way the brain appraises pain.[133] In a study exploring the impact of open presence meditation on one's pain experience, findings revealed that expert meditators had less anxiety-related baseline activity in the amygdala prior to experiencing any pain. Expert practitioners also gave lower 'unpleasantness' ratings in response to pain, suggesting that open awareness mitigates the felt experience of whatever pain we are in.

So by shifting the way the brain functions and by interfering with our habitual tendencies to throw that second dart, mindfulness

---

[131] https://www.ncbi.nlm.nih.gov/pmc/articles/PMC4941786/
[132] https://www.ncbi.nlm.nih.gov/pubmed/21055874
[133] https://www.ncbi.nlm.nih.gov/pmc/articles/PMC3787201/

and meditation play a key role in shifting our experience of pain. When pain arises, we might consider the following practice to help mindfully address our relationship to it:

## Pain Presence Body Scan

When pain arises, many of us want to pull away from it – to curl up, to contract, or to push it away. However, pain does not respond to these pleas for release. Instead, we might open our awareness to what is here – to see if rather than begging for *it* to change *we* might shift our way of being with it.

1. Come into a seated or lying down position, whatever brings you as much comfort as is possible in this moment. Close your eyes and take three full, deep breaths to ground yourself.

2. With open awareness, observe where physical pain is present in the body. Note what the mind might have to say about this pain and put the thought aside. Instead, witness this area of the body with non-judgmental, compassionate awareness.

3. Hone your attention on a single point of difficulty for you. Without forcing this experience to be other than it is, begin breathing into this area of tension. With each inhalation, invite an expansion into the area of concern – and with each exhalation, see if it might be possible to naturally soften. This might be softening of the specific area that is in pain or of a surrounding area that is tensing up due to the pain that exists elsewhere.

4. Continue for 5-10 minutes – or for longer if this feels supportive. Notice any shifts that occur in either mind or body. Even if the pain is still present to some degree, how has the mind's appraisal of it shifted?

### Finding Peace Amidst Terminal Illness Diagnosis

Beyond facilitating our ability to navigate the raw experience of any illness (i.e. anxiety attacks, chronic pain, digestive issues, and so on), mindfulness holds a very important role in addressing broader issues that rise alongside our health concerns. Particularly where we ourselves or a loved one receive diagnosis of a terminal illness (i.e. advanced stages of cancer, progressive neurodegenerative diseases), we are called to radically address our relationship to life, death, and all in-between.

As we've explored, there have been a substantial number of studies conducted that reflect the ability of mindfulness to reduce stress, anxiety, fear, and to ease the weight of difficult emotions. Limited studies have looked into the effect of mindfulness specifically in relation to palliative care and terminal illness. However, one study suggests that even five minute mindful breathing sessions can help to reduce stress in palliative care patients and their caregivers.[134]

As mindfulness encourages one to continually return to the present moment, it makes sense that it can have a strong impact on our ability to cope with dying. This does not mean it protects us from the very real, very challenging experience of sorrow, pain, and fear that can arise towards the end of life, although, it helps us to develop a new relationship with these experiences and with the nature of reality itself.

> *"But the wise do not grieve, having realized the nature of the world."*
> Translated from the Pali[135] by John D. Ireland

Death is a part of life; they are two sides of the same coin. Meditation on dying, or on death awareness, is a powerful place to start if we are willing to turn towards this inevitably of life. In fact, death awareness meditation has long been a part of the Buddhist tradition. Like other ancient traditions, Buddhism does not view

---

[134] https://journals.sagepub.com/doi/abs/10.1177/1049909115569048
[135] https://www.accesstoinsight.org/tipitaka/kn/snp/snp.3.08.irel.html

death to be the end of consciousness. Rather, it is a dissolution of the physical aspect of one's being.[136]

Mindfulness of death meditation, or *maranasati*, is that encouragement to face death.[137] We can move into this awareness by considering Buddha's five contemplations:[138]

1. I am subject to aging. Aging is unavoidable.

2. I am subject to illness. Illness is unavoidable.

3. I am subject to death. Death is unavoidable.

4. I will grow different, separate from all that is dear and appealing to me.

5. I am the owner of my actions, heir to my actions, born of my actions, related through my actions, and live dependent on my actions. Whatever I do, for good or for ill, to that will I fall heir.

Now, for those just beginning their mindfulness meditation practice, contemplation of death may not be the first place to start. Being present with the breath, the body, and then our emotional landscape prepares us for these deeper inquiries. Exhibit care for your personal mindfulness journey, deepening where it feels like a safe step for you to do so.

Where contemplation of death is not within reach or intuitive for you at this time, hone in on mindfulness of your emotions. Note what arises from a place of curiosity and compassion. Note what stories arise in the mind (often similar to pain), such as:

- "This isn't fair."

- "This shouldn't be happening."

- "I will never be able to accept this."

[136] Evans-Wentz, W., 2000. *The Tibetan Book Of The Dead*. New York: Oxford University Press.
[137] https://www.buddhistinquiry.org/article/shining-the-light-of-death-on-life-maranasati-meditation-part-i/
[138] Rosenberg, L. and Guy, D., 2000. *Living In The Light Of Death*. Boston: Shambhala Publications.

- "The world is cruel."

- "I cannot bear this."

Become an external witness to these or any other thoughts that arise for you. Breathe them out with each exhale as you come back to the raw nature of your experience. As always (and especially during challenging times), harness compassion for yourself and for all involved.

## Dealing with Compassion Fatigue

Another issue that many of us face in relation to health challenges is compassion fatigue. Particularly in cases where an adult child is caring for both their children and their elderly parents, it is not uncommon to feel overwhelmed, anxious, and exhausted due to the immense support we offer our loved ones.

However, this is not the only case where compassion fatigue arises. Caring for a chronically sick child, a dependent partner, and even the welfare of suffering animals can create this exhaustion and depletion. Healthcare workers are also greatly susceptible to this fatigue.

In the words of Dr. Charles Figley, director of the Tulane Traumatology Institute:

> "Compassion Fatigue is a state experienced by those helping people or animals in distress; it is an extreme state of tension and preoccupation with the suffering of those being helped to the degree that it can create a secondary traumatic stress for the helper."[139]

If we are unaware of our own needs and personal limits, we can reach a point of complete exhaustion where we are no longer able to care for ourselves or another. Where we aren't forced to stop (which can happen if we become ill ourselves), this immense

---

[139] https://compassionfatigue.org/

offering of support carries on, frequently leading to subconscious trauma within our own body. When we lack the rest our own body and mind requires, we are unable to restore as is required. Sooner or later, this manifests as illness within our own being.

Addressing compassion fatigue first requires our awareness of where we are depleting ourselves. The sooner we can catch it, the easier it will be to break the cycle and to explore the balance between what we give to others and what we give to ourselves. If you feel that this balance needs to be addressed personally, consider the following reflective practice to gain insight into how you might nourish yourself in tandem with your concern for others.

## Self-Care Contemplation

Complete this journal exercise to explore where you might be out of balance in terms of the compassion and care you grant to others and the attention you devote to yourself. This exercise is designed for enhancing self-awareness and can be used as a tool to guide you forward in self-nourishing ways.

1. In what ways do you care for others? Consider physical care as well as mental and emotional care.

2. Of the above expressions of care, which do you also grant to yourself?

3. What are your own needs at present? How might you honor these today?

4. How might you make self-care a habit? What practices can you schedule into each and every day to nurture yourself?

## Additional Mindfulness Exercises for Supporting Health

Depending on your primary health concerns, there are a variety of exercises you can explore to support yourself. Remember that the mind and body are inextricably interconnected, so mindfully nurturing one supports the other as well. Consider the following exercises as tools to enhance both physical and mental well-being.

## Intuitive Movement

What each of us needs in any moment is unique. Sometimes, slow and subtle movement is more supportive of well-being while at other times what we intuitively yearn for is more dynamic movement. This intuitive movement exercise helps us deepen our connection to the physical body as we listen to its calls more closely.

1. Begin in a comfortable seated position on a yoga mat or other soft surface where you will have space to move freely. You can sit on a chair or cushion if that supports you.

2. Close your eyes as you take 5-10 grounding breaths. Soften the forehead and the belly as you sink into this practice.

3. Remaining still for a few more moments, quietly listen for any parts of the body that might be yearning for movement. There is no need to rush this practice; take your time to listen.

4. When the call arises, explore whatever part of the body is calling to be engaged or stretched. This could include (but is certainly not limited to):

   - Neck rolls

   - Seated side stretches

   - Forward bends

   - Cat-cow stretches

   - Shoulder rolls

5. As you explore whatever movements you feel called towards, ensure that you move slowly, retaining mindfulness

of each shift. Move slower than feels comfortable, listening to whatever the body has to 'say'.

6. You might stay seated, remain low on your mat, or even rise to your feet. Explore this fluid, intuitive movement for 10 minutes – or for as long as you'd like. You might also play instrumental music during this practice to invite greater fluidity or a particular energy to your movements.

7. To finish your practice, return to a seated position or rest on your back. Notice what is present in the body with curiosity and compassion.

## Five-Minute Breath Presence

When stress, anxiety, or a down-mood washes over you, you might explore a five minute breathing practice to simply give both mind and body a chance to rest. During the entirety of this practice, let your breathing be your anchor.

1. Practice this in a seated or lying down position. Resting on your back is fine so long as you are able to remain attentive to the breath.

2. Set a timer for five minutes, ensure that you are comfortable, and then close your eyes. Draw your attention to the natural rhythm of the breath.

3. Observe whatever sensations arise with each inhalation and each exhalation. You might also note a second's pause at the end of each inward and each outward movement. Until the alarm sounds, follow the breath like a wave that ebbs and flows through your body.

4. If the mind wanders, remain compassionate towards this tendency and then come back to the breath. It does not matter how many times you need to redirect your attention.

5. When the timer rings, keep your eyes closed for a few more moments as you notice any inner shifts that have occurred. Is there a greater sense of calm and ease? Do you feel more present with yourself and with your environment? When you are ready, slowly open your eyes to re-enter the world.

## Visualizing Pain

Visualization is another useful tool for a range of health concerns, including pain. This practice guides you more intently and compassionately towards your experience of painful sensations. Explore it from a place of care and curiosity.

1. Begin by resting on your back if this is comfortable for you. If not, make your way into any position that supports you in this moment. Close your eyes and take a few slow breaths to ground yourself.

2. With the breath remaining in the background of your awareness, shift your attention to a single area where you are experiencing pain. *Note that this practice is not for use when immediate medical attention is required.*

3. Holding your attention on the area of your pain, soften your stomach as you take three full, deep breaths into the area of concern. Imagine that your breath reaches into this area to soften, cleanse, or nourish it.

4. After those three breaths, begin to visualize that this pain you are experiencing is a ball of energy. Feel into this visual presence, noting what it might look like: How large is it? What color is it? What is its texture? Does it have a particular shape? Simply notice what comes up for you.

5. Stay with this visual as you continue to breathe mindfully; however, be open to the fact that this ball's appearance can change. Note where it changes color, texture, size, or shape.

6. What happens when you stay with this 'pain ball' for one minute? Three minutes? Ten minutes? How does your experience of pain shift?

7. When you feel ready to finish this visualization, come back to the flow of your breath. Take three more deep breaths into the belly and then slowly open your eyes to the world around you. Note what that experience was like for you.

## Health and Healing today

In this chapter, we have looked at some supporting techniques for creating space around our health challenges. I want to spend just a little time talking about another phenomenon of health that is both aspirational and mysterious at the same time. It's the context of "healing".

Over the last few years at the clinic of my partner, I routinely noticed that when people came in with chronic physical health conditions, almost always there was an emotional issue at the core of it. And it was made ever more complex by habits, beliefs and past experiences. As I began to discuss this subject with other experts in integrative and holistic medicine, I realized that almost all masterful practitioners have come to realize that "healing the person" is so much more than "treating the disease" and that healing the person is more sustainable. Prior to the advent of allopathic medicine (in US we call it modern medicine), most of the developed systems of medicine ranging from ancient traditions like Ayurveda, Traditional Chinese Medicine (TCM) or contemporary traditions like European Biological Medicine, Homeopathy, Anthroposophical medicine, etc. have had a huge focus on "healing" as the ultimate goal. With the state of being "disease free" almost as an automatic outcome.

This realization, combined with my previous experience with energy medicine, which combines meditations and energy work, and more recent work with trauma has set me on a path on which I still find myself a beginner but extremely interested – of being able to create mindfulness and meditation modalities that awaken the innate healing capacity of the body. Some of my early experiments are now available in the *AYAM app* and the eLearning platform. The feedback received so far has been very encouraging and I am hopeful that this area will continue to grow, allowing us to go deeper into the work of self-care and wellbeing with meditation and mindfulness. I will keep you all posted.

**Suggested ayam**[TM] **Practice:**

Programs: Overcoming Crises, Meet Your Beautiful Self, ayam for life(available live only)

Meditations: Self Healing, Sleep Well, Calm

# CHAPTER 16

Building a Mindful Organization: The Art of Mindful
Leadership

Many of you must be wondering about the title of this chapter, given
that in a previous chapter (14) we already discussed mindfulness at
the workplace, then why revisit this again – it's a fair question, so let
me begin with attempting to answer this. The previous chapter was
written with the point of view of an individual practitioner. Basically
how 'you', regardless of what role or level you operate in within the
organization, can bring mindfulness to the workplace. Sort of, be the
'change or influencer' from within, which can be a powerful way to
start, for it takes only one Galileo to ask if, "...the sun really goes around
the earth." That being said, for some of us who are in leadership roles
and need to think beyond individual capacities and capabilities, we
need to enquire into what could be an intervention from a strategy,
policy, framework point of view that would eventually transform the
organization from within.

It's a complex question, with no straight path as an answer, or as my
strategy professor from business school would say – it's one of those
questions, where the answer is "...it depends." Much work has been
done in this area in recent years and at *ayam* as I discussed in the
previous chapter, we have curated a collection of 10 week programs
both for workplace settings and the general population to support
this intention. This chapter, however, takes a somewhat diagonal cut
at the solution. It is written from the vantage point of a leadership
role which suggests simple practices and tools that are a blend of
policy and framework intervention and also personal practice and
lead by example type interventions.

This subject of creative-stress and toe-tickle-tango that comes with
both building a personal practice of mindfulness and meditation,

while also trying to advocate, evangelize, promote, institutionalize or support (as the case may be for you) in the workplace is an interesting one. Rarely if ever are both these journeys a straight line. The process is always iterative and with some ups and downs. So there may be moments where your personal practice may be doing very well, whereas workplace adoption may be facing headwinds of the human elements of change, or vice versa. In such cases (and many others), it may be helpful to make this "creative fork" between your personal journey and that of the organization – which is a sum total of so many people and variables. Hence, this chapter – to think more focused about the organization from a leadership vantage point.

## Today's workplace context

Modern day organizations are changing as fast as the rest of society is. Our workplaces are not exempt from the quickening pace and increasing stress of the world around us. Though each workplace is unique, there are various factors that are creating difficulty for organizations across the board.

Some of the challenges faced by modern day organizations and their employees today include:

- Increased stress due to heavy competition, 'races to the top', and a performance-centric atmosphere

- Decreased human connection and fewer in-person interactions due to remote working, automation, and cubicle desk spaces

- Less security and no safety blanket due to the gig economy

- 'Survival of the fittest' mentality and appreciation for the Type A personality

- Physical, emotional, and mental burnout amongst employees

Each industry is unique, and so the degree to which we experience these challenges varies. For instance, in some workplaces, physical burnout might rank higher than mental burnout while for others, the experience is quite the opposite. Often, the two go hand in hand.

But the question we need to ask ourselves is this:

### Does it have to be this way?

Can work be a place we enjoy going to? Can it be a source of personal growth, nourishment, and inspiration? Can performance be free from added stress? Can excellence and achievement be a team sport? Can success be shared by all? Can trust be a currency that everyone trades in? Can communication be something that unites rather than divides?

While the answers to some of these questions might feel out of reach or difficult to achieve, we might consider that workplaces haven't always been this way – that the setup of our world (workplaces included) is not fixed or static. In the same way that we open up to new ways of relating in partnership, our organizations are capable of taking on new forms and ways of being.

If we consider that the answer to the above questions is 'yes' even if we aren't quite sure how we will arrive there, we open ourselves up to what we might describe as the 'mindful organization'.

## Three Levels of Organization

Before we bring mindfulness into the equation, it is important to understand what an organization is. We often consider that it's equivalent to a company or a business – and in some ways it is. However, what the word organization reflects is a 'network of conversations' or a 'network of relationship-processes'. In other words, it's more than the company it appears to be on the surface. Beneath that outer layer, it is made up of the relationships between each individual that plays a role in it.

A mindful organization then is a network of relationship-processes that has mindfulness interwoven into its fabric. It is the white of the whiteboard, the backdrop upon which everything else presents itself. Mindful organizations are not about hosting a yearly meditation session for all employees; they are organizations that explore, encourage, and commit to mindfulness as a way of being. Through mindful conversations at all levels of the organization, mindfulness soon becomes an integral foundation of the company's culture.

As we work to bring mindfulness into any organization, we can consider three different levels or layers within the organization. We will dive into more specific practices further in the chapter, but these are some of the ways that mindfulness can manifest itself in various levels:

1.  The individual level

    At the individual level, we consider the way that mindfulness can support each player in any relationship-process. Examples of ways we can enhance mindfulness at this level include live training sessions and workshops as well as resources to support employees in developing and sustaining their mindfulness practices. Resources could include anything from mindfulness handouts to yoga studio memberships for staff.

2.  The functional level

    At the functional level, we look at the way mindfulness works within and between teams, departments, and other groups. Inviting mindfulness into this level includes exploring practices involving listening, gratitude, positive language, and mindful communication. This is also the level at which kindness and transparency are interwoven into processes such as brainstorming sessions, groups meetings, and performance reviews.

3. The organizational level

Lastly, the organizational level involves developing and embodying the persona of the behaviors that are recognized as being conducive to mindfulness, such transparency, kindness, and compassionate listening. At this level, the top must lead from the front, helping to unite the organization as a community of one. This is about walking the talk.

When we bring all three of these levels into consideration, our endeavor to create a mindfulness organization is at its fullest. No parts of the equation are left out. By addressing mindfulness as it pertains to individuals, to relationships within the organization, and to the culture of the organization as a whole, mindfulness starts to embed itself in the complex web of individuals, interactions, and energies that make it what it is.

## The Organization as Community

This complex web that makes up the organization is similar to what makes up a community. To this point, we can look at the organization we are a part of as a traditional community where each person in the village has a role to play. Not only does each have a role to play, but each contributes to the overall well-being of the community. In the same fashion, the culture of the community influences the well-being of the individuals within it. It is a symbiotic relationship.

When we consider the organization as a community, it might be easier for us to sense why each interaction and each individual is important – and why each is a reflection of the health of the company as a whole. Consider a small village in the mountains to solidify this image in your mind. Then consider:

*Why is community important?*

Communities create a sense of belonging. Through shared bonds and a common purpose, a community allows for its members to focus on and work towards a shared goal while knowing they are supported in doing so. Furthermore, communities are resilient; when one member or corner of the community struggles, the others are there to lift it back up. When mindfulness, care, and compassion are interwoven into the community (or organization), a natural dance towards greater meaning and success unfolds. Well-being blossoms and strength, commitment, and trust in the whole are able to take root.

Values of a mindful community include trust, compassion, kindness, acceptance, and gratitude. When these virtues are cultivated in organizations, the company and its individual constituents thrive.

## Qualities of a Mindful Leader and Organization

The mindful leader (or the mindful leadership style) is a catalyst of cultural transformation. When mindfulness is honored, embodied, and expressed through the actions of leadership, the company sends a clear message to its members, which impacts the processes amongst individuals and various departments or groups.

Some of the qualities that a mindful leader and organization embody are list below, along with examples of what this might look like in action:

- Transparency – i.e. being clear and upfront about the present market conditions

- Presence – i.e. listening to an employee's concerns with curiosity and non-judgment

- Flexibility – i.e. being able to change direction or approach when it is needed

- Compassion – i.e. having heartfelt concern for those one works with

- Honesty – i.e. clearly and compassionately broaching difficult conversations and staying true to what needs to be said

- Curiosity – i.e. asking questions before jumping to conclusions

- Non-Judgment – i.e. taking in various data points and refraining from making assumptions based on personal biases

- Openness – i.e. welcoming new ideas from all team members

- Kindness – i.e. offering thoughtful, uplifting words, bonuses, or resources to employees without expecting anything in return

- Gratitude – i.e. feeling and expressing appreciation for all those in the workplace

- Trust – i.e. having faith and confidence in the expertise of employees and departments and therefore not 'micromanaging'

This list is not exhaustive, but it highlights some of the qualities we can work on cultivating as a leader within a mindful organization. It is important to keep in mind that each one of us is unique, and that some of these will come more naturally for us than for others. Likewise, some of these qualities may be difficult for us to embody naturally.

For instance, one leader might have an innate ability to be trusting of its employees while some might need to explore and examine where trust is not present. Mindfully reflecting upon these values is one way of increasing self-awareness. It probes us into deeper questions rather than conclusions, questions such as:

- *Is there a way I can surrender my tendency to micromanage? What might support me in this endeavor?*

- *Where am I not as present with my team members as I could be? How might I learn to listen with greater presence?*

- *How might I express my gratitude for my colleagues? Or, how might I become more appreciative of all those I work with?*

It is important to remember that we do not need to (nor should we) *force* ourselves to change. Coercion is an ineffective way of experiencing real change. Rather, by becoming mindful of where we can grow as leaders and by making a heartfelt commitment to compassionately and patiently exploring this process, we slowly come into the insights and tools we require to evolve.

In place of the pursuit of perfection, we might aim instead to be honest, open, and vulnerable. These qualities bring us back to our humanity, which is where real change and innovation occurs.

By sharing who we are with those we work with, we start to shift the culture of the organization in inspiring and empowering ways. In the words of Brené Brown[140]:

> *"Vulnerability is the birthplace of innovation, creativity, and change."*

### Ways to Implement Mindfulness

So what would an organization rooted in mindfulness do differently than one that has not yet delved into this way of relating? The main task at hand would be to rethink your core process in such a way that they become rooted in mindfulness. The whole organization should then stand in mindfulness as a way of thinking, acting, and breathing. By rethinking and reworking these processes (outlined below), you shift the relationship-processes in meaningful ways.

The core processes that need to be reviewed, as a start are:

I.   Hiring and firing

II.  Performance appraisal

---

[140] https://blog.ted.com/vulnerability-is-the-birthplace-of-innovation-creativi-ty-and-change-brene-brown-at-ted2012/

III.   Customer communication

IV.   Learning and development (L&D)

## Hiring and Firing

Both hiring and firing are important processes for an organization. This is when we welcome someone into the corporate community or decide to let them go. Each of these tasks requires openness and sensitivity for the individual we are engaging with to feel fully seen – whether they are on their way in or out of the organization.

When it comes to hiring, many organizations make their selections based on personality tests, standardized interview questions, and other easily-measurable criteria. While all of these have their place in assessing the skills of a candidate, mindful hiring requires that we remember: this is a relationship we're building.

It is important therefore to bring the human element into this interaction. A few of the ways you can do this include:

◊ **Grounding yourself before beginning the interview**

You can ground yourself by taking a few deep breaths, exhaling any tense, nervous, or otherwise difficult feelings or energies you may be experiencing. If your day is busy, make a commitment to be entirely present throughout the interview or by being honest about the feeling of stress you are experiencing given the demands of the day. Practice honesty, vulnerability, and transparency as much as is appropriate.

◊ **Coming from a place of non-judgment**

Chances are you have already received and read through a resume before the interview takes place. While you will undoubtedly have some prior conceptions about what this person will bring to the table, remain curious and unassuming about who they are and what they have to offer. This will help to remove any cognitive biases that might lead you to make a choice that isn't in the best interest of the organization – whether that means hiring or not hiring someone.

◊ **Asking a variety of questions – and going off-script**

While there will indeed be certain questions you'll want to ask, remember that you are interacting with someone who is rich with experience unlike anyone else who will come to the table. Ask a mix of questions, including less traditional ones like, "What do you read in your time off?" or "What qualities do you think are important for workplace well-being?" Assure them that these questions are not a 'test'; they are simply to get to know them better.

When it comes to letting people go, the same degree of awareness about our shared humanity is essential. This is a vulnerable position for anyone to be in and as such, it must be approached with kindness, care, and compassion. Furthermore, firing and letting go of staff impact not only the person leaving the organization. These actions send a ripple effect through an organization, which can either increase trust and respect or decrease the well-being of the culture.

Some of the ways you might mindfully approach a situation where you must fire or let go of a staff member include:

◊ **Ensuring to the best of your ability that the end of employment does not come as a surprise to the person being let go**

Where the end of employment is due to major shifts in the economy or other unpredictable circumstances and not because of poor performance, it might not be as possible for this to not come as a surprise. However, where the firing or letting go is due to less than ideal performance, it is important that the employee has received feedback prior to this termination. This can be achieved through greater transparency, honesty, and compassionate communication.

◊ **Rooting yourself in mindful presence as this could be challenging for you as well**

Grounding yourself in mindful presence means being aware of what emotions are present within you and perhaps settling the mind through either a simple body scan practice or breath awareness meditation. This will help you to navigate the situation from a place of greater ease, kindness, and acceptance of the situation.

◊ **Remembering that this is a vulnerable and uncomfortable position for the employee to be in**

Regardless of the circumstances of termination, being fired or let go is very difficult. It is important to remember this – that regardless of what was or wasn't done to lead to this ending, the employee you are facing shares the same emotions and feelings as you. Approaching this interaction from a place of compassion is fundamental in ensuring mindfulness is retained here. This is about putting yourself, as they say, in another person's shoes. If it were you, how would you like for this to be managed?

◊ **Ensuring this interaction is held in a private space, adding to the employee's sense of safety and comfort**

Keeping the above in mind, you can further approach this with care by making sure that this conversation is held in a private conference room or office. You might also like to have a third party present – another manager or supervisor – who can help to address any questions or concerns the employee might have. This could be an HR specialist.

◊ **Ensuring that communication of the termination to remaining team members maintains an appropriate level of transparency, respect, and compassion**

Remaining employees will all have different reactions to the termination of a particular employee. To ensure the response is as supportive as possible, communicate what happened with compassion and honesty while remaining respect for the person who was let go. Let the team know that you are open to discussing this termination with anyone who has concerns or difficult feelings in relation to the event.

Since hiring and firing is a nuanced process that shifts according to the situation and the people involved, your approach will be just as personal and unique from moment to moment. Before beginning any of these processes, refer back to the list of mindful leader qualities to see which you might consciously harness as you prefer to bring someone into the team or to let someone go.

## Performance Appraisal

Performance reviews can trigger stress and anxiety in both the employee and the employer. No matter how we approach it, these situations will conjure up the fears of judgment and of 'not measuring up'. Mindfulness of this energy that is inherent in performance reviews can help the process to be as effective and smooth as possible.

Some basic mindfulness interventions you can explore during performance appraisals include:

◊ **Coming to the table prepared**

Preparing for an employee's performance review is two-fold. First, it involves careful preparation in regards to collecting the stats, accomplishments, and difficulties that have come up in regards to this employee over the time frame in question. Second, it means preparing yourself mentally. If the mind is racing or caught up in assumptions and judgments, close your eyes and spend a few minutes focusing on your breath before the interaction.

◊ **Rooting yourself in compassion**

Regardless of how the employee has performed since the last review, ensure you are coming to the table from a place of kindness, care, and compassion. As was noted in the suggestions for hiring and firing, it is important to tap into the humanity you share with the person sitting across from you.

◊ **Being generous and uplifting in your assessments**

Ensure that you have plenty of uplifting and positive comments to add to your performance review, even if the employee has much to work on. In some cases, it might be difficult for you to find the strengths of a particular employee – which is okay. In this case, connect with other supervisors and managers prior to the review to see what other eyes see. As we know, our own cognitive biases impact the data we collect, and so it is important to search for the data that others pick up on, too.

◊ **Avoiding words that trigger the sympathetic nervous system (SNS) response**

As we explored in chapter six, the words we use have a direct impact on our physiology. To be conscious and considerate of the well-being of the person receiving the feedback, avoid using words such as: try, control, effort, work, hard, push, must, and should. For instance, rather than saying, "We would like to see you put in more effort…" you might opt for something more soothing and open-ended like, "What might support you in moving closer towards our goals?"

Like hiring and firing, performance appraisals are not something that come with a clear rulebook because each situation is unique. However, by referring back to the qualities you want to lay as the framework for your organization, you set yourself up for success.

## Customer Communication

Relationship processes of an organization go far beyond what occurs within the bricks and mortar of the company. Like communities, the well-being of an organization is also dependent upon how healthy its relationships are with those outside of it. No community and no organization can thrive in isolation, which is why customer communication is a crucial consideration in developing a culture of mindfulness.

When interacting with customers, the same basic principles of mindfulness apply. It is important to support and nourish a mutually beneficial relationship between the provider and the purchaser. If one side does not have its needs met, the relationship will suffer and could eventually deteriorate all together.

Some of the ways you can ensure that your company's mindfulness culture ripples out to its customers include:

◊ **Listening with curiosity and non-judgment**

When a customer approaches the organization with a concern and complaint, it is important that the staff managing the relationship approaches the customer with curiosity, openness, compassion, and non-judgment. It is easy to become defensive when we feel we are being judged or attacked or when someone raises their voice. Ensuring staff are trained in mindful customer service goes a long way in helping employees to notice when defenses arise and what can be done about it.

◊ **Practicing honesty and transparency**

Honesty and transparency must extend beyond the walls of the organization for them to be authentic. Being clear and upfront in your communications via product labels, newsletters, advertisements, and any other form of marketing helps to build a strong, respectful foundation.

This helps to build trust both within the organization and outside of it.

◊ **Expressing gratitude**

To take mindfulness a step further in customer relations, gratitude can be expressed in any number of ways. Through newsletters, follow-up letters, and at the point of service, sharing appreciation for the support of your customers acts as a gift to both the purchaser and yourself. When customers feel appreciated, they are more likely to come back again.

Bringing the same care and attention to your customer base as you explore within the organization goes a long way. It helps your customers to feel good about giving you their business, it deepens your roots within the community you are a part of, and it reminds us that we are all in this together. Without our customers, we would not be able to do what we do. Mindfulness helps us to bridge the apparent gap between us and them so that we can start to really see ourselves as one.

## Learning and Development (L&D)

A focus of human resources, learning and development is where we offer our employees the chance to gain new skills that we hope will drive performance. In a mindful organization, learning and development is not solely focused on the outcome it will have for the business, but it also acts as an opportunity for personal growth.

We must remember that those who work for us are not exclusively project leaders, health and safety managers, or sales people. They are humans with a wide range of experience, emotions, feelings, interests, and needs.

Learning and development within a mindful organization can (and should) therefore expand beyond traditional training programs that have a direct connection to business success. When you encourage holistic growth of your employees, you will discover a positive ripple effect that enhances business performance as well. However, helping our employees to succeed without expecting certain payoffs is how we connect with the heart of the humans within our organization. It is not just about us; it is about them as individuals, too.

In fact, it might be helpful to break up your training programs into two distinct categories: one focused on professional development and the other on personal growth and well-being. This will help employees decipher between what they should bring to the table. For instance, in a personal growth and well-being program they might let themselves open up to the training in a different way than if the program is focused on professional development.

Various themes of trainings and workshops you might consider for mindfulness-based learning and development programs include (but are not limited to):

- **Professional Development**

  o Mindful customer service training

  o Mindful teamwork training

  o Creativity workshops

  o Compassionate communication workshops

  o Mindful team coaching (with training themes including focus, motivation, and performance)

  o Guest speakers to cover any range of topics, including but not limited to vulnerability, transparency, communication, motivation, purpose, etc.

- **Personal Growth & Well-Being**

  o Stress reduction trainings

  o Mental health talks and workshops

o   Yoga, Tai Chi, or Qigong programs

o   Meditation intensives

o   Compassion and/or self-compassion workshops

o   Breathwork trainings

o   Team wellness retreats

o   Mindful eating workshops

The structure of how these are offered will vary from organization to organization. Some might be best suited as a weekly session while others might be offered less frequently or as a special event. For best results, mindfulness learning and development programs should be a standard part of the company culture. Why? Because mindfulness is not something we master after one, ten, or twenty sessions. It is something that takes time to fully work itself into the core of our being.

**Myths About Mindfulness and Work**

It is important that we address a common myth that often arises when 'mindfulness' and 'workplace' land in the same sentence. Many people misunderstand what mindfulness offers us, believing that it makes us passive, laid back, or non-reactive. None of these assumptions could be further from the truth.

First, mindfulness helps us to remove the mental distractions that make it difficult for us to focus on the task at hand. Oftentimes, when we struggle to get things done, it is not because we are lazy or have poor intentions; it is simply because the mind has not yet been trained to focus. To this point, mindfulness has indeed been found to increase focus and attention in various studies.[141]

Furthermore, when practiced under the guidance of a knowledgeable teacher, mindfulness increases vitality and positively impacts

[141] https://www.ncbi.nlm.nih.gov/pmc/articles/PMC6088366/

productivity measures. Research has shown it can improve team atmosphere, organizational atmosphere, and personal performance.[142] It makes 'success without stress' possible.

Finally, mindfulness does indeed have a role to play in our reactions – and to this point, it does decrease them. However, what it increases in place of our reactions is our responses. We learn to mindfully respond rather than to unconsciously react to the people and circumstances around us. This is what we want in a mindful organization; thoughtful responses to override unthoughtful reactions.

## Routine Exercises for the Mindful Organization

In addition to the suggestions already listed, routine exercises can be adopted by the organization to further enhance how deeply mindfulness is interwoven into its foundation. Depending on the type of company in question, these might be implemented in different ways. Furthermore, not all of these are required for a company to become more mindful. They are simply starting points for enhancing the presence of mindfulness within the organization.

Some of the implementations and exercises you might consider include:

• Scheduled breaks for meditation and mindful movement

• A designated meditation and movement room

• On-demand access to resources, such as online workshops, worksheets, and meditation recordings

• Short sits (mindful pauses) before meetings commence

• Gratitude sharing before morning meetings

• Mindful pauses for silent reflection in the middle of meetings

• Creative contemplation sessions before group brainstorming

---

[142] https://www.frontiersin.org/articles/10.3389/fpsyg.2018.00195/full

Again, the practices you choose to implement will be unique to your organization. There are no rules to this. Commit first to embracing and exploring mindfulness qualities (such as compassion, openness, honesty, and acceptance) and then consider how these might naturally work themselves into your relationship processes.

Remember to consider the three levels of your organization: the individual, functional, and organizational. Adding mindfulness training and practices to each of these levels will help you to lay the groundwork for a culture that is immersed in the qualities of the heart-mind and the qualities of our shared humanity.

## A note to the leader

Whenever we talk about leaders and leadership there is always a background question of who is a leader and what the heck leadership is! Thousands of books have been written over the last few decades and thousands more will be written about this esoteric art and phenomenon. I was enthused enough that I wrote a whole doctoral dissertation around this subject but admittedly, I am not any more of an expert on this than I was before I started. One thing however I have learnt in the process is that, it's possible to define a leader and leadership in a specific context in a way that people can self identify with it, if they fit the role. And therefore, in case of participating in building a mindful organization, I would like to define it as; *"Leader is anyone who creates a dynamic in an organization."* Of itself, I don't think this definition is very original; if I recall it correctly, I heard it or some version close to it from my culture professor at business school. However, over time this definition has grown on me. In the context of our discussion, it rings especially true because "mindfulness" is a transformative dynamic that can facilitate and intermediate many other changes in the environment.

So you could be a sales manager or CFO or Office Manager or a Board Member, as long as you have a personal influence sphere where you work with colleagues and spark conversations and impact how they engage with each other, or demonstrate by example – you are pretty much a leader. They key question is – are you a "mindful leader" which by corollary asks are you adding to the dynamic of mindfulness in a positive way. I don't think of this as a normative discussion of "good way or bad way", rather simply as are you *being mindful about being mindful.*

Mindfulness above all else is not a 'thing to do' or a mountain to scale – rather is a way of being to cultivate. It's a journey of life long evolution, a journey of nurturing wholesome qualities and a journey in which no one ever arrives. This journey comes with gradual unfoldment of profound joy, compassion, peace and fulfillment. And that is a worthy outcome for any person, leader or organization to aspire for all of whom they touch!

**Suggested ayam(TM) Practice:**

Programs: ayam for leaders (available Live only), Meet Your Beautiful Self

Meditations : Calm, Focus, Abundance, Sleep Well

# CHAPTER 17

Meditation & Mindfulness: At the Frontiers of Health and Wellness

When we think about the use of meditation and mindfulness in everyday life, many of us unconsciously consider that these practices are primarily or most effectively drivers of spiritual growth and antidotes to stress and anxiety. Less often do we think about (or even consider) the other ways in which these techniques are beneficial in promoting health.

Even where we've heard that mindfulness and meditation have been studied for their usage in cancer, depression, and pain treatment (to name a few), we (collectively speaking) don't often give these ideas or their findings too much weight. And yet, it has been scientifically shown that these interventions indeed play a role in treating some of the most difficult conditions of the human experience. Both clinically and in a supporting role, mindfulness and meditation find their effective place in a range of health and wellness issues.

Initially, due to having an "over exposure" to the spiritual seeker community where "awakening and transcendence" tend to be the major goals of meditation, I also had a limited exposure to the more direct health benefits and the research in this area.

But fortunately for me, I had an extended period in my life when I was on the Board of a global foundation that was at the forefront of using Energy Medicine to combat medically non-responding disease. True to the mission of the Foundation, all trustees needed to be trained in the modalities so that they had a deep, personal experience to bring to their oversight roles. For me, this meant traveling through Africa and South America to become trained and accumulate fieldwork experience as well.

A fascinating experience which included missed flights, almost getting kidnapped at gunpoint etc., but the memory that stuck with me most about this phase was an observation of *"significantly better response and recovery"* amongst people that actively participated in meditation with us as opposed to others who did not, even though both were receiving the same modalities and had similar levels of health conditions.

Around this time, there were also a few experiences that had a hugely moving effect on my life, one of which I would like to share with you. It relates to an uncle of a close friend of mine. The uncle had been diagnosed with stage IV cancer, but not wanting to worry his family, he wouldn't make a big deal about the pain he was going through. In those days, I was studying with a mentor who was also a world renowned energy healer, so my friend sought me out to ask if there was anything I or my mentor could do at this stage.

This was not an unusual question for me at all, given the social context we were living in at that time, so I gave him the truthful answer; *"not much."* A few days later, he called me again, asking me if I was willing to see them anyway for a session, saying that it would mean a lot to him and his family to know that they had tried. How could I say no? So I agreed and his cousin (the son of the uncle) and the uncle himself came to see me. I did the best I could in a 'healing session' as I had been taught and, following the session, we meditated together for about 15-20 minutes.

At the end of the session, the uncle asked me a very difficult question; *when could he see me again?* I hesitated a bit, but there is only so much objectivity you can have when a kind, 70+ year old man is asking to see you again for what he believes has some hope for him. I agreed to see him the next week and continued to do so for regular sessions for the next few weeks until it was time for me to go back to the US. During one of these sessions, I saw his uncle recording it, which I didn't think much about at that time.

Anyhow, before leaving the country, I had a heart to heart with his son and wished them well.

A few months later, I received the sad news of his passing and had the chance to offer my condolences to my friend in person on my next visit. A couple of years later, I received a text from his son on the anniversary of his father's death expressing gratitude for my work with him. I called him back and we had a little chat. He mentioned to me that, even after I had left, his father would listen to the recorded meditation almost daily, right up to his last days. And on one occasion, after the meditation, his father confided to him that he knew he was terminally ill and that it was a matter of time. He also knew the healing sessions were of no 'healing' use anymore, but he was still following through with them because the closing meditation had a hugely relieving effect on him. It gave him 2-3 hours of pain-free rest, which was very valuable to him, and he was very grateful that my friend had introduced us and enabled him to access "these islands of peace."

I was stunned upon hearing that and had real trouble holding back my tears... repeating to myself in my mind "...had I only known." Let's just say that it was the last time that I ever said no to offering a healing session to anyone who believed it could benefit them in any way, and I also agreed to look beyond what I thought were the boundaries of positive health effects meditation can have on people!

This is just one anecdote; I have many more stories of similar nature but, despite that, I realized that my sample set was very small and the observations hardly scientifically rigorous. It did however make enough of an impression on me that I made myself a promise that when this phase of fieldwork was over, I would do more research on this correlation. This later took the form of my pursuing formal education and research in related areas, and certainly brought much more insight.

Additionally, over the last decade or so in my practice, I have seen a gradual but substantial shift in the mix of people seeking out meditation and mindfulness. Previously, the vast majority used to be "spiritual seekers" and now, I find corporate professionals looking for life balance and people wanting to support their health making up a large part of attendees both in retreats and classes. So this conversation is more relevant today than ever before.

This book would not therefore be complete without a discussion of some meaningful depth around the clinical grade interventions that have emerged from this field which we can easily access. And to serve this purpose, in this chapter we will explore some of these health applications of mindfulness and meditation and two major modalities that have been developed over the past half century. We'll also highlight some emergent technologies that integrate the principles of mindfulness and meditation so that we may harness the full healing potential that these practices have to offer.

## Beyond Spiritual Growth

Spiritual growth or 'advancement' is indeed, in and of itself, an admirable and life-enhancing pursuit. As we open ourselves up to a deeper or higher understanding of our spiritual nature, we naturally begin to get more out of life. However, it is important to note that spiritual growth is not all we can hope for when we pursue mindfulness and meditation. Though these traditions speak primarily to measures of well-being such as freedom, contentment, and peace, science is now beginning to understand how much more significant the benefits of these practices are.

Empirical research on the physiological impact of these modalities began in the 1950s.[143] Since then, countless studies have been conducted to better understand the relationship between such ancient practices and well-being on multiple fronts. This work has shed light on what might otherwise be considered 'mystical', leaving no doubt that the implications of practicing mindfulness and meditation are far-reaching.

[143] https://www.semanticscholar.org/paper/Meditation-and-the-Neuroscience-of-Consciousnes-s%3A-Lutz-Dunne/7b06c2f9ec346ded9d5f901908b49f7427bb153e

From pain and depression to addiction and beyond, what we do with the mind has a direct impact on the body. As we know, the mind and body are inextricably interconnected. We've talked about the stress response, which illuminates how our thoughts (and even certain words themselves) can spark a cascade of physiological responses that together are known as the fight, flight, or freeze response.

If we extrapolate from here, we might then consider that our hormones (a part of the stress response) plays a direct role in the maintenance and well-being of nearly every organ system.[144] The systems that cortisol is known to impact (due to glucocorticoid receptors that are present in nearly all of our bodily tissues) include:

- The nervous system

- The immune system

- The cardiovascular system

- The respiratory system

- The reproductive system

- The musculoskeletal system

- The integumentary system

As we know, cortisol increases when we are stressed. This increase is likely to affect each of the above systems in one way or another. When stress is acute, cortisol is beneficial as it does indeed play an adaptive role. However, when stress is chronic, we end up in a state of imbalance. Consider for a moment how this imbalance might impact each one of these systems. If we have too much or too little of something in our bodies (or if something is over or underactive), what do we expect the long term impact to be if nothing changes? When we consider this, it becomes clear that the potential decline in health due to chronic stress is widespread.

---

[144] https://www.ncbi.nlm.nih.gov/books/NBK538239/

Since we now know that mindfulness and meditation play a role in easing stress and may even down-regulate the activity of major stress axes in the human body,[145] we can understand how these techniques would play a tangible role in preventing and/or alleviating many stress-induced conditions.

However, the stress mechanisms in the body are not the only areas where mindfulness and meditation intervene. These practices also impact our neurobiology, which dictates our cognitive and behavioral functions. Through these and many other mechanisms, such practices that have stood the test of time impact the very real sense of well-being that we embody.

To take a brief look at some of the findings, outlined below are about a dozen of the hundreds of studies that have revealed the widespread impact of these interventions:

## Cancer

- One study revealed that mindfulness-based stress reduction (MBSR) programs were helpful in improving psychological functioning in both cancer patients and their partners. It showed that this intervention created significant reductions in mood disturbances, muscle tension, and neurological and upper respiratory symptoms.[146]

- A review of 13 studies to assess the evidence for using mindfulness-based interventions in cancer care suggested that these interventions resulted in significant improvements in anxiety, depression, stress, sexual difficulties, immune function, and physiological arousal.[147]

- Another review of multiple studies suggests that mindfulness meditation may be effective in managing pain in cancer

---

[145] https://www.ncbi.nlm.nih.gov/pmc/articles/PMC4940234/
[146] https://pubmed.ncbi.nlm.nih.gov/19918956/
[147] https://www.researchgate.net/publication/45509491_What_is_the_evidence_for_the_use_of_mindfulness-based_interventions_in_cancer_care_A_review

patients as it moderates the emotional appraisal of pain by reducing attention from the unpleasant sensation.[148]

## Mental Health

- A 2009 pilot study exploring the effectiveness of mindfulness-based cognitive therapy (MBCT) in treating patients with chronic-recurrent depression revealed that self-reported symptoms of depression decreased from severe to mild. There was also an observed reduction in the number of participants who met the full criteria for depression.[149]

- In the early stages of psychosis, mindfulness has been found to improve emotional regulation. It has also been observed that, in regards to schizophrenia, mindfulness-based interventions can reduce rehospitalization rates.[150]

- Meditation practice has also been suggested as an intervention to help reduce cognitive decline. This might delay the onset of dementia or reduce the risk of it all together.[151]

- Another study revealed that MBCT is effective in lowering intolerance of uncertainty in those with a panic disorder.[152]

## Immunity

- A study looking at 20 randomized controlled trials (RCTs) revealed that mindfulness meditation is connected to reductions in proinflammatory processes, increases in cell-mediated defense markers, and increases in enzyme activity that protect against cell aging.

---

[148] https://www.ncbi.nlm.nih.gov/pmc/articles/PMC6371675/
[149] https://www.sciencedirect.com/science/article/pii/S0005796709000333
[150] https://www.ncbi.nlm.nih.gov/pmc/articles/PMC4591204/
[151] https://www.ncbi.nlm.nih.gov/pmc/articles/PMC6015474/
[152] https://www.ncbi.nlm.nih.gov/pmc/articles/PMC4823195/

- One review suggests that mindfulness meditation, Transcendental Meditation, and Qigong can have a positive impact on one's natural killer cell activity, as well as B-lymphocyte numbers and telomerase activity.[153]

## Digestive System

- Mindfulness-based interventions have been found to improve inflammatory biomarkers in patients diagnosed with Crohn's disease or ulcerative colitis.[154]

- MBSR was found to improve the quality of life of those with inflammatory bowel disease, as well as decrease the severity of their symptoms.[155]

## Addiction

- One study looked at the impact of mindfulness-based relapse prevention and discovered a significantly reduced risk of relapse to drug and heavy alcohol use in those who received the training, compared with those who had 'treatment as usual'. Follow-ups were six and twelve months later.[156]

- Research has also shown that mindfulness-based interventions can help to reduce substance misuse and craving. This occurs by its modulating effects on internal processes related to self-regulation and reward processing.[157]

## Pain

- A randomized study looking at the impact of MBSR and cognitive behavioral therapy (CBT) on 342 adults with

[153] https://www.ncbi.nlm.nih.gov/pmc/articles/PMC4097901/
[154] https://www.nature.com/articles/s41598-020-63168-4
[155] https://www.ncbi.nlm.nih.gov/pmc/articles/PMC6178327/
[156] https://www.ncbi.nlm.nih.gov/pmc/articles/PMC4489711/
[157] https://ascpjournal.biomedcentral.com/articles/10.1186/s13722-018-0115-3

chronic lower back pain showed that both MBSR and CBT resulted in considerable (and comparable) improvement in the experience of back pain. After 26 weeks, 43.6% of participants in the MBSR group and 44.9% of participants in the CBT group reported meaningful improvement in their symptoms.[158]

- Research also looked at the impact of a 10-week stress reduction and relaxation program on 90 patients with chronic pain. The results showed statistically significant reductions in measures of present-moment pain, mood disturbance, psychological symptoms, and inhibition of activity due to pain.[159]

These highlights are just some of the many studies that have revealed the power and potential of mindfulness and meditation. The major point that I am trying to make is simply that *"the body and mind are interwoven with one another to a degree far greater than the mind might imagine. What we do with our mind has a direct impact on what happens in the body."*

The impact of these techniques are not new. Mindfulness and meditation practitioners have long understood the great effect that these practices can have. What's changed? Simply that science has become interested and is now catching up. As technologies develop, it is becoming easier to gain a measurable understanding of how these practices affect us. As time rolls forward, so too will our realizations about the great potential of these ancient understandings.

To gain a better sense of the applications of these practices, we will take a look at two primary clinical modalities that have been the foundation of research in this field. We'll go on to explore related technologies that have emerged out of this research, which shed light on how we can enhance our mindfulness and meditation practices with the integration of real-time data.

---

[158] https://pubmed.ncbi.nlm.nih.gov/27002445/
[159] https://link.springer.com/article/10.1007/BF00845519

## Two Primary Clinical Modalities

Effective and significant data collection relies largely on standardized research methods. Having clear models that can be reproduced in various test settings can strengthen our understanding of the true impact of whatever method we are investigating. For this reason, two primary clinical modalities have taken center stage in research related to mindfulness and meditation: Mindfulness-Based Stress Reduction (MBSR) and Mindfulness-Based Cognitive Therapy (MBCT). These clearly defined and reproducible programs have made it easier for us to dig deeper into what these practices can offer.

## Mindfulness-Based Stress Reduction

Developed in 1979 by Dr. Jon Kabat-Zinn, Mindfulness-Based Stress Reduction is an 8-week program that constitutes 2.5 hours of practice per week, plus a single daylong retreat[160]. Originally developed for stress and chronic pain management,[161] the program was, in its earliest stages, offered as a 10-week 'Stress Reduction and Relaxation Program'. Overtime, it became known as MBSR: a standardized 8-week mindfulness-based intervention. Its applications have been broadened through years of research and it is now used in the treatment of conditions such as anxiety, depression, immune disorders, hypertension, and diabetes.

The program includes:[162]

- The body scan

- Sitting meditation (attention to breathing, thoughts, sounds, emotions, and bodily sensations)

- Simple movement practices (i.e. walking, standing, or lying down, yoga exercises)

---

[160] https://www.ncbi.nlm.nih.gov/pmc/articles/PMC3336928/
[161] https://www.sciencedirect.com/science/article/abs/pii/0163834382900263
[162] https://www.ncbi.nlm.nih.gov/pmc/articles/PMC5783379/

- Informal meditation practices (i.e. awareness of eating, showering)

The primary intention of the program, developed at the University of Massachusetts Medical School, is "to create a structured pathway to relieve suffering and increase well-being for people facing a host of challenges arising from a wide range of medical and psychological conditions and the demands and stressors inherent in the everyday lives of human beings."[163] And although it is rooted in the universal dharma teachings of Buddhism, it is not designed to teach Buddhism, nor does it contain any cultural, religious, or ideological factors associated with this tradition.[164]

Widely applicable and accessible to people of all walks of life, these programs are offered in an array of different settings. From hospitals and clinics to schools, prisons, and workplaces, the MBSR program is adaptable to a range of environments.[165] And though the setting might vary from study to study, the standardized program remains the same.

Listed below are some of the measured and self-reported results discovered through MBSR studies. This is just a handful of the many studies that reveal the power of mindfulness-based interventions:

- Mindfulness meditation training can buffer CD4+ T lymphocyte decreases in adults with HIV-1.[166]

- MBSR was found to be associated with greater glycemic control in those with type 2 diabetes mellitus.[167] A reduction in depression, anxiety, and general psychological distress was also noted.

---

[163] https://www.umassmed.edu/globalassets/center-for-mindfulness/documents/mbsr-curriculum-guide-2017.pdf
[164] https://onlinelibrary.wiley.com/doi/full/10.1093/clipsy.bpg016
[165] https://onlinelibrary.wiley.com/doi/full/10.1093/clipsy.bpg016
[166] https://www.ncbi.nlm.nih.gov/pmc/articles/PMC2725018/
[167] https://pubmed.ncbi.nlm.nih.gov/17900040/

- In students, MBSR has been found to enhance emotional regulation, improve mood, and decrease stress, anxiety, and fatigue.[168]

- Trauma-sensitive MBSR was found to be associated with significant reductions in PTSD and depressive symptoms in a study focused on female survivors of interpersonal violence. Anxious attachment was also reduced. [169]

- MBSR has also been found to enhance distress tolerance and overall resilience.[170]

In clinical settings, MBSR is indeed a forerunner. However, it is not alone in taking center stage in this field. Inspired and informed by the findings of MBSR over the years, another mindfulness-based clinical intervention was developed: Mindfulness-Based Cognitive Therapy.

## Mindfulness-Based Cognitive Therapy

Some decades after MBSR made its name in clinical health research and application, Mindfulness-Based Cognitive Therapy was created by cognitive behavioral therapists Dr. Mark William, Dr. John Teasdale, and Dr. Zindel Segal. Known as MBCT, this mindfulness intervention is the integration of MBSR and Cognitive Behavioral Therapy (CBT), which was originally developed to help those suffering from depression.[171]

Similar to MBSR in structure, MBCT is an 8-week program that meets once per week with a mindfulness teacher trained in the method. It incorporates mindfulness practices such as meditation, breathing exercises and stretching, which help to enhance mindful awareness of thoughts, feelings, and sensations within the body.[172]

---

[168] https://link.springer.com/article/10.1007%252Fs12671-012-0094-5
[169] https://www.ncbi.nlm.nih.gov/pmc/articles/PMC4806391/
[170] https://www.researchgate.net/publication/292071709_Mindfulness-based_stress_reduction_MBSR_enhances_distress_tolerance_and_resilience_through_changes_in_mindfulness
[171] https://www.bangor.ac.uk/mindfulness/what-is-mindfulness.php.en
[172] https://www.oxfordmindfulness.org/issues-landing-page/depression/

While the structure of MBSR and MBCT are similar, there are key differences in the techniques and application of the mindfulness practices. Some of those differences are:[173]

- MBSR is more generic in its application, whereas MBCT focuses on specific conditions (such as depression).

- Though MBCT shows benefits in a range of health conditions, it is primarily focused on treating mental health conditions.

- MBCT, in comparison to MBSR, puts a greater amount of focus on exploring and working with the psychological and cognitive components that contribute to our experience.

- As it is indeed interwoven with CBT, MBCT incorporates techniques and practices from this field of knowledge. It also includes teaching points related to the specific condition which one is experiencing.

Much of the clinical research on MBCT is focused on mental health measures. The findings noted below highlight some of the observed benefits of this intervention as it applies to this area of focus:

- MBCT was found to significantly reduce the risk of relapse in patients with 3 or more previous episodes of depression.[174]

- One study revealed that MBCT can reduce suicidal ideation.[175]

- MBCT has also been associated with reductions in anxiety in those with generalized anxiety disorder.[176]

---

[173] https://www.bangor.ac.uk/mindfulness/what-is-mindfulness.php.en
[174] https://content.apa.org/record/2000-05084-010
[175] https://www.sciencedirect.com/science/article/pii/S0010440X14002351
[176] https://pubmed.ncbi.nlm.nih.gov/17765453/

- In those with bipolar disorder, a preliminary MBCT study found immediate effects of this mindfulness intervention on reducing anxiety and depressive symptoms.[177]

- Another study revealed that MBCT is connected to a reduction in anxiety, worry, and depression and an increase in mindfulness and self-compassion where perinatal anxiety is present.[178]

## Outside of MBSR and MBCT

It is important to note that MBSR and MBCT are not the only meditation techniques that have provided health and healing to those who practice them. Transcendental Meditation, Qigong, Vipassana, and mindfulness practice outside of MBSR and MBCT all contribute to an increase in individual well-being. Qigong, for instance, has been observed to reduce anxiety and balance the autonomic nervous system.[179] Additionally, Transcendental Meditation has been noted for its ability to prevent and treat cardiovascular disease.[180]

The importance, however, of having standardized, clinically applicable modalities such as MBSR and MBCT ensures that the health and healing benefits of mindfulness and meditation as a whole are brought to light. No longer can it be argued that these practices are spiritual nonsense. The evidence for their validity in mainstream health settings is indeed in the research.

## Mindfulness and Meditation Technologies for Health Promotion

As modern technologies continue to be enhanced exponentially, various tools are being developed that take mindfulness and meditation to another level of application. No longer is real-time

---

[177] https://www.sciencedirect.com/science/article/pii/S0165032707003060
[178] https://link.springer.com/article/10.1007/s00737-013-0402-7
[179] https://www.hindawi.com/journals/ecam/2018/4960978/
[180] https://www.ncbi.nlm.nih.gov/pmc/articles/PMC2211376/

data reserved for clinical settings; we can hold the numbers in our own two hands.

The following technologies reveal how mindfulness and meditation can indeed be interwoven with the world of technology. These immersions bring meditation out of the spiritual domain and into the field of scientific, non-secular wellness training.

## Brain Entrainment Program

Brain entrainment is the application of precisely engineered audio frequencies in the form of binaural beats. Binaural beats are generated when two sine waves (one going into each ear) are of slightly different frequencies[181] (i.e. 300 Hz and 330 Hz). A beat of 30 Hz is then perceived by the listener, which is said to shift our brain waves. Research of this technology is in its early stages, but studies focused on auditory beat stimulation suggest that its application can modulate cognition, reduce anxiety, and enhance mood states.[182]

## Neurofeedback

Another modality that is being interlaced with mindfulness and meditation is that of neurofeedback. A form of biofeedback, this technology measures brain waves through electro-encephalography (EEG) and produces a signal that we can then use to moderate our brain function. This helps to enhance our ability to self-regulate. The Muse™ headband, for instance, measures brain waves and charts them for viewing after the session. In addition, it moderates the audio when certain changes are detected, such as shifting the audio stream to that of stormy weather when it senses the mind has wandered.[183] This cue guides us to come back to the breath or to whatever other mindfulness technique we are exploring. It is a perfect example of real-time neurofeedback.

---

[181] https://www.ncbi.nlm.nih.gov/pmc/articles/PMC4428073/
[182] https://www.ncbi.nlm.nih.gov/pmc/articles/PMC4428073/
[183] https://choosemuse.com/how-it-works/

## LED Light Therapy

A third immersion of technology and meditation involves LED light therapy. Light, as an external stimulant, has the capacity to evoke certain moods and feelings.[184] By measuring real time data while meditating (such as heart rate variability) and altering ambient light according to this data, it would become possible to trigger behavioral shifts. In other words, if certain wavelengths or colors of light are equated with stress and the applied sensors pick up that the heart rate is increasing, it could alter the light applied accordingly.

## Heart Rate Variability (HRV)

Heart rate variability biofeedback is a way of measuring what is happening in the nervous system from moment to moment. Low HRV is associated with various psychological disorders, whereas high HRV is connected to cardiovascular health and resilience.[185] Heart monitoring for these intervals of variability are used in a variety of mental training technologies, such as EliteHRV and HRV4Training, to help users monitor and self-regulate through meditative practices such as focused breathing. The power of this technology is that it increases awareness and makes us more adaptive to, and empowered to manage life's stressors.

Some of these applied technologies are newly emerging, and yet each highlights the great potential that technology has for contributing to health promotion through mindfulness and meditation. As we become equipped with more knowledge through the application of these technologies, we will deepen our understanding of our own reactions and responses to life. In turn, we will enhance our ability to consciously direct our attention and our behaviors in ways that nourish, heal, and uplift us – one breath at a time.

---

[184] https://link.springer.com/article/10.1007/s00779-018-1141-6
[185] https://www.frontiersin.org/articles/10.3389/fpsyg.2019.02172/full

## Where Do We Go From Here?

One of the reasons why I have dealt with this subject at some length is essentially to normalize the conversation around reaching out to Mindfulness and Meditation as an effective intervention, especially in brain and behavioral health conditions.

Our health is our greatest asset and building a healthy lifestyle includes taking care of not only our body but also our emotional and mental well-being. We don't have to wait till we have manifested clinically significant symptoms to take action: we can begin by integrating the practice of mindfulness and meditation into our life that allow naturally for a healthy unfoldment of new decades of our life. This can include simple subscription to a mindfulness app that we can spend 10-15 minutes with daily, to signing up for a studio membership or going on retreats to nurture ourselves. And think of this as an investment into living the greatest life possible for ourselves.

For those of us who are facing some mental health challenges or struggling with substance abuse etc., it's also worth looking into our communities to find practitioners (including Psychiatrists, Psychologists, Therapists and Counselors) who are trained and certified in clinical grade interventions like MBSR/MBCT etc. This may well be a viable option for staying off the other drugs that can be habit forming and detrimental to other aspects of health, but then again, it's a conversation that is deeply personal which you need to have with a health professional. I just wanted to let you know there are other choices!

## The Synthesis

In the spirit of nurturing self-care and welling practice, when we developed the *ayam meditation collection* and the *ayam for leaders/ ayam for work* programs, the goal was to create a paradigm of synthesis. A synthesis of ancient wisdom, emerging research from cognitive sciences, neuro-biology and life tools that we can very easily integrate in our lives.

While these programs are not meant to be clinical interventions (at least not yet) they do provoke the innate healing and balancing response that will benefit most of us.

Now that being said, a large majority of you may be thinking that these techniques are great, but wondering; how do I weave them into my life?

The next section is dedicated exclusively to the theme of building a personal practice.

I look forward to continuing this conversation!

**Suggested ayam$^{(TM)}$ Practice:**

Programs: ayam for life; ayam for work (both available live only); Overcoming Crises

Meditations: Sleep Well, Self Healing, Gratitude, Calm, Love and Compassion

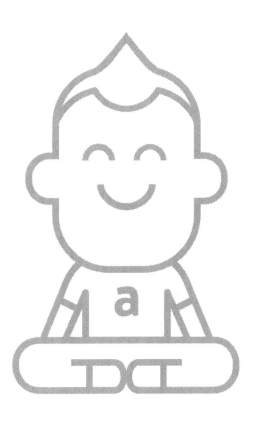

# SECTION 5

Crafting your own journey with
ayam™ meditations

Now we have reached that section of the book where I will vax eloquently about the ayam platform because it's the best ever! *OK I am just kidding or am I ?* The truth is it doesn't matter.

I want to devote this section to helping you get the maximum value out of a daily practice. I am using ayam as a reference tool but you could pretty much use the same principles to work with any platform you chose or on your own without any platform.

One of the things I learnt early on in my meditation training was the value of disciplined practice. The cornerstone of it was – making a determination to devote whatever time works for your life to the practice of meditation. After all, it's part of your "me" time – allocated to self-care and well-being.

Initially, I thought that the longer I meditated, the better it would be for me. There was a short phase in my monk life when I meditated for over 14 hours a day. That was a lot and honestly, looking back in the rear view mirror, not all that helpful. It does not leave any time for you to do anything meaningful with your life beyond meditation, including even studying! At other times in my life I have devoted 1.5-2hrs every day to my practices as well, a more doable rhythm but still not practical for most people.

With experience of personal practice, as well as training others, I have now come to the conclusion that *"duration"* is not the only important thing; the *"regularity of practice"* is equally important. What does that mean ? I guess what I am trying to say is this: practicing meditation for 10 mins a day is better than practicing 1 hour every week.

So how long is enough? A common question I am asked literally everyday and my answer is the same; *as long as it works for you and you enjoy it.* To start with, if you can allocate 3-5 mins everyday for basic mindfulness practices, it's already a good start. Growing it slowly to a 20 min formal practice or mindfulness and meditation is actually a very rich practice, if you can do it daily.

Ideally, allocating sometime in the morning and evening works best, allowing you to begin your day with vitality and alignment and closing your day with gratitude and peace.

## My personal practice

My personal practice is of making a 20 mins or so of time commitment every morning, consisting of some mindful movement, breathing exercises and a formal sitting. In the evenings, I usually make time for 10 mins before I go to sleep to properly close my day and put my mind to rest. Sometimes, when I have the opportunity, I prefer to go for a mindful walk for 20-30 mins in the evening, especially when the weather is nice.

My lifestyle allows me to allocate this 30-40 min total everyday towards my practice. But for some of us who are very busy or just getting started, even 3-5 mins a day – once a day is a good start.

In addition to the daily meditation practice, I also make time on most weekends for 1-1.5 hr for a contemplative silence, allowing myself to focus on whatever is on my mind so I don't carry it into the next week. And instead of thinking about 'solutions', I tend to approach them as 'enquiry' of what is present in my mind or emotions. Personally, I find it very helpful in staying focused on the here and now instead of being burdened by memories of the past or apprehension/excitement of the future.

I also take an annual retreat of 3-5 days to disconnect from whatever is going on in life and focus literally on 'where I want to go with life next'.

These practices are not 'gold standard', neither something I prescribe to others. Everyone is unique; their life circumstances are unique and so their practices are unique. I have shared with you my practice to just give a view of the balance I have found which works for me. I am hoping you will make your own experiments and find your own unique self expression and balance.

# ayam

## Essentials:

Daily essentials are just that; 'meditations for daily essential needs of modern life'. These are short practices of meditation that you could build a daily practice around.

The three practices of Breath Awareness, Peace & Calm and Vitality, essentially use the same foundational techniques with different visualizations and hand positions to provoke specific results. These meditations take less than 10 mins and you can do them anytime in day – be it at the start of your day or even before you sleep. **Best time for Breath Awareness practice:** *Mornings, or middle of your day when you need a boost.*

Goodwill meditation is a great way to start your day by expressing goodwill to all beings that you engage with in life. This meditation uses advanced techniques of meditation that allow for you to engage your whole self (both along the vertical and horizontal axis). This meditation lays the foundation for a day full of flow, as you start it with goodwill that is what you will receive from others also during the day. A daily practice of this will have a profound impact on ease and grace you feel in your life.

**Best time for Goodwill meditation practice:** *Mornings before you start your day.*

Gratitude meditation allows you to express gratitude for things you have received in your day and in your life at large. It provides an opportunity to experience how truly blessed we are even when we have had an otherwise challenging day – it's a great alignment of perspective! It's one of my favorite meditations from the ayam collections.

**Best time for Gratitude practice** : *Evenings before you close your day.*

## Meditations

ayam meditations collections has 8 core meditations that have been carefully curated based on the most common needs of modern life. Each one of them has specific content that is tailored to meet the promise the title suggests. For example, the Calm meditation is focused on developing a lasting state of peace and calm in your being, whereas Self Healing meditation is designed for allowing us to heal from a range of experiences in our life and move forward with full self expression.

These meditations can be practiced anytime. The easiest way to select which one is by answering the question: *what do I want in my life right now?* And the answer can range from Sleep to Abundance... and you can pick the meditation that your heart most desires.

I strongly recommend allocating time on at least a twice weekly basis to do these longer meditations.

## Programs

On the *ayam platform*, both on the app and eLearning solution, there are a number of programs that have been developed essentially for study, skill development and going deeper with your meditation practice.

While the app is a great place to start, at some point you may feel the inner desire to "become masterful" at these meditations and also understand how they function and what effects they have on your well-being beyond what you may have already noticed. The programs aim to do just that – educate you, provide advanced practices and explain in detail how meditations work.

The main 5 program and their objects are very easy to understand from the titles themselves:

◊ **Your First Meditation:** *Getting Started*

This program helps you get started with your first ayam meditation ever. This is equally well suited for people who have never mediated, as well as people who want to take the first step of formally learning a meditation practice. A great place to start!

◊ **Your First Week with ayam:** *Developing a Daily Practice*

This program builds on the foundation of the earlier program and handholds you in developing a daily practice by progressively deepening the level of meditations over 7 days and introducing all the key building blocks that you will need for most advanced ayam meditations.

◊ **Powerfully Overcoming Crises**

This program addresses how to use meditations and mindfulness to build resilience in challenging times in life, that we sometimes call crises. The program features specific meditations that can unlock our hidden reserve of patience, resilience and vitality that will enable us to sail through these crises with greater ease.

◊ **Deepening Your Practice**

This program is a deep dive into learning the art and science of mediation. You will receive a step by step introduction in how to craft profound meditative experiences, including the opportunity to learn the design of the ayam™ meditations and the underling scientific principals that make it so effective. This program is a must watch for you if you are seeking a firm grounding on the path of mindfulness and mediation.

◊   **Just Meet Yourself: 8 Key Meditations to Transform Your Life**

This program takes a deep dive into the contextual and ontological formulations of the 8 core meditations of ayam app. This program is a blended mix of education, life coaching and guided practice around what we can successfully argue are the foundational and aspirational benefits to be expected from the practice of meditation. I Hope you enjoy the programs!

## Broadcasts and Live Events

Broadcasts and live events available within the ayam platform are a key part of the engagement that we aim to offer to our users. A sense of community and practicing/meditating together creates a very unique limbic tango that enables the whole group to go deeper and walk away with richer insights. We have attempted to create variety in terms of styles and facilitators to enable this to become a rich and fulfilling experience. We look forward to welcoming you there!

## Walking The Path: Unfolding Tranquility and Wisdom

I would like to use the last few words of the book to take a deeper cut at the questions of *what is the purpose of practicing meditation and mindfulness anyway?* Throughout this book, we have explored various themes and ideas ranging from letting off stress and anxiety, impacting the brain and behavioral health, cultivating love, joy, compassion and including finding a sense of meaning, purpose and true fulfillment. And these are certainly the benefits one could receive from meditation. The question that remains is *"do they qualify as purpose?"*

The truth is I don't know a final answer to the question. I am like you, a student of this path. I am not even sure at this stage if a causal purpose is actually necessary. As one could also turn around and ask, *what is the purpose of the universe to exist?* So I will not speculate on a boundary definition of that purpose. I will however leave you with a thought of what is possible, if you engage in a regular practice of mindfulness and meditation - *unfoldment of tranquility and wisdom.*

What do I mean by that? I mean a state of calm, unconditional mind that has been lost to people, no wobbling at the behest of emotions, a sharpness of perception and a way of being sourced from a state of deep empathy, compassion, unconditional service and above all, freedom to be. Wisdom adds to it a level of inner knowing where questions don't arise from inquisitiveness but insight arises from practicing with a beginners mind, offering us a quick peek into the nature of life itself and reality of living thereof.

To me walking on this path, undertaking a journey of unfoldment has been a great reward – there is no ultimate reward I seek, but the bliss of continuing the path. I hope you can craft your own path too. It is my most sincere wish and good will for you. Enjoy the journey as its own reward!

**#self-care and well-being is the foundation of a fulfilling life!**

Made in the USA
Coppell, TX
03 December 2021